Zofia A. Brzozowska, Mirosław J. Leszka

Maria Lekapene, Empress of the Bulgarians

Neither a Saint nor a Malefactress

BYZANTINA LODZIENSIA

Series of the Department of Byzantine History of the University of Lodz

Founded by

Professor Waldemar Ceran

in

1997

№ XXXVI

BYZANTINA LODZIENSIA
XXXVI

Zofia A. Brzozowska, Mirosław J. Leszka

Maria Lekapene, Empress of the Bulgarians

Neither a Saint nor a Malefactress

Translated by
Marek Majer (VII.1)
Artur Mękarski (II; III.1; III.3; III.4; VI; VIII; Appendix)
Michał Zytka (I; II; III.2; III.3; III.5; IV; V; VI; VII.2; VIII)

WYDAWNICTWO
UNIWERSYTETU
ŁÓDZKIEGO

Zofia A. Brzozowska – University of Łódź
Faculty of Philology, Department of Slavic Studies
171/173 Pomorska St., 90-236 Łódź (Poland)
slawistyka@uni.lodz.pl

Mirosław J. Leszka – University of Łódź
Faculty of Philosophy and History
Institute of History, Department of Byzantine History
27a Kamińskiego St., 90-219 Łódź (Poland)
bizancjum@uni.lodz.pl

Published by Łódź University Press & Jagiellonian University Press

First edition, Łódź–Kraków 2017
W.08458.17.0.K

ISBN 978-83-8142-028-0 – paperback Łódź University Press
ISBN 978-83-233-4441-4 – paperback Jagiellonian University Press
ISBN 978-83-8142-029-7 – electronic version Łódź University Press
ISBN 978-83-233-9810-3 – electronic version Jagiellonian University Press

Łódź University Press
8 Lindleya St., 90-131 Łódź
www.wydawnictwo.uni.lodz.pl
e-mail: ksiegarnia@uni.lodz.pl
phone: +48 (42) 665 58 63

Distribution outside Poland

Jagiellonian University Press
9/2 Michałowskiego St., 31-126 Kraków
phone: +48 (12) 631 01 97, +48 (12) 663 23 81, fax +48 (12) 663 23 83
cell phone: +48 506 006 674, e-mail: sprzedaz@wuj.pl, www.wuj.pl

Contents

Chapter VIII

Appendix

Introduction

According to some of the scholars attempting to recreate the biographies of Bulgarian tsaritsas, the character of the relevant medieval sources can be most fully summarized with the principle: *do not mention them, or speak of them poorly*[1]. This also applies to Maria Lekapene, wife of tsar Peter. While the former part of the statement seems to pertain primarily to contemporary authors, the latter is common among modern historians, constructing their narratives based on exceedingly small source material and accusing the tsaritsa of an unambiguously negative impact on the events taking place in the Bulgarian state during the 10th century[2].

---

[1] *В данните от изворите и от специализираната литература по отношение на повечето от българските владетелки важи принципът "Или нищо, или лошо". Поемайки тежестта на короната, те сякаш се дематериализират до степента на безплътни сенки на своите съпрузи или пък се митологизират като разюздани юди самовили, обсебени от сатанински егоцентризъм, алчност, коварство и всякакви низки щения* (В. И г н а т о в, *Българските царици. Владетелките на България от VII до XIV в.*, София 2008, p. 6).

[2] В.И. З л а т а р с к и, *История на българската държава през средните векове*, vol. I/2, *Първо българско Царство. От славянизацията на държавата до падането на Първото царство (852–1018)*, София 1927, p. 535–536; П. М у т а ф ч и е в, *История на българския народ (681–1323)*, София 1986, p. 201.

According to scholars of the caliber of Vasil Zlatarski and Petar Mutafchiev, the tsaritsa exerted major influence on her husband's foreign policy, even acting as an 'agent' of Constantinople at the Preslav court and indirectly contributing to the collapse of Bulgarian statehood in 971. Moreover, some historians are also willing to blame Maria for carrying out an ideological transfer of some kind, i.e. for infecting Old Bulgarian culture with elements of Byzantine political ideology – a 'plague' from which (as per the uncompromising Petar Mutafchiev) the medieval Bulgarians never recovered.

Much more balanced assessments regarding Maria's influence on the direction of the foreign and internal policies of her husband, as well as the dissemination of Byzantine culture in Preslav, can be found in the works of later historians, e.g. Vasil Gjuzelev[3] or Jonathan Shepard[4]. These scholars stress that the exceptionally scanty source material makes it impossible to formulate unequivocal conclusions concerning this matter.

Maria Lekapene has also attracted the attention of scholars working on the Bulgarian ideology of power and the system of the monarch's self-representation in the 10th century, i.e. titles, seals and insignia (Georgi Atanasov[5],

---

[3] В. Гю з е л е в, *Значението на брака на цар Петър (927–969) с ромейката Мария-Ирина Лакапина (911–962)*, [in:] *Културните текстове на миналото – носители, символи, идеи*, vol. I, *Текстовете на историята, история на текстовете. Материали от Юбилейната международна конференция в чест на 60-годишнината на проф. д.и.н. Казимир Попконстантинов, Велико Търново, 29–31 октомври 2003 г.*, София 2005, p. 27–33.

[4] J. S h e p a r d, *A marriage too far? Maria Lekapena and Peter of Bulgaria*, [in:] *The Empress Theophano. Byzantium and the West at the turn of the first millennium*, ed. A. D a v i d s, Cambridge 1995, p. 121–149.

[5] G. A t a n a s o v, *On the Origin, Function and the Owner of the Adornments of the Preslav Treasure from the 10th century*, "Archaeologia Bulgarica" 3.3, 1999, p. 81–94; i d e m, *Инсигниите на средновековните български владетели. Корони, скиптри, сфери, оръжия, костюми, накити*, Плевен 1999; i d e m, *Печатите на българските владетели от IX–X в. в Дръстър (Силистра)*, [in:] *От тука започва България. Материали от втората национална конференция по история, археология и културен туризъм "Пътуване към България", Шумен 14–16.05. 2010 година*, ed. И. Й о р д а н о в, Шумен 2011, p. 286–293.

Georgi Bakalov[6], Ivan Jordanov[7], Angel Nikolov[8], Todor Todorov[9]). Of course, Peter's spouse also appears in studies devoted to Bulgarian female royalty and the role of women in medieval Bulgaria (Judith Herrin[10], Sashka Georgieva[11], Magda Hristodulova[12]).

The paucity of source material pertaining to Maria is most likely the primary reason why the empress has not yet been the subject of a separate, monographic study. The goal of the present book is to fill this gap in historiography. Starting with the assumption that the history of medieval Bulgaria cannot be considered in isolation from the history of the neighboring Byzantine empire, and being aware that it is in the transmission of Byzantine spiritual and material culture that Maria Lekapene's influence could be seen most clearly, we decided to analyze the life of our protagonist against a wider cultural background. Therefore, we present

---

[6] Г. Бакалов, *Царската промулгация на Петър и неговите приемници в светлината на българо-византийските дипломатически отношения след договора от 927 г.*, "Исторически преглед" 39.6, 1983, p. 35–44; idem, *Средновековният български владетел. Титулатура и инсигнии*, София 1995.

[7] И. Йорданов, *Корпус на печатите на Средновековна България*, София 2001; idem, *Corpus of Byzantine Seals from Bulgaria*, vol. iii/1, Sofia 2009; idem, *Корпус на средновековните български печати*, София 2016.

[8] А. Николов, *Политическа мисъл в ранносредновековна България (средата на IX–края на X в.)*, София 2006.

[9] Т. Тодоров, *Константин Багренородни и династичният брак между владетелските домове на Преслав и Константинопол от 927 г.*, "Преславска книжовна школа" 7, 2003, p. 391–398; idem, *България през втората и третата четвърт на X век: политическа история*, София 2006 [unpublished PhD thesis]; idem, *Владетелският статут и титла на цар Петър I след октомври 927 г.: писмени сведения и сфрагистични данни (сравнителен анализ)*, [in:] *Юбилеен сборник. Сто години от рождението на д-р Васил Хараланов (1907–2007)*, Шумен 2008, p. 93–108.

[10] J. Herrin, *Theophano. Considerations on the Education of a Byzantine Princess*, [in:] *The Empress Theophano. Byzantium and the West at the turn of the first millennium*, ed. A. Davids, Cambridge 1995, p. 64–85 [= J. Herrin, *Unrivalled Influence. Women and Empire in Byzantium*, Princeton 2013, p. 238–260].

[11] S. Georgieva, *The Byzantine Princesses in Bulgaria*, "Byzantinobulgarica" 9, 1995, p. 163–201; eadem, *Жената в българското средновековие*, Пловдив 2011.

[12] М. Христодулова, *Титул и регалии болгарской владетельницы в эпоху средневековья (VII–XIV вв.)*, "Études Balkaniques" 1978, 3, p. 141–148.

her biography in comparison with those of the Byzantine empresses of the 4th–10th centuries, describing the model of the *imperial feminine* they had created and the ways in which it had changed over the course of the centuries (until it was successfully transplanted onto Bulgarian soil by Peter's wife). The image is further enriched by the occasional appearance in the pages of this monograph of two other female royals, Maria's contemporaries. Kievan Rus', by accepting Christianity from Constantinople and adopting the Old Church Slavic language and writing, became a state culturally related to Bulgaria. Accordingly, in this book, the reader shall find references to the Kievan princess Olga, as well as to Anna Porphyrogennete (a fairly close relative of the Bulgarian tsaritsa).

* * *

We would like to thank the whole team of the Waldemar Ceran Research Centre for the History and Culture of the Mediterranean Area and South-East Europe (*Ceraneum*) at the University of Lodz for the highly supportive attitude towards our work. We thank Professor Maciej Kokoszko, director of *Ceraneum*, and Professor Georgi Minczew, deputy director and head of the International Advisory Board of *Ceraneum*. We would also like to extend our special thanks to Professor Joanna Jabłkowska, Dean of the Faculty of Philology (University of Lodz) and to Professor Maciej Kokoszko, Dean of the Faculty of Philosophy and History (University of Lodz), for supporting our research.

Particular thanks are due to Dr. Karolina Krzeszewska, employed at the office of *Ceraneum*, for her efficient assistance with numerous formal tasks associated with carrying out the project. As always, we were able to count on the support of our Colleagues from *Ceraneum* and from our two parent research units at the University of Lodz – the Department of Byzantine History and the Department of Slavic Studies: Prof. Teresa Wolińska, Prof. Sławomir Bralewski, Prof. Ivan Petrov, Dr. Paweł Filipczak, Dr. Agata Kawecka, Dr. Andrzej Kompa, Dr. Kiril Marinow, Dr. Małgorzata Skowronek, and Dr. Jan M. Wolski. We thank

Professor Ireneusz Milewski from the University of Gdańsk for the meticulous and positive editorial review. We thank Dr. Marek Majer for editing and proofreading the English text. We would also like to give thanks to Elżbieta Myślińska-Brzozowska for providing the illustrations (drawings) for this volume.

* * *

This book was written as part of a research project financed by the National Science Centre (Poland). Decision number: DEC-2014/14/M/HS3/00758 (*The Bulgarian State in 927–969. The Epoch of Tsar Peter I the Pious*).

I

Zofia A. Brzozowska

Sources

Most of the information regarding the life and activities of Maria Lekapene has come to us from Byzantine authors. Crucially, many of the accounts which we are going to examine here were written during Maria's life, or soon after her death. The most detailed description of the developments of 927, i.e. the negotiations leading to the conclusion of peace between the empire and Bulgaria (the guarantee of which was to have been the marriage between Peter and the granddaughter of Romanos I Lekapenos), is found in a narrative written down in the 10th century in Constantinople. It was created by authors from the so-called 'circle of Symeon Logothete': the Continuator of George the Monk (Hamartolos), Symeon Logothete, Leo Grammatikos and Pseudo-Symeon Magistros[1].

---

[1] The reader may find a review of Byzantine historiographical texts focusing on Maria and the events of 927 in such works as: В. Г ю з е л е в, *Значението на брака на цар Петър (927–969) с ромейката Мария-Ирина Лакапина (911–962)*, [in:] *Културните текстове на миналото – носители, символи, идеи*, vol. I, *Текстовете на историята, история на текстовете. Материали от Юбилейната международна конференция в чест на 60-годишнината на проф. д.и.н. Казимир Попконстантинов, Велико Търново, 29–31 октомври 2003 г.*, София 2005, p. 32; А. Н и к о л о в, *Политическа мисъл в ранносредновековна България (средата на IX–края на X в.)*, София 2006, p. 233–236; Т. Т о д о р о в, *България през втората и третата четвърт на X век: политическа история*. София 2006 [unpublished PhD thesis], p. 150–152;

The output of the anonymous Continuator of George the Monk includes the description of events from 842 onwards – from the point at which George's narrative ended. The fragments devoted to Peter and Maria are practically identical with the relevant passages in the *Chronicle of Symeon Logothete*. The text is known in two variants. Redaction A, older, written down before 963, describes the events prior to 948, i.e. the death of Romanos I Lekapenos. The later redaction B includes the history of Byzantium up to 963 (enhanced with certain additional details). The older version of the *Chronicle of Symeon Logothete* is highly similar to redaction A of the *Continuation of George the Monk*, while the newer version closely resembles redaction B. In this monograph, I am not going to differentiate between the redactions A and B, as the passages relating to Maria Lekapene in both variants are identical. They include first and foremost an unusually extensive and detailed narrative of the events of 927[2], as well as a mention of the Bulgarian tsaritsa's visits to Constantinople in the later period[3].

Textologically separate, but related in content, are the *Chronicle of Pseudo-Symeon Magistros* and the *Chronicle of Leo Grammatikos*. Their descriptions of the developments of 927 are similar to the ones discussed above, but presented more concisely[4].

The second, later redaction of the *Chronicle of Symeon Logothete*, completed ca. 963, most likely served as the basis for the anonymous author of the first part of book 6 of the *Continuation of Theophanes*, written at roughly the same time. It is hardly surprising, therefore, that this work's account of the circumstances in which the Bulgarian-Byzantine peace treaty of 927 was concluded is also highly similar to the descriptions mentioned above. It also includes a strikingly close depiction of the marriage

---

i d e m, *Владетелският статут и титла на цар Петър I след октомври 927 г.: писмени сведения и сфрагистични данни (сравнителен анализ)*, [in:] *Юбилеен сборник. Сто години от рождението на д-р Васил Хараланов (1907–2007)*, Шумен 2008, p. 94–95.

[2] Continuator of George the Monk, p. 904–907; Symeon Logothete, 136, 45–51, p. 326–329.

[3] Continuator of George the Monk, p. 913; Symeon Logothete, 136, 67, p. 334.

[4] Leo Grammatikos, p. 315–317; Pseudo-Symeon Magistros, 33–34, p. 740–741.

between Maria and Peter, as well as a record of the tsaritsa's several journeys to Constantinople, where, accompanied by her children, she paid
visits to her relatives[5].

Some information on Maria Lekapene was also included in the works
of later Byzantine chroniclers: John Skylitzes and John Zonaras. Both
of these authors included a description of the facts of 927, based on the
above-mentioned earlier accounts but presented in a more condensed
form[6]. Moreover, they also noted an event that, for obvious reasons, could
not have been mentioned by the authors of the earlier historiographical
works (concluded in the early 960s) – i.e. the death of Maria[7].

The works of Constantine VII Porphyrogennetos deserve particular
attention. He was of a similar age to Peter and his spouse and was married to her aunt – Helena Lekapene; he also participated in the events
of 927 and most likely knew Maria personally. However, the 'purple-born'
author is not objective: he is unsympathetic to our heroine's family
and does not conceal his outrage that she, a granddaughter of emper-
or Romanos I Lekapenos, married a foreign, Slavic ruler. Constantine
included an evaluation of this marriage in chapter 13 of the treatise *On the
Governance of the Empire*[8]. Another of his works, the *Book of Ceremonies*,
may also prove a valuable source. While it would be futile to search the
pages of this text for direct remarks on Maria, it does provide us with

[5] Continuator of Theophanes, VI, 22–23, 35, p. 412–415, 422.

[6] John Skylitzes, p. 222–224; John Zonaras, XVI, 18–19, p. 473–475.

[7] John Skylitzes, p. 255; John Zonaras, XVI, 23, p. 495.

[8] Constantine VII Porphyrogennetos, *On the Governance of the
Empire*, 13, p. 72–74. For the opinion of Constantine VII on the Bulgarians, as well as
on the causes of this ruler's negative attitude towards the Lekapenos family and their
dynastic marriage of 927, see: Г. Литаврин, *Константин Багрянородный о Болгарии
и Болгарах*, [in:] *Сборник в чест на акад. Димитър Ангелов*, ed. В. Велков, София
1994, p. 30–37; F. Tinnefeld, *Byzantinische auswärtige Heiratspolitik vom 9. zum
12 Jahrhundert*, "Byzantinoslavica" 54.1, 1993, p. 21–22; Т. Тодоров, *Константин
Багренородни и династичният брак между владетелските домове на Преслав
и Константинопол от 927 г.*, "Преславска книжовна школа" 7, 2003, p. 391–398;
В. Гюзелев, *Значението на брака...*, p. 30–31; A. Paroń, *"Trzeba, abyś tymi oto słowami odparł i to niedorzeczne żądanie" – wokół De administrando imperio Konstantyna VII*,
[in:] *Causa creandi. O pragmatyce źródła historycznego*, eds. S. Rosik, P. Wiszewski,
Wrocław 2005, p. 345–361; A. Николов, *Политическа мисъл...*, p. 269–279.

some important information about the official status and titulature of the mid-10th century Bulgarian ruler[9].

Maria is also mentioned by a Western European author contemporary to her: Liudprand of Cremona, who came to Constantinople on a diplomatic mission twice (in 949 and in 968)[10]. The person of Maria and the circumstances of her marriage with the Bulgarian ruler drew Liudprand's attention during both of his stays in the Byzantine capital. In 968, the reasons were obvious – the goal of his visit to Constantinople was, after all, to negotiate Nikephoros II Phokas's agreement to marry a 'purple-born' Byzantine woman to the son of Otto I. The Byzantine-Bulgarian marriage of 927 may have been an important argument during these negotiations, in that the rule according to which a woman from the imperial family could not marry a foreign ruler was not strictly adhered to at the Constantinopolitan court[11]. Curiously, Liudprand is also the only author to mention that, upon entering into marriage, Maria adopted a new name (Irene, i.e. 'Peace'), symbolically underscoring the role she was to play in the Byzantine-Bulgarian relations after 927[12].

We do not know why Bulgarian medieval authors consistently fail to mention Maria Lekapene. The tsaritsa is entirely absent from Bulgarian works that refer to her husband, e.g. the *Sermon Against the Heretics* by Cosmas the Priest (10th century), or historiographical texts devoted to St. John of Rila (the so-called 'folk' life from the 11th century or the prologue life from the 13th century, or the work of Euthymios of Tarnovo). Even more surprisingly, we will not find any references to the empress in hymnographic works dedicated to Peter as a saint of the Eastern Church

---

[9] Constantine VII Porphyrogennetos, *The Book of Ceremonies*, II, 47, p. 681–682.

[10] Liudprand of Cremona, *Retribution*, III, 38, p. 86; Liudprand of Cremona, *Embassy*, 16, 19, p. 194–195.

[11] T. Wolińska, *Konstantynopolitańska misja Liudpranda z Kremony (968)*, [in:] *Cesarstwo bizantyńskie. Dzieje. Religia. Kultura. Studia ofiarowane Profesorowi Waldemarowi Ceranowi przez uczniów na 70-lecie Jego urodzin*, eds. P. Krupczyński, M.J. Leszka, Łask–Łódź 2006, p. 208–212.

[12] J. Shepard, *A marriage too far? Maria Lekapena and Peter of Bulgaria*, [in:] *The Empress Theophano. Byzantium and the West at the turn of the first millennium*, ed. A. Davids, Cambridge 1995, p. 126–127; B. Гюзелев, *Значението на брака...*, p. 30.

(e.g. in the *Officium* from the 13th-century *Menaion of Dragan* or in the troparion from the 1330 *Lesnovo Prologue*). The laudatory part of the *Synodikon of Tsar Boril* omits Lekapene completely; it does, however, include praises of numerous Bulgarian royals of both sexes (among them another Maria, the last empress consort of the first state – 1018), of several later tsaritsas, and of Peter himself[13]. Given that the *Synodikon* has not reached us in its complete form, we may venture a hypothesis that some mention of Maria Lekapene may have been present in the part that is now lost. Rather symptomatic, on the other hand, is the account from the *Tale of the Prophet Isaiah*, a 12th-century compilation: according to its anonymous author, Peter purportedly died without having known either sin or a wife/woman (гр҃ѣха не имѣе ни жени)[14].

Against this backdrop of medieval Bulgarian literary tradition, one entry, added as a gloss to the 14th-century Slavic translation (completed in Bulgaria) of the *Chronicle of Constantine Manasses*, seems unique: сего ц҃рѣ [i.e. Romanos I Lekapenos's] внѹкѫ Петрѫ ц҃рь блъгарскы имѣ женѫ. This passage, repeated in Bulgarian and Serbian copies of this source, seems to be the only one across the entire South Slavic material that mentions Maria[15].

In a study that requires the analysis of native sources (such as e.g. research into the titulature of the Bulgarian empress consort), the historian needs to seek additional information by examining the Slavic translations of Byzantine chronicles. From among the above-mentioned Greek historiographical texts, both versions of the *Continuation of George*

---

[13] *Synodikon of Tsar Boril*, p. 149–150; Г. Б а к а л о в, *Царската промулгация на Петър и неговите приемници в светлината на българо-византийските дипломатически отношения след договора от 927 г.*, "Исторически преглед" 39.6, 1983, p. 37–38; i d e m, *Средновековният български владетел. Титулатура и инсигнии*, София 1995, p. 172; Т. Т о д о р о в, *България...*, p. 155; i d e m, *Владетелският статут...*, p. 98.

[14] *Tale of the Prophet Isaiah*, p. 17. On the portrayal of Peter in the *Tale of the Prophet Isaiah*: D. Č e š m e d ž i e v, *Bułgarska tradycja państwowa w apokryfach: car Piotr w "Bułgarskiej kronice apokryficznej"*, transl. Ł. M y s i e l s k i, [in:] *Biblia Slavorum Apocryphorum. Novum Testamentum*, eds. G. M i n c z e w, M. S k o w r o n e k, I. P e t r o v, Łódź 2009, p. 139–147.

[15] *Среднеболгарский перевод Хроники Константина Манассии в славянских литературах*, eds. Д.С. Л и х а ч е в, И.С. Д у й ч е в, София 1988, p. 232, 237.

the Monk as well as the work of John Zonaras were certainly translated into the language of the Orthodox Slavs[16].

The Slavic translation of the *Continuation of George the Monk* was completed in Bulgaria in the late 10th or early 11th century, and it was based on the newer, expanded redaction of the text (B), written after 963. Therefore, the Slavic translation dates back to merely several decades later than the original Greek version (i.e., incidentally, soon after Maria's death). According to numerous scholars, the Slavic translation is unusually faithful to the original, preserving a version of the text that is closer to the protograph than some of the extant Byzantine copies[17]. It features a thorough account of the year 927 and a reference to Maria's later visits to Constantinople[18].

Interestingly enough, another translation of the *Chronicle of Symeon Logothete* (vel *Continuation of George the Monk*), entirely independent from the translation discussed above, was produced in the 14th century in the South Slavic area. It was based on the older redaction of the Byzantine chronicle (A), covering events until 948. In the manuscripts of this translation, the work is unequivocally ascribed to Symeon Logothete[19]. Again,

---

[16] Д.И. Полывянный, *Царь Петр в исторической памяти болгарского средневековья*, [in:] *Средновековният българин и "другите". Сборник в чест на 60-годишнината на проф. дин Петър Ангелов*, eds. А. Николов, Г.Н. Николов, София 2013, p. 139.

[17] А.П. Каждан, *Хроника Симеона Логофета*, "Византийский Временник" 15, 1959, p. 126; W. Swoboda, *Kontynuacja Georgiosa*, [in:] *Słownik starożytności słowiańskich. Encyklopedyczny zarys kultury Słowian od czasów najdawniejszych do schyłku XII w.*, vol. II, eds. W. Kowalenko, G. Labuda, T. Lehr-Spławiński, Wrocław 1965, p. 468; M. Каймакамова, *Българска средновековна историопис*, София 1990, p. 170–171; A. Brzóstkowska, *Kroniki z kręgu Symeona Logotety*, [in:] *Testimonia najdawniejszych dziejów Słowian. Seria grecka*, vol. V, *Pisarze z X wieku*, ed. A. Brzóstkowska, Warszawa 2009, p. 64–66.

[18] Continuator of George the Monk (Slavic), 6–7, 10, p. 560–562, 566.

[19] Г. Острогорский, *Славянский перевод хроники Симеона Логофета*, "Seminarium Kondakovianum" 5, 1932, p. 17–37; А.П. Каждан, *Хроника...*, p. 130; W. Swoboda, *Symeon Logotheta*, [in:] *Słownik starożytności słowiańskich...*, vol. V, eds. W. Kowalenko, G. Labuda, T. Lehr-Spławiński, Wrocław 1975, p. 506–507; M. Каймакамова, *Българска средновековна историопис...*, p. 187–188; Т. Тодоров, *България...*, p. 155–156; idem, *Владетелският статут...*, p. 98; A. Brzóstkowska, *Kroniki...*, p. 66.

the fragments of the source referring to Maria Lekapene were rendered particularly faithfully, free from abbreviations or editorial interpolations[20].

The Bulgarian translation of the *Chronicle of John Zonaras* (from the second half of the 12th century) and especially the 14th-century Serbian redaction can hardly be considered complete. In the manuscripts containing the most extensive version of the Slavic text, we encounter a lacuna between the reign of Leo VI (886–912) and that of Basil II (976–1025). Accordingly, it is impossible to find any mention of Maria in the text[21]. Interestingly, information about her death and her role as a *sui generis* 'guardian of peace' between Byzantium and Bulgaria was included in the synopsis of John Zonaras's work by the anonymous author of manuscript РНБ, F.IV.307, which comprises the 14th-century Slavic translation of the *Chronicle of Symeon Logothete*: цръ же блъгарскаго Петра женѣ оумерши, иже съ Гръкы миръ оутвръждаѫ[22].

Remarks about Maria Lekapene can also be found in several Russian historiographical sources which were dependent content-wise, and sometimes even textologically, on Slavic translations of Byzantine chronicles. Thus, the highly detailed description of the events of 927 as well as the passage on Maria's later visits to Constantinople – *de facto* re-edited fragments of the *Continuation of George the Monk* – were weaved into the text of the *Hellenic and Roman Chronicle* of the second redaction[23]. The latter is a monumental relic of Rus' historiography of the late Middle Ages, compiled prior to 1453 on the basis of native accounts as well as Byzantine sources acquired in the East Slavic area (e.g. the *Chronicle of George the Monk* and the *Chronicle of John Malalas*)[24].

---

[20] S y m e o n   L o g o t h e t e (Slavic), p. 136–137, 140.

[21] О.В. Т в о р о г о в, *Паралипомен Зонары: текст и комментарий*, [in:] *Летописи и хроники. Новые исследования. 2009–2010*, ed. О.Л. Н о в и к о в а, Москва–Санкт-Петербург 2010, p. 3–101.

[22] J o h n   Z o n a r a s (Slavic), p. 146.

[23] *Hellenic and Roman Chronicle*, p. 497–498, 501; Z.A. B r z o z o w s k a, *The Image of Maria Lekapene, Peter and the Byzantine-Bulgarian Relations Between 927 and 969 in the Light of Old Russian Sources*, "Palaeobulgarica" 41.1, 2017, p. 50–51.

[24] Т.В. А н и с и м о в а, *Хроника Георгия Амартола в древнерусских списках XIV–XVII вв.*, Москва 2009, p. 9–10, 235–253; Т. В и л к у л, *Літопис і хронограф. Студії з домонгольського київського літописання*, Київ 2015, p. 372–387.

A brief entry on Maria, based on the above-mentioned Bulgarian gloss to the Slavic translation of the *Chronicle of Constantine Manasses*, can also be found in two (interrelated) 16th-century Russian compilations which contain an extensive history of the world: the *Russian Chronograph* of 1512 and the *Nikon Chronicle*[25]. The tsaritsa is mentioned in both of these sources along with the description of the reign of emperor Romanos I Lekapenos. The Russian historiographer relates that this ruler's granddaughter was the wife of Bulgarian tsar Peter: сего цара Ромона [внуку] Петръ болгарьскый цадь имѣ женѹ[26].

Noteworthy information about Maria and her position at the Preslav court can be gleaned from sphragistic material. It is beyond any doubt that, during the period 927–945, tsar Peter was depicted on official seals accompanied by his spouse. A relatively high number of artifacts of this kind have survived to our times. Ivan Jordanov, a specialist in medieval Bulgarian and Byzantine sigillography, divided them into three types[27]:

I.   *Peter and Maria – Basileis/Emperors of the Bulgarians* (after 927) – a depiction of Peter and Maria is found on the reverse. The tsar is shown on the left-hand side of the composition, the tsaritsa on the right (from the viewer's perspective). Both are portrayed in the official court dress of Byzantine emperors. The Bulgarian rulers are holding a cross between one another, grasping it at the same height. The inscription presents them as the *basileis* of the Bulgarians: Πέτρος καὶ Μαρίας βασιλεῖς τῶν Βουλγάρων[28].

---

[25] М.А. С а л м и н а, *Хроника Константина Манассии как источник Русского хронографа*, "Труды Отдела древнерусской литературы" 32, 1978, p. 279–287; А.А. Т у р и л о в, *К вопросу о болгарских источниках Русского хронографа*, [in:] *Летописи и хроники. Сборник статей*, Москва 1984, p. 20–24 [=*Межславянские культурные связи эпохи Средневековья и источниковедение истории и культуры славян. Этюды и характеристики*, Москва 2012, p. 704–708].

[26] *Russian Chronograph*, p. 358; *Nikon Chronicle*, p. 28; Z.A. B r z o z o w s k a, *The Image...*, p. 51–54.

[27] There are also some atypical artifacts. Cf. И. Й о р д а н о в, *Корпус на средновековните български печати*, София 2016, p. 269–271.

[28] И. Й о р д а н о в, *Корпус на печатите на Средновековна България*, София 2001, p. 58–59; В. Г ю з е л е в, *Значението на брака...*, p. 27; И. Б о ж и л о в, В. Г ю з е л е в,

Fig. 1. Seal depicting Peter and Maria Lekapene with the inscription:
Πέτρος βασι[λεὺς] εὐσ[εβ]ής, Bulgaria, 940–945. Drawing (reconstruction):
E. Myślińska-Brzozowska

II. *Peter and Maria – Autocrators/Augusti and Basileis of the Bulgarians*
(940s) – the depiction of the tsar and his spouse on the reverse
does not differ fundamentally from the one described above.
Because of the poor state of preservation of all specimens of this
type, the accompanying writing can be reconstructed in several
ways: Πέτρος καὶ Μαρίας ἐν Χριστῷ αὐτοκράτορες Βουλγάρων (*Peter*

История на средновековна България. VII–XIV в., София 2006, p. 275; И. Й о р д а н о в,
Корпус на средновековните български печати..., p. 86–89. All seal inscriptions in this
book quoted as reconstructed by Ivan Jordanov.

and Maria in Christ Autocrators of the Bulgarians); Πέτρος καὶ Μαρίας ἐν Χριστῷ αὔγουστοι βασιλεῖς (*Peter and Maria in Christ Augusti and Basileis*); Πέτρος καὶ Μαρίας ἐν Χριστῷ αὐτοκράτορες βασιλεῖς Βουλγάρων (*Peter and Maria in Christ Autocrators and Basileis of the Bulgarians*). According to numerous scholars, the second interpretation should be considered correct; on the other hand, in his most recent publications, Ivan Jordanov is inclined to accept the third reading[29].

III. *Peter and Maria, pious Basileis/Emperors* (940–50s) – the most common type. On the reverse of the *sigillum*, we find a depiction of Peter and Maria, portrayed similarly as in the previous types. The couple is holding a cross – the tsar from the left, the tsaritsa from the right side. However, contrary to the seal images of type I and II, the hands of the monarchs are placed at different heights. In the majority of cases, the tsar's hand is higher; however, there are also examples in which it is Maria who is holding the cross above her husband's hand. The inscription only mentions Peter, calling him a pious emperor: Πέτρος βασι[λεὺς] εὐσ[εβ]ής[30].

---

[29] J. S h e p a r d, *A marriage...*, p. 141–143; Г. А т а н а с о в, *Инсигниите на средновековните български владетели. Корони, скиптри, сфери, оръжия, костюми, накити*, Плевен 1999, p. 98–99; И. Й о р д а н о в, *Корпус на печатите...*, p. 59–60; В. Г ю з е л е в, *Значението на брака...*, p. 27; И. Б о ж и л о в, В. Г ю з е л е в, *История...*, p. 275–276; Т. Т о д о р о в, *България...*, p. 156–159; i d e m, *Владетелският статут...*, p. 99–101; С. Г е о р г и е в а, *Жената в българското средновековие*, Пловдив 2011, p. 313–315; M.J. L e s z k a, K. M a r i n o w, *Carstwo bułgarskie. Polityka – społeczeństwo – gospodarka – kultura. 866–971*, Warszawa 2015, p. 159–160; И. Й о р д а н о в, *Корпус на средновековните български печати...*, p. 90–95.

[30] J. S h e p a r d, *A marriage...*, p. 143–146; И. Й о р д а н о в, *Корпус на печатите...*, p. 60–63; В. Г ю з е л е в, *Значението на брака...*, p. 27; И. Й о р д а н о в, *Корпус на средновековните български печати...*, p. 95–110.

II

Zofia A. Brzozowska
Mirosław J. Leszka

Origins and Early Years

The Lekapenoi family, from which Maria was descended, owed its position to Romanos, the grandfather of the future tsaritsa. Romanos was born around 870 in Lekape, situated between Melitene and Samosata. He was the son of Theophylaktos, nicknamed Abastaktos (Unbearable)[1], an Armenian peasant who enlisted in the Palace Guard soon after Romanos's birth (around 871)[2]. Our knowledge of Romanos's life before his rise to power is rather limited. We know that his career in the imperial fleet (ship commander – *protokarabos*– was his first important position[3]) started during the reign of emperor Leo VI. In 911, he served as *strategos* of Samos, and some time later he was appointed fleet commander (*droungarios tou*

---

[1] *Prosopographie der mittelbyzantinischen Zeit. Zweite Abteilung (867–1025)* [cetera: *PMB*], vol. VI, ed. F. Winkelmann et al., Berlin–Boston 2013, p. 561–562, s.v. *Theophylaktos Abastaktos (#28180)*.

[2] The basic information on Romanos's origin is to be found in: S. Runciman, *The Emperor Romanus Lecapenus and His Reign. A Study of Tenth-Century Byzantium*, Cambridge 1969, p. 63; A. Kazhdan, *Romanos I Lekapenos*, [in:] *Oxford Dictionary of Byzantium*, vol. III, Oxford 1991, p. 1806; *PMB*, vol. V, ed. F. Winkelmann et al., Berlin–Boston 2013, p. 578–579, s.v. *Romanos I. Lekapenos (#26833)*.

[3] Liudprand of Cremona, *Retribution*, III, 25. Cf. J.H. Pryor, E.M. Jeffreys, *The age of dromon. The Byzantine Navy ca 500–1204*, Leiden–Boston 2006, p. 271.

ploimou)[4]. His participation in the failed expedition against Bulgaria was, paradoxically, a turning point in his career. On August 20th, 917, the Byzantine forces suffered defeat in the battle of Anchialos[5]. During the campaign, Romanos was in charge of the fleet, while the ground forces were commanded by Leo Phokas, Domestic of the Schools. The task of the fleet was to convey the Pechenegs across the river Danube; ultimately, however, the Pechenegs never took part in the campaign against Bulgaria. It is believed that one of the reasons behind their non-involvement in the fighting was the conflict between Romanos I Lekapenos and John Bogas[6]. A number of other charges were brought against Romanos in the context of this campaign. In view of Leo's defeat in the battle under discussion, Romanos, as we are informed by sources unfavorable to him, decided to sail for Constantinople, leaving behind the Byzantine survivors[7]. Regardless of his actual conduct during the campaign, empress Zoe Karbonopsina and those with whom she exercised power on behalf of emperor Constantine VII took a negative view of it. Dissatisfied with his service, she intended to punish him. It was only thanks to the support from Constantine Gongylios and *magistros* Stephen that Romanos evaded being blinded[8]. If this was indeed the way the events unfolded, then the

---

[4] Liudprand of Cremona, *Retribution*, III, 26. Cf. S. Runciman, *The Emperor Romanus...*, p. 63; *PMB*, vol. V, p. 579. Runciman believed that this took place during the reign of Alexander.

[5] On the battle of Anchialos see: M.J. Leszka, *Symeon I Wielki a Bizancjum. Z dziejów stosunków bułgarsko-bizantyńskich w latach 893–927*, Łódź p. 177–181 (the work also contains a bibliography on the battle).

[6] Continuator of Theophanes, p. 389–390; Leo Grammatikos, p. 295–296; Continuator of George the Monk, p. 882; John Skylitzes, p. 204; John Zonaras, p. 464–465; Continuator of George the Monk (Slavic), p. 547–548; Symeon Logothete, 135, 21. On other reasons why the Pechenegs decided to collaborate with the empire cf.: M.J. Leszka, *Symeon I Wielki...*, p. 171–173; A. Paroń, *Pieczyngowie. Koczownicy w krajobrazie politycznym i kulturowym średniowiecznej Europy*, Wrocław 2015, p. 306–308. John Bogas was *strategos* of Cherson. He was entrusted with the task of securing the Pechenegs' alliance against the Bulgarians.

[7] Continuator of Theophanes, p. 388; Leo the Deacon, VII, 7 (it is claimed here that Romanos went to Constantinople to seize power); John Skylitzes, p. 203.

[8] Continuator of Theophanes, p. 390; John Skylitzes, p. 205. Cf. S. Runciman, *The Emperor Romanus...*, p. 56.

empress made a mistake that soon cost her the position of regent and turned out to jeopardize the future career of her son, Constantine VII.

The regency found no fault with Leo Phokas, as evidenced by the fact that he was placed in command of the forces which were to defend Constantinople against Symeon's troops[9]. Rumors circulated around the Byzantine capital that the empress was even going to marry Leo, who had lost his second wife (most certainly the sister of *parakoimomenos* Constantine, an influential member of the regency)[10] to death some time earlier. It is difficult to say whether there was any truth to these rumors; what is certain is the fact that the plan, assuming it ever existed, was never put into effect.

Be that as it may, Leo Phokas and Romanos began to vie with one another for the imperial throne. Constantine VII – manipulated by his guardian, Theodore, and without consulting his mother – decided to turn to Romanos for protection against Leo Phokas. This significantly helped Romanos, who became the protector of the legal emperor. Upon learning about the steps taken by her son and his guardian, Zoe demanded that Romanos disband the forces that remained under his command. Romanos had no intention of complying with this order, however, and the empress found herself in a most strenuous situation. Patriarch Nicholas Mystikos, taking advantage of her difficulties, removed her from the position of the head of the regency council. He also wanted to expel her from the palace, which she managed to neutralize by appealing to her son and begging him to let her stay. The emperor acceded to her pleas[11]. Although the patriarch hardly wished to transfer the power to Romanos, he did not know how

---

[9] Leo Phokas saved himself from the massacre and fled to Mesembria, from where he sailed to Constantinople. Cf. K. M a r i n o w, *Zadania floty cesarskiej w wojnach bizantyńsko-bułgarskich (VII–XI w.)*, [in:] *Byzantina Europaea. Księga jubileuszowa ofiarowana Profesorowi Waldemarowi Ceranowi*, eds. M. K o k o s z k o, M.J. L e s z k a, Łódź 2007, p. 389.

[10] E.g.: C o n t i n u a t o r of T h e o p h a n e s, p. 390; J o h n S k y l i t z e s, p. 205, 233. Cf. R.J.H. J e n k i n s, *A "Consolatio" of the Patriarch Nicholas Mysticus*, "Byzantion" 35, 1965, p. 164–165; L. G a r l a n d, *Byzantine Empresses. Women and Power in Byzantium AD 527–1204*, London–New York 1999, p. 122.

[11] L e o G r a m m a t i k o s, p. 298; C o n t i n u a t o r of T h e o p h a n e s, p. 392; J o h n S k y l i t z e s, p. 207. Nicholas sent a man called John Toubakes to remove Zoe

Fig. 2. Solidus with an image of empress Zoe Karbonopsina and her son
Constantine VII Porphyrogennetos, Constantinople, 914–919
Drawing (reconstruction): E. Myślińska-Brzozowska

to stop him. Theodore, Constantine's guardian, stepped in again, suggesting to Romanos that he sail his fleet to the harbor at the Boukoleon
palace. Following this advice, Romanos captured the palace without any
difficulty, taking control of the whole state – initially on behalf of the
minor emperor[12]. These events took place in March 919. Shortly afterwards, in May 919, Constantine VII married Helena, Romanos's daughter;

---

from the palace. The empress reportedly begged her son to prevent this; Constantine
took his mother's side and, with tears in his eyes, he asked for permission to let her stay.

[12] Continuator of Theophanes, p. 390–392; John Skylitzes, p. 207.
For a detailed analysis of the events leading to the fall of Zoe's regency and Romanos's
rise to power cf.: S. R u n c i m a n, *The Emperor Romanus...*, p. 58–62.

thanks to this marriage, Romanos became *basileopator*[13]. In September 920, the imperial father-in-law was proclaimed *caesar*, and on December 17th, 920 – Constantine VII's co-emperor. It was still before the conferment of these titles that he had removed Phokas, whom he ordered blinded, from his way[14].

Romanos's rise to political prominence was a sentence to Zoe. Although she was allowed to stay in the palace for some time, she was deprived of any impact on the political situation. As soon as Romanos became convinced that he was no longer in danger of losing his position of power, he proceeded to dispose of his son-in-law's mother. Accused of plotting against his life, she was removed from the palace and placed in the Monastery of St. Euthymios[15]. In addition, Romanos cast away all those who were connected with the empress and her son. Consequently, Constantine found himself at his mercy.

Concerned about consolidating his power and about passing it to his sons in the future, in May 921[16] Romanos decided to proclaim the

---

[13] On the position of *basileopator* see: P. K a r l i n - H a y t e r, A. L e r o y-Mo l i n g h e n, *Basileopator*, "Byzantion" 38, 1968, p. 278–281; S. T o u g h e r, *The Reign of Leo VI (886–912). Politics and People*, Leiden–New York–Köln 1997, p. 99–100. Doubts have been raised as to how the name of the office should be understood. Perhaps it should be spelled *basileiopator*, i.e. 'father of the palace' (A. S c h m i n c k, "*Frömmigkeit ziere das Work*". *Zur Datierung der 60 Bücher Leons VI*, "Subseciva Groningana" 3, 1989, p. 108–109) rather than 'father of the emperor.'

[14] Runciman dates the marriage of Helena and Constantine VII, as well as Romanos's proclamation as *caesar* and as co-emperor, to 919; so does L. G a r l a n d, *Byzantine Empresses...*, p. 123. On the arguments for dating these events to 920 see: V. G r u m e l, *Notes de chronologie byzantine*, "Echo d'Orient" 35, 1936, p. 333sqq. On the history of the conflict between Romanos Lekapenos and Leo Phokas: I. B u r i ć, *Porodica Foka*, "Zbornik Radova Vizantološkog Instituta" 17, 1976, p. 241–245.

[15] L e o G r a m m a t i k o s, p. 303; C o n t i n u a t o r o f T h e o p h a n e s, p. 397; J o h n S k y l i t z e s, p. 211. Zoe was removed from the palace in August 920, still before Romanos was proclaimed *caesar*.

[16] C o n t i n u a t o r o f T h e o p h a n e s, p. 398. Cf. S. R u n c i m a n, *The Emperor Romanus...*, p. 65–66; A.R. B e l l i n g e r, Ph. G r i e r s o n, *Catalogue of the Byzantine Coins in the Dumbarton Oaks Collection and in the Whittemore Collection*, vol. III, *Leo III to Nicephorus III. 717–1081*, Washington 1993, p. 528.

oldest of them (Christopher – Maria's father) co-emperor[17]. Owing to this decision, his daughter would later become a suitable candidate for the wife of the Bulgarian ruler.

The most important problem that Romanos I Lekapenos had to deal with in the first years of his reign was to put an end to the conflict with Bulgaria, inherited from his predecessors. Until May 927, his opponent on the Bulgarian side was Symeon. After the latter's death, the role fell to his son, Peter – the future husband of Romanos's granddaughter. We shall deal with this conflict in more detail in the next chapter.

* * *

We do not know when Maria Lekapene was born. Given that in 927 she was considered to be of suitable age to enter into marriage, as well as to be betrothed to Peter, her birth can be tentatively dated between 907 and 915[18]. She was the daughter of Christopher Lekapenos,

---

[17] Christopher had three half-brothers: Stephen, co-emperor from December 25th, 923 (*PMB*, vol. VI, p. 83–89, *s.v. Stephanos Lakapenos, #27251*); Constantine, co-emperor from December 25th, 923 (*PMB*, vol. III, ed. F. W i n k e l m a n n et al., Berlin–Boston 2013, p. 589–594); Theophylaktos, who in 933 became patriarch of Constantinople (*PMB*, vol. VI, p. 565–572, *s.v. Theophylaktos, #28192*; G. M i n c z e w, *Remarks on the Letter of the Patriarch Theophylact to Tsar Peter in the Context of Certain Byzantine and Slavic Anti-heretic Texts*, "Studia Ceranea. Journal of the Waldemar Ceran Research Centre for the History and Culture of the Mediterranean Area and South-East Europe" 3, 2013, p. 115) and four sisters: Helena, married to Constantine VII (*PMB*, vol. II, ed. F. W i n k e l m a n n et al., Berlin–Boston 2013, p. 693–696, s.v. Helene Lakapene, #22574); Agatha, who became the wife of Romanos Argyros (*PMB*, vol. I, ed. F. W i n k e l m a n n et al., Berlin–Boston 2013, p. 106–107, *s.v. Agathe Lakapene, #20168*) and two others, whose names we do not know. Romanos Lekapenos also had a son out of wedlock (from his relationship with an unnamed woman of Slavic or Bulgarian origin), called Basil, who played a significant role in the history of the empire – especially in the first decade of Basil II's reign (*PMB*, vol. I, p. 588–598, *s.v. Basileios Lakapenos, #20925*; И. Й о р д а н о в, *Печати на Василий Лакапин от България*, [in:] *Средновековният българин и "другите". Сборник в чест на 60-годишнината на проф. дин Петър Ангелов*, eds. А. Н и к о л о в, Г.Н. Н и к о л о в, София 2013, p. 159–166).

[18] Jonathan Shepard suspects that Maria was about twelve years old in 927 (J. S h e p a r d, *A marriage too far? Maria Lekapena and Peter of Bulgaria*, [in:] *The Empress Theophano. Byzantium and the West at the turn of the first millennium*, ed.

Fig. 3. Solidus with an image of emperor Romanos I Lekapenos and his
son Christopher, Constantinople, 921–931. Drawing (reconstruction):
E. Myślińska-Brzozowska

the eldest son of emperor Romanos I and his wife Theodora (as mentioned above, Christopher was elevated to the position of co-emperor

A. D a v i d s, Cambridge 1995, p. 136), while Vasil Gjuzelev dates her birth to 911, which
would make her sixteen years old at the time of her marriage to Peter (В. Г ю з е л е в,
*Значението на брака на цар Петър (927–969) с ромейката Мария-Ирина Лакапина
(911–962)*, [in:] *Културните текстове на миналото – носители, символи, идеи*, vol. I,
*Текстовете на историята, история на текстовете. Материали от Юбилейната
международна конференция в чест на 60-годишнината на проф. д.и.н. Казимир
Попконстантинов, Велико Търново, 29–31 октомври 2003 г.*, София 2005, p. 28).
Cf. also M.J. L e s z k a, K. M a r i n o w, *Carstwo bułgarskie. Polityka – społeczeństwo
– gospodarka – kultura. 866–971*, Warszawa 2015, p. 156, where our protagonist's birth
is dated to ca. 912.

and third co-ruler of the empire in May 921[19]). As a descendant of the
Lekapenoi family, Maria had Armenian blood in her veins. However,
curiously enough, her background also includes a Slavic ancestor: according to Constantine VII Porphyrogennetos, her mother Sophia was the
daughter of Niketas Magistros, a Slav from the Peloponnesos[20]. The latter
is also mentioned in the *Continuation of George the Monk*, the *Chronicle
of Symeon Logothete*, the *Chronicle of Pseudo-Symeon Magistros* and the
Continuation of Theophanes[21].

The future Bulgarian tsaritsa was most likely the eldest child of
Christopher and Sophia, who married prior to Romanos I Lekapenos's
ascension to power[22]. Since Maria's father was crowned in 921, and her
mother was only elevated to the rank of *augusta* in February 922 (after
empress Theodora's death)[23], our heroine did not enjoy the prestigious
title of *porphyrogennete*, i.e. imperial daughter 'born in the purple'[24].

Maria had two younger brothers, neither of whom was to play any
significant political role: Romanos, who died in childhood, and Michael.
The latter had two daughters – Sophia and Helena (who married
an Armenian, Gregory Taronites)[25]. Particularly notable among

---

[19] Continuator of Theophanes, VI, 1, p. 398. Cf. S. Runciman, *The
Emperor Romanus...*, p. 65–66; A.R. Bellinger, Ph. Grierson, *Catalogue...*, p. 528.
    [20] Constantine VII Porphyrogennetos, *On the Themes*, p. 91.
Cf. В. Гюзелев, *Значението на брака...*, p. 28; А. Николов, *Политическа мисъл
в ранносредновековна България (средата на IX–края на X в.)*, София 2006, p. 273–274;
PMB V, p. 20–22, *s.v. Niketas (#25740)*.
    [21] Continuator of George the Monk, p. 905, 908; Symeon
Logothete, 135, 30, p. 309; 136, 16, 48, 54, p. 315, 327, 330; Pseudo-
-Symeon Magistros, 36, p. 742; Continuator of Theophanes, VI,
22, 25, p. 413, 417.
    [22] S. Runciman, *The Emperor Romanus...*, p. 64.
    [23] Continuator of George the Monk, p. 894; Pseudo-
-Symeon Magistros, 24, p. 733; Continuator of Theophanes,
VI, 9, s. 402; John Zonaras, XVI, 18, p. 471. Cf. S. Runciman, *The Emperor
Romanus...*, p. 67; J. Shepard, *A marriage...*, p. 136; В. Гюзелев, *Значението на
брака...*, p. 28; А. Николов, *Политическа мисъл...*, p. 274.
    [24] S. Georgieva, *The Byzantine Princesses in Bulgaria*, "Byzantinobulgarica"
9, 1995, p. 167.
    [25] S. Runciman, *The Emperor Romanus...*, p. 78, 234; J. Shepard, *A marriage...*,
p. 136.

Maria's influential relatives was her aunt, Helena Lekapene, who in 919 married Constantine VII Porphyrogennetos, remaining by his side until 959. As mentioned before, two of Maria's uncles, Stephen and Constantine, also donned the imperial purple when they were elevated by Romanos I to the position of co-rulers in 923, whereas the third uncle, Theophylaktos, became the patriarch of Constantinople (933–956)[26].

There are several key questions to be asked regarding Maria's origins, position and connections: How many years did she spend in the palace in Constantinople? What kind of education did she receive there? To what extent did she have an opportunity to familiarize herself with court ceremonies and the Byzantine ideology of power? Consequently, how justified is it to view her as consciously transplanting certain elements of Byzantine political culture onto Bulgarian soil?

Constantine VII Porphyrogennetos had told Maria's grandfather that he, born and raised outside of the imperial court, lacked a sufficient understanding of its rules and thus also the basic competencies required for being a ruler[27]. The same judgement could also be applied to Christopher Lekapenos, who crossed the threshold of the palace in Constantinople as a fully mature man, by then both a husband and a father[28]. This leads to the next question: when did Maria herself enter the palace? The latest possible date seems to be February 922, when our protagonist's mother, Sophia, was elevated to the rank of *augusta*. The ceremonial court duties associated with this promotion[29] necessitated permanent residence in the capital city and the palace. The Bulgarian tsaritsa-to-be, then, spent at least

---

[26] Cf. fn. 17.

[27] Constantine VII Porphyrogennetos, *On the Governance of the Empire*, 13, p. 72. Cf. S. G e o r g i e v a, *The Byzantine Princesses...*, p. 167; T. Т о д о р о в, *Константин Багренородни и династичният брак между владетелските домове на Преслав и Константинопол от 927 г.*, "Преславска книжовна школа" 7, 2003, p. 393.

[28] S. R u n c i m a n, *The Emperor Romanus...*, p. 64; A.R. B e l l i n g e r, Ph. G r i e r s o n, *Catalogue...*, p. 528.

[29] J. H e r r i n, *Theophano. Considerations on the Education of a Byzantine Princess*, [in:] *The Empress Theophano. Byzantium and the West at the turn of the first millennium*, ed. A. D a v i d s, Cambridge 1995, p. 72–73 [= J. H e r r i n, *Unrivalled Influence. Women and Empire in Byzantium*, Princeton 2013, p. 245].

five years at the imperial court. It is worth adding that she was a teenager
at the time – the period in life in which one's personality, habits and
preferences are shaped most deeply.

It is difficult to determine how thorough Maria's education was.
Analyzing several anonymous commemorative poetic texts written after
Christopher's death, Jonathan Shepard concluded that he valued knowledge and considered it important to ensure that his children obtain an
education worthy of their standing. Thus, Maria's curriculum during her
stay at the palace may have been extensive, covering both religious and
secular matters (fundamentals of law and general familiarity with the
imperial Byzantine court ceremonial, as well as rules of diplomacy)[30].
Judith Herrin goes even further, assuming that Maria's relatives hoped that
her marriage would render her a *sui generis* representative of Byzantine
interests at the Bulgarian court[31]. Thus, she may have been actively prepared for this role. The British scholar attempts to compensate for the lack
of source material concerning Maria by comparing her biography with
that of another Byzantine woman married to a foreign ruler – Theophano,
wife of emperor Otto II. According to Herrin, Theophano's later political
activity attests to the education she received before her marriage, one
which was intended to prepare her comprehensively for the role of an
imperial wife and mother. No less interesting (from the perspective of our
subject) seems to be the case of Agatha, one of the daughters of Helena
Lekapene and Constantine VII Porphyrogennetos: she was sufficiently
competent and knowledgeable in matters of state to assist her father
in chancery work, helping him not only as a secretary, but also as a trusted
adviser and confidant[32].

Even if Maria Lekapene was not as profoundly erudite as her cousin,
her stay at the imperial court in Constantinople must have resulted in her
gaining experience that would help her adapt to the role of the Bulgarian

---

[30] J. S h e p a r d, *A marriage...*, p. 137–138. Cf. M.J. L e s z k a, K. M a r i n o w, *Carstwo
bulgarskie...*, p. 156.

[31] *She represents the out-going Byzantine princess, who had to perform an ambassadorial
role in the country of her new husband* (J. H e r r i n, *The Many Empresses of the Byzantine
Court (and All Their Attendants)*, [in:] e a d e m, *Unrivalled Influence...*, p. 229).

[32] E a d e m, *Theophano...*, p. 248–253.

tsaritsa. Spending time in the chambers of the Great Palace, Christopher's daughter likely had numerous opportunities to familiarize herself with both the official court ceremonial and with the unwritten rules observed by those in the highest echelons of power. Our protagonist had no dearth of positive examples to follow: we must not forget that her aunt Helena, her grandmother Theodora as well as her mother Sophia all wore the imperial purple. Spending time in their company and observing them, Maria had favorable circumstances to develop an understanding of what it meant to be a Byzantine empress.

III

Zofia A. Brzozowska
Mirosław J. Leszka

The Year 927

1. Byzantine-Bulgarian Relations during the Reign of Symeon the Great (893–927)

In order to understand Peter's situation regarding his relations with the empire after his father's death, it seems advisable to begin with a general overview of his father's policy towards Byzantium.

Following Bulgaria's conversion to Christianity in 866, the Bulgarian-
-Byzantine relations, which had previously been far from harmonious, took on a peaceful, religion-based character. Nevertheless, this state of affairs did not last longer than until the beginning of the 890s: the mutual relations deteriorated under Vladimir-Rasate (889–893) and escalated into an open confrontation under Symeon I (893–927), Peter's father. Having assumed power in 893, Symeon found himself in conflict with emperor Leo VI because of changes in the regulations concerning Bulgarian trade in the empire; the animosity would ultimately result in the outbreak of war between the two countries[1]. Thus, Symeon had to elaborate a way

---

[1] On the causes and course of the war see: Г. Ц а н к о в а-П е т к о в а, *Първата война между България и Византия при цар Симеон и възстановяването на българската търговия с Цариград*, "Известия на Института за История" 20, 1968, p. 167–200; T. W a s i l e w s k i, *Bizancjum i Słowianie w IX w. Studia z dziejów stosunków*

of handling the Byzantines in the early days of his reign. It was no longer possible to pursue the strategy chosen by Boris-Michael after his conversion to Christianity in 866, aimed at preserving peace with Byzantium.

The events of 893–896 show that during the initial stage of his rule, Symeon would deal with the empire so as to defend the position to which the Bulgarian state (in terms of both territory and prestige) and its ruler had been elevated during his father's reign. The policy he pursued was informed by the belief that the empire had no right to use the common religion as a justification for its claims to sovereignty over Bulgaria. The title of ἐκ Θεοῦ ἄρχων Βουλγαρίας, for which Symeon finally settled, can be regarded as an indication of the compromise he decided to accept[2]. In the years that followed, the ruler, taking advantage of the good relations with the empire, focused on internal affairs. The development of the city of Preslav – the state's new political center – was among his main endeavors, as was his promotion of literature. The latter shows that his efforts were designed to build a sense of national pride and to provide

politycznych i kulturalnych, Warszawa 1972, p. 221–223; И. Б о ж и л о в, *Цар Симеон Велики (893–927): Златният век на Средновековна България*, София 1983, p. 87–89; i d e m, *Византийският свят*, София 2008, p. 379–381; i d e m, В. Г ю з е л е в, *История на средновековна България. VII–XIV в.*, София 2006, p. 246–247, 266–267; N. O i k o n o m i d e s, *Le kommerkion d'Abydos, Thessalonique et la commerce bulgare au IXe siècle*, [in:] *Hommes et richesses dans l'Empire byzantin*, vol. II, VIIe–XVe siècle, eds. V. K r a v a r i, J. L e f o r t, C. M o r r i s s o n, Paris 1991, p. 241–248; J. K a r a y a n n o p o u l o s, *Les causes des luttes entre Syméon et Byzance: un réexamin*, [in:] *Сборник в чест на акад. Димитър Ангелов*, ed. В. В е л к о в, София 1994, p. 52–64; В. В а ч к о в а, *Симеон Велики. Пътят към короната на Запада*, София 2005, p. 53–54; И. Б и л я р с к и, *Фискална система на средновековна България*, Пловдив 2010, p. 139–140; M.J. L e s z k a, *The Monk versus the Philosopher. From the History of the Bulgarian-Byzantine War 894–896*, "Studia Ceranea. Journal of the Waldemar Ceran Research Centre for the History and Culture of the Mediterranean Area and South-East Europe" 1, 2011, p. 55–70; i d e m, *Symeon I Wielki a Bizancjum. Z dziejów stosunków bułgarsko-bizantyńskich w latach 893–927*, Łódź 2013, p. 67–98.

[2] И. Й о р д а н о в, *Корпус на средновековните български печати*, София 2016, p. 60–68. The author indicates that, in his seal iconography, Symeon followed the path paved by his father (p. 68). Cf. also T. С л а в о в а, *Владетел и администрация в ранносредновековна България. Филологически аспекти*, София 2010, p. 236–239.

an adequate ideological framework for a country functioning in the Christian ecumene[3].

Boris-Michael's death in 907, as some scholars believe, changed Symeon's situation[4]. He regained the complete freedom to rule his country the way he wanted and was given a chance to take his relations with the empire to a new level, as he ostensibly became convinced of his right to claim the title of *basileus*. It was apparently in mid-913, as Bulgaria's relations with Byzantium under emperor Alexander deteriorated, that he decided to put this idea into action[5] and proclaimed himself *basileus*, abandoning the previous title of ἐκ Θεοῦ ἄρχων – the one approved by Byzantium[6]. In all likelihood, he realized that the Byzantines would not be willing to accept the step he took and that it would inevitably require a demonstration of military power, or even war. Thus, he attempted to take advantage of the opportunity to kill two birds with one stone. First, he utilized the fact that Alexander, by refusing to pay him tribute, had broken the terms of the existing peace treaty. The breach of the agreement

---

[3] The search for the past – necessarily pagan – coupled with the efforts to integrate it into the new Christian historical consciousness is reflected both in the small number of extant original works and in the translations. It is no coincidence that the *List of Bulgarian Khans*, containing a mythical vision of the origins of the Bulgarian state, was referred to during Symeon's reign. See e.g.: А. Н и к о л о в, *Политическа мисъл в ранносредновековна България (средата на IX–края на X в.)*, София 2006, p. 151–230; *История на българската средновековна литература*, ed. А. М и л т е н о в а, София 2008, p. 37sqq; М. К а й м а к а м о в а, *Власт и история в средновековна България VIII–XIV в.*, София 2011, p. 115–156. These works contain references to various further studies on the issue.

[4] М. В о й н о в, *Промяната в българо-византийските отношения при цар Симеон*, "Известия на Института на История" 18, 1967, p. 168sqq.

[5] For more on Alexander's policy towards Bulgaria see: Н. О в ч а р о в, *Една хипотеза за българо-византийските отношения през 912–913 г.*, "Археология" 31.3, 1989, p. 50–57; Р. Р а ш е в, *Княз Симеон и император Александър*, [in:] i d e m, *Цар Симеон Велики. Щрихи към личността и делото му*, София 2007, p. 32–41; M.J. L e s z k a, *Symeon...*, p. 118–124.

[6] А. Н и к о л о в, *Политическа...*, p. 129–139; i d e m, *"Великият между царете"*. *Изграждане и утвърждаване на българската царска институция през управлението на Симеон I*, [in:] *Българският златен век. Сборник в чест на цар Симеон Велики (893–927)*, eds. В. Г ю з е л е в, И.Г. И л и е в, К. Н е н о в, Пловдив 2015, p. 165sqq; M.J. L e s z k a, *Symeon...*, p. 129–133.

by the emperor made it possible for Symeon to shift the blame for the
outbreak of the war onto Byzantium. Second, he integrated the issue
of the recognition of his new title into the broader demand concerning
the above-mentioned tribute. In this way, he was able to avoid giving some
of the members of the Bulgarian elite a reason to accuse him of taking
up arms only in order to satisfy his personal ambitions. The Bulgarians'
march on Constantinople in the summer of 913, which turned out to
be an effective manifestation of power, was Symeon's success[7]. Not only
did the Byzantines resume paying the tribute, but they also recognized
Symeon's imperial proclamation, although the latter was illegal from
Constantinople's perspective[8]. Having accomplished all his plans, Symeon
could feel satisfied, the more so because he had achieved his goals without
shedding a drop of Christian blood. It may have been directly after August
913 that he began using the title εἰρηνοποιός βασιλεύς (peace-making *basileus*) on his seals[9], an appellation that is still the subject of an ongoing
debate. According to Ivan Duychev, the title manifested Symeon's political program, an important element of which was to establish peace both
with the empire and within his own country[10]. Ivan Bozhilov maintains
that the phrase should be understood as pointing to Symeon's plan to
establish a new order (τάξις). The latter, referred to by the scholar as the
Pax Symeonica, was in his opinion conceived as an attempt to replace or
at least balance the existing *Pax Byzantina* in the Christian ecumene. In this
plan, Symeon envisaged himself as the same kind of *pater familias* among

---

[7] On the Bulgarian expedition against Constantinople see: Д. А н г е л о в,
С. К а ш е в, Б. Ч о л п а н о в, *Българска военна история от античността до втората четвърт на X в.*, София 1983, p. 266–268; M.J. L e s z k a, *Symeon...*, p. 134–137.

[8] On the conditions of the agreement in question see: А. Н и к о л о в, *Политическа...*, p. 130–139; M.J. L e s z k a, *Symeon...*, p. 138–158.

[9] И. Й о р д а н о в, *Корпус на средновековните български печати...*, p. 68–73.
The inscription is an acclamation. The same phrase can be found in the *Book of
Ceremonies* by Constantine VII Porphyrogennetos (I, 77, p. 373). I. B o ž i l o v (*L'ideologie
politique du tsar Syméon: pax Symeonica*, "Byzantinobulgarica" 8, 1986, p. 82–83) provides
other examples of the term being used in Byzantine texts.

[10] I. D u j č e v, *Relations entre Slaves méridionaux et Byzance aux Xe–XIIe siècles*,
[in:] i d e m, *Medioevo bizantino-slavo*, vol. III, *Altrisaggi di storia, politica eletteraria*,
Roma 1971, p. 188.

the family of rulers and nations that the Byzantine emperor had been; furthermore, the Bulgarians were to assume the role of the new chosen people, who – just like the Byzantines – enjoyed God's protection and were capable of defending Christianity as well as preserving the cultural heritage of Rome and Greece[11].

Bozhilov, however, appears to be taking his idea of the *Pax Symeonica* too far: one is inclined to doubt the validity of ascribing such a deep meaning to a formula originating in imperial Byzantine acclamations, the more so because the Bulgarian scholar associates it more with Charlemagne than with Byzantium[12]. The interpretation offered by Duychev, and shared by other scholars such as Jonathan Shepard[13] and Rasho Rashev[14], is considerably more compelling. By using the term εἰρηνοποιός to refer to himself in 913, Symeon sent a clear message: he wished to be perceived as a ruler who established peace with Byzantium. It should be borne in mind that his contemporaries considered peace to be a supreme value – as Nicholas

---

[11] И. Б о ж и л о в, *Цар...*, p. 114–115; i d e m, *L'ideologie...*, p. 81–85. Symeon must have carried out the program in several stages. First, the ruler had to obtain Byzantium's consent to use the imperial title. His next steps involved marrying his daughter off to Constantine VII, being granted the status of his guardian (*basileopator*) and, consequently, acquiring influence over the empire's government. Our criticism of the view that Symeon strove to obtain the title of *basileopator* can be found in: M.J. L e s z k a, *Symeon...*, p. 144–146. See also: Н. К ъ н е в, *Стремял ли се е българският владетел Симеон I Велики (893–927 г.) към ранг на визатийски василеопатор?*, [in:] i d e m, *Византинобългарски студии*, Велико Търново 2013, p. 111–119.

[12] И. Б о ж и л о в, *Цар...*, p. 113–114; i d e m, *L'ideologie...*, p. 83–84. Bozhilov refers to the title used by Charlemagne, which included the adjective *pacificus* ('the one who brings peace'). The Bulgarian scholar claims that the title was used with reference to the Frankish Empire, which the ruler created by conquering the lands of Bavaria, Saxony and the kingdom of the Lombards, as well as by subjugating the Slavs, the Avars and the Muslims in Spain. Even if this was the case, the fact remains that Bozhilov is silent about the route by which this element of Carolingian political ideology would have reached the court in Preslav and become an inspiration to Symeon. On Carolingian political ideology see: W. F a l k o w s k i, *Wielki król. Ideologiczne podstawy władzy Karola Wielkiego*, Warszawa 2011.

[13] J. S h e p a r d, *Symeon of Bulgaria-Peacemaker*, [in:] i d e m, *Emergent elites and Byzantium in the Balkans and East-Central Europe*, Farnham–Burlington 2011, p. 52–53.

[14] Р. Р а ш е в, *"Втората война" на Симеон срещу Византия (913–927) като литературен и политически факт*, [in:] i d e m, *Цар Симеон...*, p. 94.

Mystikos put it, *it brought with it nothing but good and was pleasing to God*[15]. Symeon was perfectly aware of this, which led him to use the motive in his propaganda.

In 913, it seems, Symeon hoped to build a lasting peace with Byzantium; however, it was not long before he realized that his plans were difficult to carry out. The changes in the composition of the regency council, to be presided over by widowed empress Zoe Karbonopsina, forced him to search for new ways of securing stable, peaceful relations with Byzantium (the council ruled the empire on behalf of Constantine VII, and the changes in question were introduced at the beginning of 914). It may have been at that time that Symeon, or one of his advisers, came up with the idea of a marriage between the members of the ruling dynasties of Bulgaria and Byzantium[16]. The Byzantines did not accept the offer; nor, it seems, did they confirm the terms of the 913 agreement (although they probably did not terminate it either)[17]. Be that as it may, Symeon found himself confronted with the necessity of reorienting his plans. It appears that, until 917, he still believed that maintaining peace was possible. However, the aggressive policies of Byzantium, which resulted in the outbreak of the war[18], finally made him change his attitude towards the empire and redefine the parameters of Bulgaria's participation in the Christian community.

---

[15] N i c h o l a s   M y s t i k o s, 16, p. 108, 110; 17, p. 110; 23, p. 160. The way in which the issue of peace was treated in Byzantium has been covered by: С.Н. М а л а х о в, *Концепция мира в политической идеологии Византии первой половины X в.: Николай Мистик и Феодор Дафнопат*, "Античная Древность и Средние Века" 27, 1995, p. 19–31; J. H a l d o n, *Warfare, State and Society in the Byzantine World*, London 1999, p. 13–33; J. C h r y s o s t o m i d e s, *Byzantine Concepts of War and Peace*, [in:] *War, Peace and World Orders in European History*, eds. A.V. H a r t m a n n, B. H e u s e r, London–New York 2001, p. 91–101; P.M. S t r ä s s l e, *Krieg und Frieden in Byzanz*, "Byzantion" 74, 2004, p. 110–129; K. M a r i n o w, *Peace in the House of Jacob. A Few Remarks on the Ideology of Two Biblical Themes in the Oration On the Treaty with the Bulgarians*, "Bulgaria Mediaevalis" 3, 2012, p. 85–93.

[16] M.J. L e s z k a, *Symeon...*, p. 142–144.

[17] *Ibidem*, p. 160–163.

[18] On the causes and course of the 917 war see: В.И. З л а т а р с к и, *История на българската държава през средните векове*, vol. I/2, *Първо българско Царство. От славянизацията на държавата до падането на Първото царство (852–1018)*, София 1927, p. 380–388; Д. А н г е л о в, С. К а ш е в, Б. Ч о л п а н о в, *Българска военна...*,

Thus, Symeon took up the gauntlet thrown by the Byzantines. For more than six years, he waged war against Byzantium – in Byzantine territory[19]. His first significant victories (especially the battle of Anchialos) left him convinced that he was in the position to demand that Byzantium recognize Bulgaria's unique status in the Christian world. A symbolic representation of the way in which his approach had changed was his assumption of a new title – *basileus Romaion* (βασιλέ[υς] Ρομέων), i.e. *Basileus* of the *Romaioi* – the same as the one borne by Byzantine rulers[20].

By proclaiming himself *Basileus* of the *Romaioi*, which must have taken place between the beginning of 921 and October–November 923, he indicated that he would neither recognize Romanos Lekapenos (whom he considered a usurper) as the leader of the Christian ecumene nor accept the role of his 'spiritual son.'

What was the meaning of Symeon's assuming the title of *basileus*? Scholars are divided on this issue. Some have claimed that Symeon strove to capture Constantinople and, by taking the place of Byzantine emperors, to build a form of universal Bulgarian-Byzantine statehood[21]. According to others, he wanted to be recognized as the ruler of the Byzantine West

---

p. 268–272; И. Б о ж и л о в, *Цар*..., p. 121–126; i d e m, В. Г ю з е л е в, *История*..., p. 255–256; J. S h e p a r d, *Symeon*..., p. 34–45; M.J. L e s z k a, *Symeon*..., p. 167–185.

[19] On this period in the Byzantine-Bulgarian relations see: Д. А н г е л о в, С. К а ш е в, Б. Ч о л п а н о в, *Българска военна*..., p. 272–277; И. Б о ж и л о в, *Цар*..., p. 126–1144; i d e m, В. Г ю з е л е в, *История*..., p. 256–260; M.J. L e s z k a, *Symeon*..., p. 187–217.

[20] И. Й о р д а н о в, *Печати на Симеон, василевс на Ромеите (?–927)*, "Bulgaria Mediaevalis" 2, 2011, p. 87–97; i d e m, *Корпус*..., p. 73–81. We have a significant number of this type of *sigilla* (27). They bear the following inscription: Συμεὼν ἐν Χρισ[τῷ] βασιλέ[υς] Ρομέων (*Symeon in Christ Basileus of the Romaioi*). Particularly noteworthy is the fact that they also contain the formula Νικοπυου λεονιπυο πολὰ τὰ ἔ[τη] (*to the Victory-maker the Lion-like many years*). Contrary to the phrase 'creator of peace,' probably introduced in 913, the new type of seals emphasizes Symeon's military victories – or, to put it more broadly, the military aspect of his imperial power. See also: К. Т о т е в, *За една група печати на цар Симеон*, [in:] *Общото и специфичното в Балканските народи до края на XIX в. Сборник в чест на 70-годишнината на проф. Василика Тъпкова-Заимова*, ed. Г. Б а к а л о в, София 1999, p. 107–112.

[21] F. D ö l g e r, *Bulgarisches Cartum und byzantinisches Kaisertum*, "Известия на Българския Археологически Институт" 9, 1935, p. 57; G. O s t r o g o r s k i, *Avtokrator i samodržac*, [in:] i d e m, *Vizantija i Sloveni*, Beograd 1970, p. 303–318.

Fig. 4. Seal depicting Symeon I the Great with the inscription: Συμεὼν
ἐν Χρισ[τῷ] βασιλέ[υς] Ρομέων, Bulgaria, ca. 921. Drawing (after R. Rašev):
E. Myślińska-Brzozowska

(the lands owned by Byzantium in Europe)[22] or even as the successor of
the Roman emperors who had ruled the western part of the Roman
Empire[23].

It does not seem likely that Symeon's goal was to capture Constantinople and to turn it into a capital city, to be used as a base from

[22] Р. Р а ш е в, *Втората...*, p. 93.

[23] В. В а ч к о в а, *Симеон...*, *passim*.

which his Slav-Greek state would be governed. Even in the period of his greatest victories, he did not undertake any serious operation that could lead to the seizure of Byzantium's capital (his plan to threaten it by forging an alliance with the Arabs went awry[24]). He considered Preslav the center of his state. He put a lot of effort into developing and beautifying the city; collecting relics was one of the ways in which he tried to raise it to the position of a religious center[25]. Would he have acted in this way if he had been blinded by the idea of taking over the Byzantine capital?

Or should Symeon's use of the title in question be interpreted in terms of an appeal to the tradition of an emperor independent of Constantinople, conventionally referred to as the Emperor of the West[26]? Unfortunately, it is impossible to give a positive answer to the question either – there is no evidence indicating that the Bulgarian ruler attempted to invoke the tradition of a western center of imperial power. The lack of such evidence has even been noted by Veselina Vachkova[27], who recently advanced the notion of Symeon as a ruler of the West (in the sense of the western part of the Roman Empire).

---

[24] К.С. К р ъ с т е в, *България, Византия и Арабският свят при царуването на Симеон I Велики*, "Bulgaria Mediaevalis" 3, 2012, p. 371–378; M.J. L e s z k a, *Symeon...*, p. 200–201.

[25] This aspect of Symeon's policy is stressed by: A. N i k o l o v, *Making a New Basileus. The Case of Symeon of Bulgaria (893–927). Reconsidered*, [in:] *Rome, Constantinople and Newly-Converted Europe. Archaeological and Historical Evidence*, vol. I, eds. M. S a l a m o n et al., Kraków–Leipzig–Rzeszów–Warszawa 2012, p. 101–108. Preslav became the center of the cult of Boris-Michael, Bulgaria's first Christian ruler, canonized soon after his death. His grave, it is believed, was located in the chapel of the so-called Royal Church (М. В а к л и н о в а, И. Щ е р е в а, *Княз Борис I и владетелската църква на Велики Преслав*, [in:] *Християнската култура в средновековна България. Материали от национална научна конференция, Шумен, 2–4 май 2007 г., по случай 1100 години от смъртта на св. Княз Борис-Михаил (ок. 835–907 г.)*, ed. П. Г е о р г и е в, Велико Търново 2008, p. 185–194).

[26] It is quite remarkable that the sphragistic material at our disposal offers no hint that Symeon used the title of *Basileus* of the *Romaioi* and the Bulgarians; still, it needs to be stated that this title did reflect the reality, as the Bulgarian ruler's subjects included both *Romaioi* and Bulgarians.

[27] В. В а ч к о в а, *Симеон...*, p. 84. Cf. П. П а в л о в, *Християнското и имперското минало на българските земи в ойкуменичната доктрина на цар Симеон Велики (893–927)*, [in:] *Източното православие в европейската култура. Международна конференция. Варна, 2–3 юли 1993 г.*, ed. Д. О в ч а р о в, София 1999, p. 112–114.

On the other hand, a view that can be justified is that Symeon strove to weaken Byzantium's position in the Balkans and aimed to capture space in which Bulgaria could play a dominant role. It is in this context that the term 'West' (*dysis*) appears[28], found in the correspondence of Nicholas Mystikos[29] and in the letters of Romanos I Lekapenos. In the fifth letter, the Bulgarian ruler is accused of plundering the 'whole West' and taking its people into captivity; Romanos adds that, because of his misconduct, Symeon cannot be called Emperor of the *Romaioi*[30]. The issue of the 'West' appears in the sources once more in the account of the circumstances of Symeon' death. His statue, which is believed to have stood on the hill of Xerolophos, had its face turned westwards[31]. By the 'West,' the three sources in question seem to mean Byzantium's European territories or, more broadly, Byzantium's sphere of influence in the Balkans. Only the first two accounts (not without certain reservations)[32], coupled with the analysis of certain steps taken by the ruler towards the Serbs and the Croats, can be used to support another view: that Symeon sought the Byzantines' approval of his rule over the territories they had lost to

---

[28] On the meaning of the terms *dysis* ('West') and *hesperia* ('western lands') see: В. В а ч к о в а, *Симеон*..., p. 76; e a d e m, *Понятието "Запад" в историческата аргументация на средновековна България*, "Studia Balcanica" 25, 2006, p. 295–303.

[29] N i c h o l a s   M y s t i k o s, 27, p. 190. In the letter, the patriarch suggests that Symeon wanted to rule over the whole West – which, in the patriarch's opinion, was not possible because *the sovereignty of all the West belongs to the Roman Empire* (transl. p. 191).

[30] T h e o d o r e   D a p h n o p a t e s, *Letters*, 5, p. 59.

[31] C o n t i n u a t o r   o f   T h e o p h a n e s, p. 411–412; J o h n   S k y l i t z e s, p. 221; J o h n   Z o n a r a s, p. 473; P s e u d o - S y m e o n   M a g i s t r o s, p. 740.

[32] One is advised to exercise great caution in using the letters of Nicholas Mystikos and Romanos I Lekapenos to determine Symeon's actual demands, as the letters reflect Symeon's diplomatic war with Byzantium. In diplomatic wars, one puts forward far-reaching bids in order to achieve specific goals. Besides, the letters written by Byzantine authors do not necessarily reflect the thoughts expressed in the Bulgarian ruler's original writings. It is worth noting that Nicholas Mystikos is the only author who explicitly addresses Symeon's attempts to establish his rule over the West. All that Romanos I Lekapenos says in his letter, on the other hand, is that he who ravages the lands of the *Romaioi* cannot be called their emperor: hence, the letter concerns not so much the attempt to rule the West as the use of the title. If Symeon had actually wanted to take over the *all the West*, why would he have demanded that the Byzantines concede to him lands (known as the *mandria*) which formed a part of this West?

him, as well as their abandoning the competition for influence over the areas inhabited by the Serbs and Croats[33].

We do not consider it likely that Symeon planned to take over the whole Byzantine west. Rather, in our opinion, he merely wanted to be recognized as a ruler equal to Byzantine emperors in the Balkan sphere; his assumption of the title in question should be regarded as a manifestation of this intention. On November 19th (most probably 923[34]), he met with Romanos I Lekapenos to make peace. Although it seems that the rulers failed to come to a final agreement, they managed to resolve some of the contentious issues, which sufficed for Symeon to cease his hostilities against Byzantium[35]. No source mentions Symeon's aggressive steps against the southern neighbor. Quite on the contrary, there is evidence to suggest that the ruler made active attempts to reach a final settlement with the empire. According to Todor Todorov[36], this is indicated by a passage in

---

[33] Cf. J. S h e p a r d, *Bulgaria. The Other Balkan "Empire"*, [in:] *New Cambridge Medieval History*, vol. III, ed. T. R e u t e r, Cambridge 2000, p. 567–585.

[34] Although Byzantine sources appear to be very precise in specifying the year, the month, the day of the week and even the hour of the event, the date is open to debate (cf. S. R u n c i m a n, *The Emperor Romanus Lecapenus and his Reign. A Study of Tenth-Century Byzantium*, Cambridge 1969, p. 246–248). J. H o w a r d - J o h n s o n (*A short piece of narrative history: war and diplomacy in the Balkans, winter 921/2 – spring 924*, [in:] *Byzantine Style, Religion and Civilization. In Honour of Sir Steven Runciman*, ed. E. J e f f r e y s, Cambridge 2006, p. 348) recently expressed his view on this matter, making a strong case for dating Symeon's meeting with Romanos to Wednesday, November 19th, 923.

[35] According to J. H o w a r d - J o h n s t o n (*A short piece...*, p. 352), Symeon reached agreement with Romanos on several issues: 1. the war was ended; 2. Lekapenos was recognized by Symeon as Byzantium's legal ruler; 3. Symeon was granted the status of brother of the Byzantine emperor and was given the right to bear the title of *basileus* (of the Bulgarians); still, Symeon's claims to the title of *Basileus* of the *Romaioi* were not accepted. Certain other matters, especially those regarding Byzantium's territorial concessions, were left for further negotiations. The Bulgarians laid claim to the areas referred to in one of Romanos's letters as the *mandria*. Most likely, the disputed territories included cities on the Black Sea coast, along with their surrounding areas, which – were they to remain in Byzantine hands – would pose a threat to the very core of the Bulgarian state.

[36] Т. Т о д о р о в, *"Слово за мир с българите" и българо-византийските отношения през последните години от управлението на цар Симеон*, [in:] *България, българите и техните съседи през векове. Изследвания и материали од научна

the oration *On the Treaty with the Bulgarians*, in which Symeon is compared to the Old Testament king David, while the peace with Byzantium is likened to the Temple in Jerusalem[37]. The idea of the erection of the temple was put forth by David/Symeon, but it was implemented by Salomon/Peter. According to the Bulgarian scholar, the author of the oration hinted that it was Symeon who had entered into negotiations with the Byzantines and laid foundations for the prospective peace, while Peter/Salomon (the future husband of this book's protagonist) simply concluded what his father had started[38]. The marriage between Peter and Maria, a Byzantine princess, was one of the key elements of the peace treaty under discussion. Symeon had once rejected the idea of becoming related to the Lekapenoi[39]; nonetheless, after 923, seeing no prospect of forging bonds with the Macedonian dynasty, he changed his stance and was ready to establish kinship with the Lekapenoi. Thus, Peter not only did not betray his father's wishes, but he in fact brought his plans to successful completion. However, that did not happen until a later stage of his rule. Right after his father's death and his rise to power, he took certain steps to show that he was ready to resume hostilities against Byzantium – a move designed to make Romanos I Lekapenos, Maria's grandfather, agree to what Peter considered the most favorable peace settlement[40].

конференция в памет на д-р Христо Коларов, 30–31 октомври 1998 г., Велико Търново, ed. Й. А н д р е е в, Велико Търново 2001, p. 141–150.

[37] *On the Treaty with the Bulgarians*, 16. Cf. K. M a r i n o w, *In the Shackles of the Evil One. The Portrayal of Tsar Symeon I the Great (893–927) in the Oration On the Treaty with the Bulgarians*, "Studia Ceranea. Journal of the Waldemar Ceran Research Centre for the History and Culture of the Mediterranean Area and South-East Europe" 1, 2011, p. 187–188. In some sources, Symeon is compared with king David due to his fondness for books (on this issue see: P. P а ш е в, *Цар Симеон – "нов Мойсей" или "нов Давид"*, [in:] i d e m, *Цар Симеон...*, p. 60–72). What Symeon and David were to have in common was the fact that neither of them transferred their power to the eldest son.

[38] Cf. the discussion of the topic in: K. Ma r i n o w, *In the Shackles...*, p. 187–188.

[39] N i c h o l a s M y s t i k o s, 16, p. 10.

[40] It is worth noting that, in the light of recent research, it is no longer possible to claim that Symeon was preparing another expedition against Constantinople shortly before his death. Cf. M.J. L e s z k a, *Symeon...*, p. 225–227.

2. Peter's Way to the Bulgarian Throne

Peter, Maria Lekapene's future husband, took the reins of power after his father's death, near the end of May 927. There is no doubt that this violated the rule of primogeniture observed in Bulgarian succession[41], for Peter was not Symeon's oldest son. Apart from Peter, the ruler had three other sons: Michael, John and Benjamin (Bayan), but the question of seniority among them is not entirely clear. Only a single tradition provides us with a source regarding this matter; it is of Byzantine provenance. In the *Continuation of Theophanes*, we read:

---

[41] We do not know the reasons behind Symeon's decision. It is fairly commonly held that it was influenced by Peter's mother – the Bulgarian ruler's second wife – as well as by her brother, George Sursuvul. E.g. Г. Б а к а л о в, *Царската промулгация на Петър и неговите приемници в светлината на българо-византийските диплома-тически отношения след договора от 927 г.*, "Исторически преглед" 39.6, 1983, p. 35; J.V.A. F i n e, *The Early Medieval Balkans: a Critical Survey from the Sixth to the Late Twelfth Century*, Ann Arbor 1983, p. 160; P. **Georgiev** (П. Г е о р г и е в, *Превратът през 927 г.*, "Преславска Книжовна Школа" 10, 2008, p. 433) suggests that it was a coup of sorts on the part of George Sursuvul, who, taking advantage of Symeon's illness, convinced him to cede power to Peter. The latter thus became his father's co-ruler. A similar surmise is offered by Plamen Pavlov (П. П а в л о в, *Векът на цар Самуил*, София 2014, p. 15–16). Another view present in current scholarship is that Symeon had proclaimed Peter his co-ruler several years before his death, drawing from the Byzantine government tradition. See: Т. Т о д о р о в, *За едно отражение на съвладетелската практика в Първото българско царство през втората половина на IX–първите десетилетия на X в.*, [in:] *България, българите и Европа – мит, история, съвремие*, vol. IV, *Доклади от Международна конференция в памет на проф. д.и.н. Йордан Андреев "България, земя на блажени..."*, В. Търново, 29–31 октомври 2009 г., ed. И. Л а з а р о в, Велико Търново 2011, p. 173–181. Peter had reportedly served in this role since 924. On the subject of the transfer of power in Bulgaria see Г.Г. Л и т а в р и н, *Принцип наслед-ственности власти в Византии и в Болгарии в VII–XI вв.*, [in:] *Славяне и их соседи*, vol. I, Москва 1988, p. 31–33; Г. Н и к о л о в, *Прабългарската традиция в христи-янския двор на средновековна България (IX–XI в.). Владетел и престолонаследие*, [in:] *Бог и цар в българската история*, ed. К. В а ч к о в а, Пловдив 1996, p. 124–130; Т. Т о д о р о в, *Към въпроса за престолонаследието в Първото българско царство*, "Плиска–Преслав" 8, 2000, p. 202–207; П. Г е о р г и е в, *Титлата и функциите на българския престолонаследник и въпросът за престолонаследието при цар Симеон (893–927)*, "Исторически преглед" 48.8/9, 1992, p. 10–11; П. П а в л о в, *Братята на цар Петър и техните заговори*, "История" 7.4/5, 1999, p. 2.

...Symeon died in Bulgaria; overcome by dementia and ravaged by a heart attack, he lost his mind and unjustifiably violated the law, putting forward his son Peter, born from his second wife, the sister of George Sursuvul, as the archont; he also made him the guardian of his sons. Michael, his son from his first wife, he ordered to become a monk. John and Benjamin, in turn, the brothers of Peter, still wore Bulgarian dress (στολῇ Βουλγαρικῇ)[42].

Although apparently well-versed in these events, the anonymous author of this account (found in the sixth book of the *Continuation of Theophanes*) followed the trend visible in Byzantine literature and limited themselves to the basic information only[43]. From the Byzantine author's perspective, the key point was that there had been a conflict over the matter of succession after Symeon. For some reason, the latter decided to remove Michael – his eldest son (by his first wife) and the original heir[44] – from the line of succession[45]. To prevent Michael from making potential claims to the throne, Symeon had him become a monk, following the

[42] Continuator of Theophanes, p. 412. Cf. Symeon Logothete, 136.45; John Skylitzes, p. 225.

[43] On the subject of the authorship and source base of the sixth book of the *Continuation of Theophanes* see: chapter I.

[44] Apart from narrative sources (Continuator of Theophanes, p. 412; Symeon Logothete, 136.45; John Skylitzes, p. 225), the sigillographic material also confirms that Michael had been designated as heir by Symeon – И. Йордаа-нов, *Корпус...*, p. 140–143. There are seven seals associated with Michael. Unfortunately, they are not well preserved, so that it is not easy to decipher and interpret their inscriptions, as well as to determine their definitive association with Michael. This matter was recently analyzed e.g. by Т. Тодоров, *България през втората и третата четвърт на X век: политическа история*, София 2006 [unpublished PhD thesis], p. 86–88; Б. Николова, *Печатите на Михаил багатур канеиртхтин и Йоан багатур канеиртхтин (?). Проблеми на разчитането и атрибуцията*, [in:] *Средновековният българин и "другите". Сборник в чест на 60-годишнината на проф. Дин Петър Ангелов*, eds. А. Николов, Г.Н. Николов, София 2013, p. 127–135; И. Йорданов, *Корпус...*, p. 140–143. The latter author, despite the stated reservations, concluded (p. 143) that they most likely belonged to the *baghatur* and heir to the throne – *kanartikin* (βαγατουρ κανε ηρτχι θυινος) – and not to the *baghatur* of the heir to the throne or to the *baghatur* of *khan* 'Irtchithuin.'

[45] We do not know the name of his mother or the date of his birth. He must have been born after 893, and perhaps prior to 907 (П. Георгиев, *Превратът...*, p. 429).

Byzantine custom in this matter[46]. He also designated Peter, his son by his second wife, as the heir. Since at the moment of his father's death Peter was very young[47] and relatively inexperienced, he was entrusted to the care of George Sursuvul, Symeon's brother-in-law and collaborator. From the Byzantine perspective, John and Benjamin (Bayan) – the other two sons of Symeon – took no part in this contest for their father's power.

As regards the order in which Symeon's sons entered the world, the account only provides us with a sufficient basis to state that Michael was the firstborn son of the Bulgarian ruler. It does not offer any indication as to the order of seniority among the remaining three sons. One might only speculate that John – since he was mentioned first – was older than Benjamin. Whether Peter was older or younger than his brothers, or whether he was born between them, is impossible to determine. The account in question does not rule out the possibility that the other three sons were full brothers rather than half-brothers. The Byzantine author, as we emphasized above, only stated that Michael's mother was the first wife of Symeon, and Peter's – the second. Unlike Michael, John and Benjamin are unambiguously described as Peter's brothers, which might suggest that Michael's relation to Peter differed from that of the other two. Nonetheless, one should probably not ascribe particular significance to this. Besides, it should be borne in mind that, having eliminated Michael, Symeon could designate any of his sons as his successor, regardless of his age.

---

[46] We do not know when this happened. It has been suggested that this event was associated with the supposed disagreement between Symeon and his eldest son, caused by another escalation of the conflict with Byzantium in 924–925 (or rather in 923–924). The available source material does not, however, allow the verification of this conjecture. On this subject see e.g.: П. Г е о р г и е в, *Титлата*..., p. 10–11; П. П а в л о в, *Братята*..., p. 2; Т. Т о д о р о в, *България*..., p. 88–100. As regards the monastery in which he lived, it may have been the one in Ravna, which had strong ties to the ruling dynasty. It was located relatively close to Pliska (specifically, 25 km to the south-east). On this monastery see: Б. Н и к о л о в а, *Монашество, манастири и манастирски живот в средновековна България*, vol. I, *Манастирите*, София 2010, p. 188–255.

[47] There are no sources to answer the question of when Peter was born. Given the fact that in 927 he was still unmarried, but on the other hand old enough to get married and seize power (formally he was allowed to do this at the age of 16), he must have been born in the early 910s at the latest. P. G e o r g i e v (*Превратът*..., p. 429) believes that he was born in 911.

The passage under examination closes with the surprising statement that John and Benjamin continued to wear Bulgarian dress. It is commonly thought that it was an expression of their attachment to the Proto-Bulgar tradition[48]. If we accept this information at face value – as Kirił Marinow recently suggested – we could consider it as the reason for which the two sons got stripped of their power by their father: by cultivating the Old Bulgarian tradition, they would have opposed Symeon's efforts to shape Bulgaria after the Byzantine model, even if they shared their father's vision of fighting the southern neighbor. The younger Peter may have been more enamored with Byzantine culture, so dear to his father. However, according to this scholar, we such an assumption is highly hypothetical – whereas, in fact, it seems that a far more prosaic explanation for the passage is at hand. It may be that the Byzantine authors, who favored Peter, intended to discredit his brothers by pointing out their barbarity. In this manner, they could justify the fact that he came to power instead of his brothers[49]. Moreover, it cannot be ruled out that we simply do not understand the nature of this passage, which may be of idiomatic or proverbial nature.

It follows from the above considerations that John was most likely the second or third son of Symeon. After Michael was removed from the line of succession, he was not designated as his father's heir any longer. While the opinion that Symeon did appoint him as his successor (*kanartikin*) is present in the scholarship on the subject, it should be stated outright that the basis for such a hypothesis is fairly shaky[50]. Another view, advanced

---

[48] It is also associated with the account of Liudprand of Cremona (L i u d p r a n d o f C r e m o n a, *Retribution*, III, 29), which mentions that Bayan was supposedly a user of magic and could turn himself into a wolf.

[49] M.J. L e s z k a, K. M a r i n o w, *Carstwo bułgarskie. Polityka – społeczeństwo – gospodarka – kultura. 866–971*, Warszawa 2015, p. 152, fn. 13.

[50] К. П о п к о н с т а н т и н о в, *Епиграфски бележки за Иван, Цар Симеоновият син*, "Българите в Северното Причерноморие" 3, 1994, p. 72–73. This is to be seen from the sphragistic material, i.e. the seals associated with John (И. Й о р д а н о в, *Корпус...*, p. 135–139; П. Г е о р г и е в, *Титлата...*, p. 9sqq). See also: П. Г е о р г и е в, *Превратът...*, p. 432–433. He may have held the dignity of *kanartikin* as early as 926, and was previously titled *boilatarkan*, as was usually the case with the ruler's second son. The question of the reliability of the sigillographic sources related to John has been

by Todor Todorov, holds that John may have been appointed heir to Peter. Based on the same sphragistic material as the aforementioned hypothesis, the claim is likewise rather doubtful.

3. Peace Negotiations

The first and most important task faced by Peter after his rise to power was to establish peace with Byzantium. However, he and George Sursuvul, his guardian and adviser, did not decide to enter (continue?) the peace talks right away. Quite on the contrary, they renewed hostilities against Byzantium, with the purpose of strengthening their negotiating position during the future peace talks[51]. Both sides of the conflict soon realized that the cost of continuing the war would be too high. Peter, taking advantage of his first victories, sent monk Kalokir[52] to present Romanos I Lekapenos with the proposal of opening peace negotiations[53]; the emperor accepted

---

analyzed by Bistra Nikolova (Б. Н и к о л о в а, *Печатите...*, p. 127–135). The author points out the uncertainty of their readings as well as their very association with John. She concludes, as do the present authors, that the *sigilla* associated with John should instead be linked with some dignitary by the same name from the 9th or 10th century.

[51] In the summer, perhaps at the beginning of August, Bulgarian forces entered eastern Thrace. Cf. C o n t i n u a t o r o f T h e o p h a n e s, VI, 22, p. 412; Т. Т о д о р о в, *България...*, p. 123.

[52] C o n t i n u a t o r o f T h e o p h a n e s, VI, 22, p. 412; J o h n S k y l i t z e s, p. 228. It is quite remarkable that his mission was to be carried out in secret; this may suggest that Peter and George were wary of how their troops might react to their plan. Kalokir carried a chrysobull, presumably containing the conditions upon which Bulgaria was prepared to conclude peace. On Kalokir's mission see: Т. Т о д о р о в, *България...*, p. 123; П. А н г е л о в, *Духовници-дипломати в средновековна България*, "Studia Balcanica" 27, 2009, p. 145.

[53] According to Byzantine chroniclers, one of the reasons which led the Bulgarian authorities to embrace a conciliatory approach towards Byzantium in 927 was the danger of invasion from Bulgaria's neighbors – the Croats, Turks (Hungarians) and others (S y m e o n L o g o t h e t e, 136.46–47; C o n t i n u a t o r o f T h e o p h a n e s, VI, 22, p. 412; J o h n S k y l i t z e s, p. 222). However, according to Marinow, these opinions do not bear scrutiny. The essential argument against them lies in the anti-Byzantine military

the offer[54]. There is no reason to doubt that the peace talks were initiated by the Bulgarian ruler; nor should we call into question that his move was well-prepared and carefully thought out[55]. The Bulgarian society was exhausted by the long period of wars waged by his father – the sources record a severe famine suffered by the people and the threat posed by the country's neighbors[56]. Peter knew he was left with no other option but to make peace – his father, who had not escalated the conflict with Byzantium for a few years, must have made him understand the need to end the war – but wanted its terms to be as favorable as possible for Bulgaria. As a way of suggesting his readiness to renew the war on a large scale,

---

operation itself: it could not have taken place if Bulgaria's other borders had not been secure. More to the point, the information about the simultaneous invasion by Bulgaria's neighbors would suggest the existence of a coalition created, in all probability, by the Byzantines, from whom the Bulgarians should also fear hostile actions. The existence of any agreement with the empire seems to be at odds with the Hungarians' rejection of the Byzantine proposal to form an alliance with the Pechenegs, which happened in the same year (G. M o r a v c s i k, *Byzantium and the Magyars*, Budapest 1970, p. 54). Perhaps the only real move which the Byzantines did make was to spread rumors inside the Bulgarian court regarding Byzantium's military action against Bulgaria. Based on this interpretation, the Bulgarian operation against Byzantium could be interpreted in terms of a reaction to the news of the formation of an anti-Bulgarian coalition, that is, a demonstration of force and a proof that Symeon's ancestor was not afraid of Byzantium's intrigues. However, the Byzantine authorities' swift assent to the peace proposal, coupled with the absence of any anti-Bulgarian action by Bulgaria's neighbors both in that year and in the years that followed, prove that Bulgaria was not facing any external threat (И. Б о ж и л о в, В. Г ю з е л е в, *История*..., p. 272–273; Х. Д и м и т р о в, *Българо-унгарски отношения през средновековието*, София 1998, p. 71–72; Т. Т о д о р о в, *България*..., p. 119; M.J. L e s z k a, K. M a r i n o w, *Carstwo bułgarskie*..., p. 155–156, 167).

[54] C o n t i n u a t o r   o f   T h e o p h a n e s, VI, 22, p. 412.

[55] However, it should be noted that this view is not universally accepted. Pavlov (П. П а в л о в, *Векът*..., p. 16–17), for example, claims that the relevant sources are tendentious, blowing things out of proportion. Thus, the theory holds that it was the Bulgarians who positively responded to the peace proposals put forward by the Byzantines. However, Pavlov seems to be going too far in his interpretation of the events.

[56] Assuming that the sources do not draw on the topos referring to the circumstances of the peace concluded by khan Boris in the 860s, connected with his baptism (M.J. L e s z k a, K. M a r i n o w, *Carstwo bułgarskie*..., p. 155, fn. 26). Cf. the reservations of И. Б о ж и л о в, В. Г ю з е л е в, *История*..., p. 272–273; П. П а в л о в, *Векът*..., p. 16–17.

he decided to launch an attack upon Byzantine territory. The action he took was intended to force the Byzantines into concessions; besides, Peter may have wanted to strengthen his position within his own country, especially in view of the possible opposition from his brothers, whom he had removed from power. The conclusion of peace with Byzantium would have given him more freedom of action in Bulgaria, in addition to enabling him to secure Byzantine military support[57]. Romanos I Lekapenos, too, neither wanted to nor was able to continue this long war and was prepared to make the concessions that he had refused when dealing with Peter's father. It was certainly easier for the Byzantines to make peace with Peter than with Symeon, from whom they had suffered numerous defeats: Peter was a blank slate for them. It is hardly surprising that the author of the oration *On the Treaty with the Bulgarians* claimed that God had removed Symeon and replaced him with Peter to enable the latter to establish peace. In this way, Peter became a tool in God's hands[58].

In response to Peter's peace proposal, Romanos I Lekapenos sent two envoys, monk Theodosios Abukes and court priest Constantine of Rhodes, to Mesembria, where peace talks were to be held. It was agreed that the final settlement would be negotiated in Constantinople. The Bulgarian delegation headed by George Sursuvul arrived in the Byzantine capital[59]; the envoys negotiated the preliminary terms of the prospective peace and informed Peter of the decisions taken during their negotiations.

---

[57] M.J. L e s z k a, K. M a r i n o w, *Carstwo bugarskie...*, p. 155.

[58] *On the Treaty with the Bulgarians*, 7, p. 264.159–162; 276.362–278.382; R.J.H. J e n k i n s, *The Peace with Bulgaria (927) Celebrated by Theodore Daphnopates*, [in:] *Polychronion. Festschrift F. Dölger*, ed. P. W i r t h, Heidelberg 1966, p. 293, 297.

[59] S y m e o n L o g o t h e t e, 136.46–47; C o n t i n u a t o r o f T h e o p h a n e s, VI, 22, p. 412; J o h n S k y l i t z e s, p. 222. The Bulgarian delegation also included Symeon, *kalutarkan* and *sampsis* (κουλου τερκανὸς, κάλου τερκάνος), who may have been husband of Symeon I the Great's sister, Anna; Stephen the Bulgarian (probably *kauchan*), perhaps a nephew of the late tsar; as well as three dignitaries whose names remain unknown, namely the *kron* (κρόνος), *magotin* (μαγοτῖνος) and *minik* (μηνικός). On the Bulgarian delegation see: В.И. З л а т а р с к и, *История...*, p. 523–524. It should be stressed that the delegation consisted of men who were Peter's close collaborators, comprising the ruler's council (known as the great *boyars*). On the course of the peace negotiations see: J. S h e p a r d, *A marriage too far? Maria Lekapena and Peter of Bulgaria*, [in:] *The Empress Theophano. Byzantium and the West at the turn of the first millennium*,

It follows, then, that the sequence of events from Maria Lekapene's life best illuminated by the sources comes from the period during which she became married (October 8th, 927). The matrimonial knot was to guarantee the peace concluded several days earlier between the empire and Bulgaria. Interestingly, as correctly observed by Jonathan Shepard, Maria was the only 10th-century Byzantine woman of high status who married a foreign ruler, and whose marriage was not only noted by the native historiographers, but also described by them in detail[60]. In comparison, the marriage of Anna Porphyrogennete (*nota bene*, the daughter of Maria's cousin – Romanos II) to Kievan prince Vladimir I is only mentioned by John Skylitzes in his chronicle in passing, where the author states that emperor Basil II made the ruler of Rus' his brother-in-law in order to secure his military support[61].

Therefore, we get to know Maria at a time when she is being presented to the Bulgarian envoys as a potential wife for their ruler. The anonymous Continuator of George the Monk – as well as other Byzantine writers following in his footsteps – noted that Christopher's daughter filled George Sursuvul and his companions with delight[62]. This statement, however, should not be used to draw far-reaching conclusions concerning her appearance or other qualities. Quite simply, it seems, it would have been inappropriate for foreign guests to display any other emotions during a meeting with an imperial descendant and relative, who was soon to become their own ruler. We could hardly expect the Byzantine authors to characterize Maria in a negative manner.

Interestingly, the mission of bringing Peter to Constantinople was entrusted to Maria's maternal grandfather – the aforementioned Niketas

---

ed. A. D a v i d s, Cambridge 1995, p. 122sqq; И. Б о ж и л о в, В. Г ю з е л е в, *История...*, p. 273–274; Т. Т о д о р о в, *България...*, p. 123–134.

[60] J. S h e p a r d, *A marriage...*, p. 127.

[61] J o h n   S k y l i t z e s, p. 336. Cf. J o h n   Z o n a r a s, XVII, 7, p. 553. The chronicler also mentions the marriage of Anna and Vladimir I as well as the death of the Porphyrogennete in another part of his narrative: J o h n   S k y l i t z e s, p. 367.

[62] C o n t i n u a t o r   o f   G e o r g e   t h e   M o n k, p. 905; S y m e o n   L o g o t h e t e, 136, 48, p. 327; L e o   G r a m m a t i k o s, p. 316; C o n t i n u a t o r   o f   T h e o p h a n e s, VI, 22, p. 413. J o h n   S k y l i t z e s (p. 223), contrary to the earlier chroniclers, directly stated that Maria was indeed exceptionally beautiful.

Magistros[63]. Our heroine was not present for her fiancé's ceremonious welcome in the Byzantine capital (which took place in the northern part of the city, Blachernai); neither did she take part in the peace negotiations.

4. Peace Treaty

Once it was given its final form, the peace treaty was signed. What were its provisions? Unfortunately, the text of the agreement itself is not extant; for this reason, we must rely on its approximate reconstruction[64]. The only thing we know for certain is that it provided for the marriage between the Bulgarian monarch and Maria, daughter of Christopher, Romanos I Lekapenos's son and co-ruler. It is also likely that the Byzantines would have recognized Peter's right to bear the title of *basileus* (Emperor of the Bulgarians)[65]. Both sides agreed on the exchange of war prisoners

---

[63] Continuator of George the Monk, p. 905; Symeon Logothete, 136, 48, p. 327; Continuator of Theophanes, VI, 22, p. 413.

[64] The terms of the Bulgarian-Byzantine agreement of 927 are analyzed by: S. P e n k o v, *Bulgaro-Byzantine Treaties during the Early Middle Ages*, "Palaeobulgarica" 5.3, 1981, p. 48–49; В.Д. Н и к о л а е в, *Значение договора 927 г. в истории болгаро-византийских отношений*, [in:] *Проблемы истории античности и средних веков*, ed. Ю.М. С а п р ы к и н, Москва 1982, p. 89–105; J.V.A. F i n e, *The Early...*, p. 160–162, 214–216; E. A l e k s a n d r o v, *The International Treaties of Medieval Bulgaria (Legal Aspects)*, "Bulgarian Historical Review" 17.4, 1989, p. 41, 42, 44, 48; Т. Т о д о р о в, *България...*, p. 127–133; S. P i r i v a t r i ć, *Some Notes on the Byzantine-Bulgarian Peace Treaty of 927*, "Byzantinoslovaca" 2, 2008, p. 40–49; С. З в е з д о в, *Договорът от 927 година между България и Византия*, "History. Bulgarian Journal of Historical Education" 23.3, 2015, p. 264–277.

[65] βασιλεὺς Βουλγάρων/Βουλγαρίας – cf. Г. Б а к а л о в, *Средновековният български владетел. Титулатура и инсигнии*, ²София 1995, p. 169–172; Г. А т а н а с о в, *Инсигниите на средновековните български владетели. Корони, скиптри, сфери, оръжия, костюми, накити*, Плевен 1999, p. 96–99; А. Н и к о л о в, *Политическа...*, p. 234; Т. Т о д о р о в, *Владетелският статут и титла на цар Петър I след октомври 927 г.: писмени сведения и сфрагистични данни (сравнителен анализ)*, [in:] *Юбилеен сборник. Сто години от рождението на д-р Васил Хараланов (1907–2007)*, Шумен 2008, p. 93–108.

– in particular, the Byzantine captives were to be allowed to return home[66]. The treaty must have addressed the issue of the border between the two states, although scholars are not in agreement as to how this issue was resolved. Most subscribe to the view that the border was redrawn along the same line that had separated the two states before 913, which means that the empire regained the lands it had lost as a result of the defeats following the battle of Anchialos in 917[67]. It can also be assumed that the agreement contained provisions regarding the tribute to be paid to the Bulgarians (a point traditionally addressed in Bulgarian-Byzantine treaties)[68], principles regulating trade relations between the two countries[69], as well

---

[66] Constantine VII Porphyrogennetos, *On the Governance of the Empire*, 13, p. 74 (159–160): *so many Christian prisoners were ransomed* (transl. p. 75). Such a provision is alluded to in the oration *On the Treaty with the Bulgarians*, 5, p. 260. 105–110. See also: Т. Т о д о р о в, *България*..., p. 128, 139; M.J. L e s z k a, K. M a r i n o w, *Carstwo bułgarskie*..., p. 155.

[67] The issue is discussed in detail by Petar Koledarov (П. К о л е д а р о в, *Политическа география на средновековната българска държава*, vol. I, *От 681 до 1018 г.*, София 1979, p. 50–51). A different opinion is expressed by Plamen Pavlov (П. П а в л о в, *Векът*..., p. 20), according to whom the Bulgarians returned to the Byzantines only those territories that formed something of a temporary military zone (for example, the fortress of Viza), while the empire preserved the areas extending from the Strandzha mountains in the east to Ras (today's Novi Pazar in Serbia) in the west, including such centers as Vodena, Moglena, Kastoria and others; Byzantium also retained parts of the so-called Thessalonike Plain, northern Epiros, as well as today's Albania and Kosovo. See also: Т. Т о д о р о в, *България*..., p. 127–128; M.J. L e s z k a, K. M a r i n o w, *Carstwo bułgarskie*..., p. 155, fn. 33.

[68] A hint of such an obligation is to be found in a passage from the work by Leo the Deacon, where the author mentions that the Bulgarians called for Nikephoros II Phokas to pay *the customary tribute* (IV, 5; transl. p. 109). Some scholars (S. R u n c i m a n, *The Emperor Romanus*..., p. 99; J.A.V. F i n e, *The Early*..., p. 181) claimed that under the 927 treaty, Byzantium, instead of paying an annual tribute, agreed to transfer a certain amount of money for Maria, Peter's wife, each year. It seems that Todorov (Т. Т о д о р о в, *България*..., p. 129–130) is right in claiming that until Maria's death, the Byzantines' commitment to pay her a certain amount of money existed side by side with their obligation regarding the annual tribute.

[69] There is no overt evidence to confirm that trade issues were dealt with in the agreement in question, but bearing in mind the fact that these issues were under dispute at the beginning of Symeon's reign, and that they were also the reason for the outbreak of the war of 894–896 to some extent, their omission from the treaty would be unexpected. Cf. Т. Т о д о р о в, *България*..., p. 130–131.

as Bulgaria's (and perhaps also Byzantium's) obligation to provide the ally with military assistance[70].

In addition, the 927 treaty is believed to have covered a number of religious issues. The Bulgarian church was granted full autonomy and the archbishop who stood at its head was given the right to bear the title of patriarch.

No source containing the information about the autocephaly of the Bulgarian church and the elevation of the Bulgarian archbishop to the position of patriarch (we mean here the *List of Bulgarian archbishops*[71],

---

[70] Д. С т о и м е н о в, *Към договора между България и Византия от 927 г.*, "Векове" 17.6, 1988, p. 19–22. According to this author, the existence of the military alliance is attested to by the Bulgarians' participation in the campaigns carried out by the Byzantines against the Arabs in the years 954–955 and 958. Doubts as to the Bulgarians' participation in these campaigns have been raised by Todorov (T. Т о д о р о в, *България*..., p. 131–132). The fact mentioned in support of the existence of the alliance is that Nikephoros II Phokas called for the Bulgarians to stop the Hungarian invasions of the lands of the empire (J o h n Z o n a r a s, XVI, 27, 14–15, p. 513). This argument, too, is open to debate, cf. T. Т о д о р о в, *България*..., p. 132. Although the arguments in favor of the view that the 927 treaty involved provisions regarding military assistance are insecure, the inclusion of this issue in the treaty cannot be entirely excluded.

[71] *List of Bulgarian Archbishops*, p. 102, 18–23: [...] *Damian, in Dorostolon, the present Dristra. During his reign Bulgaria was honoured with autocephaly* [or attained autocephaly – M.J.L.] *and the Byzantine Senate, following Romanos Lekapenos' orders, granted him the title of patriarch. He was then deposed by John Tzimiskes.* For more on the source see: W. S w o b o d a, *Bułgaria a patriarchat konstantynopolitański w latach 870–1018*, [in:] *Z polskich studiów slawistycznych*, vol. IV, *Historia*, Warszawa 1972, p. 57–58; В. Т ъ п к о в а - З а и м о в а, *Дюканжов списък*, "Palaeobulgarica" 24.3, 2000, p. 21–49; И. Б о ж и л о в, *Българската архиепископия XI–XII в. Списъкът на българските архиепископи*, София 2011, p. 93–101. On Damian cf.: W. S w o b o d a, *Damian*, [in:] *Słownik starożytności słowiańskich. Encyklopedyczny zarys kultury Słowian od czasów najdawniejszych do schyłku XII w.*, vol. VIII, eds. A. G ą s i o r o w s k i, G. L a b u d a, A. W ę d z k i, Wrocław 1991, p. 13–14; Г.Г. Л и т а в р и н, *Христианство в Болгарии 927–1018 гг.*, [in:] *Христианство в странах восточной, юго-восточной и центральной Европы на пороге второго тысячелетия*, ed. Б.Н. Ф л о р я, Москва 2002, p. 141–142; Г. А т а н а с о в, *Християнският Дуросторум-Дръстър. Доростолската епархия през късната античност и Средновековието IV–XIV в. История, археология, култура и изкуство*, Варна 2007, p. 158–160; i d e m, *Първата българска патриаршеска кафедра в Дръстър и патриарх Дамян*, [in:] *Изследвания по българска средновековна археология. Сборник в чест на проф. Рашо Рашев*, ed. П. Г е о р г и е в, Велико Търново 2007, p. 179–196. Cf. also S. A n g e l o v a, G. P r i n z i n g, *Das mutmassliche*

Michael of Devol's *Gloss to the Synopsis of Histories* by John Skylitzes[72] as well as the text *On Justiniana Prima's canonical position*[73]) links these facts with the treaty of 927. The three sources mentioned above connect the autocephaly with emperor Romanos I Lekapenos (920–944). In the last text, the issue is placed in the context of an agreement to which Peter was to be a party. The conferment of the title of patriarch on the archbishop of Bulgaria is referred to only in the *List of Bulgarian Archbishops*, where it is linked with the autocephaly. Thus, these religious issues can be assumed to have been dealt with in a peace treaty signed during the reigns of Peter and Romanos I Lekapenos. It so happens that the 927 treaty is the only such document that we know of. According to some scholars, this is at odds with the information to be found in the so-called

---

Grab des Patriarchen Damian: zu einem archäologischen Fund in Dristra/Silistria, [in:] *Средновековна християнска Европа. Изток и запад. Ценности, традиции, общуване*, eds. В. Гюзелев, А. Милтенова, София 2002, p. 726–730.

[72] John Skylitzes, p. 365, 8–11. Michael of Devol writes that emperor Basil II confirmed the autocephaly of the Bulgarian bishopric, which it had enjoyed already during the reign of the old Romanos (I Lekapenos). This information was recorded at the beginning of the 12th century. On the notes which bishop Michael of Devol added to John Skylitzes's work see: J. Ferluga, *John Scylitzes and Michael of Devol*, [in:] idem, *Byzantium on the Balkans. Studies on the Byzantine Administration and the Southern Slavs from the VIIth to the XIIth Centuries*, Amsterdam 1976, p. 337–344.

[73] Cf. *On Justiniana Prima's canonical position*, p. 279, 37–42. The source states that the Bulgarian Church was autocephalous and that the privileges it enjoyed were not derived only from Basil II and Romanos I Lekapenos, dating back to the period during which the agreement with tsar Peter was signed. They also had their origin in the old laws. On the source see: G. Prinzing, *Entstehung und Rezeption der Justiniana Prima-Theorie im Mittelalter*, "Byzantinobulgarica" 5, 1978, p. 269–278; Т. Кръстанов, *Испански бележки за translatio на Justiniana Prima с българската църква преди 1018 г.*, "Шуменски Университет Епископ Константин Преславски. Трудове на Катедрите по история и богословие" 6, 2004, p. 80–84; idem, *Титлите екзарх и патриарх в българската традиция от IX до XIX в. Св. Йоан Екзарх от Рим и патриарх на българските земи*, [in:] *Държава & Църква – Църква & Държава в българската история. Сборник по случай 135-годишнината от учредяването на Българската екзархия*, eds. Г. Ганев, Г. Бакалов, И. Тодев, София 2006, p. 79–80. The source claims that the Bulgarian Church inherited *Justiniana Prima*'s church laws. The issue of *Justiniana Prima*'s archbishopric established during the reign of Justinian I was recently discussed by: S. Turlej, *Justiniana Prima: An Underestimated Aspect of Justinian's Church Policy*, Kraków 2016.

Beneševič's Taktikon, a source contemporary with Romanos I Lekapenos's reign but variously dated – either to 921/927 or to 934/944. In this source, the head of the Bulgarian Church is referred to as Bulgaria's archbishop (ἀρχιεπίσκοπος Βουλγαρίας)[74]. Thus, it appears that dating the *Taktikon* to 934/944 – as per its publisher Nicolas Oikonomides – would be tantamount to excluding 927 as the date of Constantinople's recognition of the Bulgarian archbishop as patriarch[75]. However, other scholars claim that the *Taktikon*'s characterization of the issue in question may be inaccurate, and it seems that they are closer to the truth[76].

As should be apparent from the discussion above, the sources we have at our disposal do not allow us to state categorically that the questions of autocephaly and the title of patriarch were dealt with in the 927 peace negotiations. Still, given everything we know about the Byzantine-Bulgarian relations during the reign of Romanos I Lekapenos, it is logical to assume that this was actually the case. What can be said based on the surviving sources is that the issues were covered by an agreement signed by Peter and Romanos I Lekapenos, that is, in the period between 927 and 944. The point is that, as we mentioned above, we do not know of any other arrangement made by these two rulers save for the 927 treaty. Lately, Todor Todorov put forth the idea that the events in question may have taken place soon after Theophylaktos Lekapenos's rise to the position of patriarch of Constantinople (933)[77]. Todorov links these facts with the presence of papal envoys in Constantinople and Maria's visit to Romanos I Lekapenos's court. To the Bulgarian scholar, the Bulgarian archbishop's receiving the right to bear the title of patriarch was *the last*

---

[74] *Beneševič's Taktikon*, p. 245, 17.

[75] Cf. Б. Н и к о л о в а, *Устройство и управление на българската православна църква (IX–XIV в.)*, София 2017, p. 49.

[76] N. O i k o n o m i d è s, *Les listes de préséance byzantines des IXᵉ et Xᵉ siècles*, Paris 1972, p. 237–238. Cf. И. Б о ж и л о в, *Българската архиепископия...*, p. 40; Г. А т а н а с о в, *Християнският Дуросторум-Дръстър...*, p. 150–154). See also: В. Т ъ п к о в а - З а и м о в а, *Превземането на Преслав в 971 г. и проблемите на българската църква*, [in:] *1100 години Велики Преслав*, vol. I, ed. Т. Т о т е в, Шумен 1995, p. 178; S. P i r i v a t r i ć, *Some Notes...*, p. 44–45.

[77] Т. Т о д о р о в, *България...*, p. 213–214.

wedding gift for the couple ruling in Preslav[78]. This is an interesting hypothesis, but underlying it is the controversial view, to be found in Bulgarian scholarly literature, according to which the Bulgarians were planning to seize control of Constantinople and build a Slav-Greek empire; this plan was known as the 'great idea' of 10th-century Bulgaria[79]. According to Todorov, the project was championed by Symeon I and abandoned by Peter in 931, after the death of Christopher – Peter's father-in-law as well as Romanos I Lekapenos's son and co-ruler. This fact meant that neither Peter nor his sons, whom he had by Maria, could lay claim to Christopher's power. Without engaging in a polemic with this view, it is worth noting that to accept it is to make Peter fully responsible for the elevation of the Bulgarian archbishop to the position of patriarch against the intention of his father, Symeon.

Furthermore, Todorov recently formulated an interesting view concerning the Byzantine-Bulgarian negotiations held in Constantinople in October 927. The scholar is of the opinion that two distinct documents were signed during that time: the peace treaty, resolving the political conflicts between the empire and Bulgaria, as well as a distinct marriage arrangement. What issues were addressed in the latter? Todorov is inclined to believe that the provisions regarding the marriage introduced a fundamental change in the status of the Bulgarian ruler in relation to the emperors in Constantinople and determined the rank of the envoys sent to the Bosporos from Preslav. In addition, the document may have resolved the issue of Maria Lekapene's dowry, which was given the form of an annual financial subsidy to be paid by Constantinople to the Bulgarian tsaritsa throughout her life[80].

---

[78] *Ibidem*, p. 215. Papal legates were present in the city in connection with their participation in the elevation of Theophylaktos Lekapenos to the patriarchal throne, but they may have also brought Rome's consent to the change in the status of the Bulgarian bishop.

[79] For a polemic with this view cf.: M.J. L e s z k a, *Symeon...*, p. 236–247.

[80] T. T o д o p o в, *България...*, p. 133.

5. Wedding

On the day of her marriage – October 8th, 927 – Maria Lekapene proceeded to the church in the Monastery of the Holy Mother of the Life-Giving Spring, located beyond the Theodosian walls, accompanied by *protovestiarios* Theophanes, patriarch of Constantinople Stephen II, as well as numerous state dignitaries and courtiers[81]. Interestingly, the church chosen may have reminded the Byzantines and the Bulgarians of their earlier, troubled relations: after all, the temple had been set on fire on Symeon's orders, and it was in its vicinity that the peace negotiations between this ruler and Romanos I had taken place in 923[82]. Furthermore, it was Maria's grandfather who ordered the rebuilding of the ravaged church[83]. The marriage ceremony between the church's restorer and Symeon's son, then, may have had a clear propaganda significance. It suggested that Romanos I Lekapenos was the one who managed to neutralize the Bulgarian threat and perhaps – to some extent – repair the damage the Bulgarians had inflicted on the empire's lands in the past[84].

The Byzantine chroniclers agree that the rite of the sacrament of marriage was personally performed by patriarch Stephen II. He blessed Maria and Peter and put the marriage crowns on their heads (this is sometimes

---

[81] Continuator of George the Monk, p.905; Symeon Logothete, 136, 49, p.327–328; Leo Grammatikos, p.317; Pseudo-Symeon Magistros, 34, p.741; Continuator of Theophanes, VI, 23, p. 414; John Skylitzes, p. 223.

[82] Continuator of George the Monk, p. 893–894; Symeon Logothete, 136, 31, p. 321–322; Pseudo-Symeon Magistros, 29, p. 736; Leo Grammatikos, p. 311; Continuator of Theophanes, VI, 15, p. 406; John Skylitzes, p. 219; John Zonaras, XVI, 18, p. 470–471. Cf. M.J. Leszka, *Wizerunek władców pierwszego państwa bułgarskiego w bizantyńskich źródłach pisanych (VIII–pierwsza połowa XII w.)*, Łódź 2003, p. 118; idem, *Symeon...*, p. 207; idem, K. Marinow, *Carstwo bułgarskie...*, p. 157.

[83] A. Kompa, *Konstantynopolitańskie zabytki w Stambule*, [in:] *Z badań nad wczesnobizantyńskim Konstantynopolem*, eds. M.J. Leszka, K. Marinow, A. Kompa, Łódź 2011 [= "Acta Universitatis Lodziensis. Folia historica" 87], p. 167.

[84] J. Shepard, *A marriage...*, p. 129.

interpreted in historiography as the crowning ceremony of the newly-wed couple)[85]. The ceremony was witnessed by George Sursuvul and *protovestiarios* Theophanes. A wedding feast followed, after which Maria returned to the palace accompanied by Theophanes[86].

On the third day after the wedding, Romanos I Lekapenos organized another reception, which took place on a magnificently decorated ship anchored off the Pege coast. The anonymous Continuator of George the Monk stresses that the emperor feasted at the same table as Peter, his son-in-law Constantine VII Porphyrogennetos and his own son, Christopher. The participating Bulgarians are reported to have asked Romanos I for a favor: if we are to believe the chronicler, they wanted the father of their new tsaritsa proclaimed second co-ruler of the empire. The emperor readily agreed to elevate the status of his eldest son (likely having suggested the request to his guests himself, during the earlier talks), thus reducing Constantine VII Porphyrogennetos to the third position among the empire's rulers[87]. We do not know whether Maria was present at this reception. Considering the requirements of the Byzantine court

---

[85] В. Гюзелев, *Значението на брака на цар Петър (927–969) с ромейката Мария-Ирина Лакапина (911–962)*, [in:] *Културните текстове на миналото – носители, символи, идеи*, vol. I, *Текстовете на историята, история на текстовете. Материали от Юбилейната международна конференция в чест на 60-годишнината на проф. д.и.н. Казимир Попконстантинов, Велико Търново, 29–31 октомври 2003 г.*, София 2005, p. 29; Т. Тодоров, *България...*, p. 169–173.

[86] Continuator of George the Monk, p. 905–906; Symeon Logothete, 136, 49, p. 327–328; Leo Grammatikos, p. 317; Pseudo-Symeon Magistros, 34, p. 741; Continuator of Theophanes, VI, 23, p. 414; John Skylitzes, p. 223.

[87] Continuator of George the Monk, p. 906; Symeon Logothete, 136, 49–50, p. 328; Leo Grammatikos, p. 317; Pseudo-Symeon Magistros, 34, p. 741; Continuator of Theophanes, VI, 23, p. 414; John Skylitzes, p. 223–224; John Zonaras, XVI, 19, p. 474–475. Cf. J. Shepard, *A marriage...*, p. 132; Т. Тодоров, *Константин Багренородни и династичният брак между владетелските домове на Преслав и Константинопол от 927 г.*, "Преславска книжовна школа" 7, 2003, p. 396; П. Павлов, *Години на мир и "ратни беди" (927–1018)*, [in:] Г. Атанасов, В. Вачкова, П. Павлов, *Българска национална история*, vol. III, *Първо българско царство (680–1018)*, Велико Търново 2015, p. 412.

etiquette, we may assume that she was elsewhere at the time, in the quarters reserved exclusively for ladies – celebrating her marriage in the company of her mother Sophia, aunt Helena and other female relatives and high-ranking women.

Once all the wedding-related events were over, the newlyweds departed for Bulgaria. Christopher, Sophia and *protovestiarios* Theophanes accompanied them to the Hebdomon, where the imperial couple ate their final meal with their daughter and son-in-law. Afterwards came the time for the sorrowful parting: Maria's tearful parents hugged her, bade farewell to Peter, and returned to the city. The newlyweds, in turn, made their way to Preslav. As mentioned by the Continuator of George the Monk, Maria brought with her innumerable riches[88]; besides, she was likely accompanied by several trusted people who would advise and assist her in the new environment[89].

[88] Continuator of George the Monk, p. 906–907; Symeon Logothete, 136, 51, p. 328–329; Leo Grammatikos, p. 317; Continuator of Theophanes, VI, 23, p. 414–415; John Skylitzes, p. 224.
[89] M.J. Leszka, *Wizerunek...*, p. 125; В. Гюзелев, *Значението...*, p. 29.

IV

Zofia A. Brzozowska

The Marriage with the Bulgarian Ruler – Honor or Degradation?

Curiously, in the account of the authors contemporary to the events of 927, there is a unique passage related to Maria's farewells with her parents. The Byzantine chroniclers attempt to describe Maria's internal experiences and present her personal views on her marriage with the Bulgarian ruler, discussing her mixed feelings during the journey to her new country. Maria was sad to be separated from her mother, father, relatives and the palace in Constantinople, which she by then considered her family home. At the same time, however, she was filled with joy – not only because she had married a man of imperial status, but also because she had been proclaimed a Bulgarian ruler herself[1].

The titulature and status of Peter's wife at the Preslav court will be discussed in detail in a later part of this monograph. At this point, however, it is interesting to point out a different circumstance. According to the Byzantine sources, Maria was far from perceiving her marriage with the Bulgarian monarch as a misalliance unacceptable for a woman of her standing, nor did she see it as dictated by the need of reaching a compromise. Moreover, she did not consider Symeon's son a barbarian, and

---

[1] Continuator of George the Monk, p. 906–907; Symeon Logothete, 136, 51, p. 329; Continuator of Theophanes, VI, 23, p. 415.

departing for Bulgaria by no means filled her with dread. It is useful to compare the passage under discussion with the narrative about another 'female experience,' associated with an analogous situation from the 10th century – Anna Porphyrogennete's attitude towards her prospective marriage with Vladimir I, as portrayed in the Old Rus' historiographical text known as the *Russian Primary Chronicle*. The text as we know it today was redacted in the 1110s, i.e. at a time when, in Rus', Svyatoslav's son was considered worthy of comparison with Constantine I the Great – a thoroughly Christian ruler. Thus, the source informs us that the sister of Basil II and Constantine VIII was most reluctant to wed the Kievan ruler, arguing that such marriage meant a fate little better than captivity, or perhaps even death. According to the anonymous author, Anna's two brothers pleaded with her to act according to their will, and even had to force her to board the ship that was to take her to Cherson. Much like our protagonist, the Porphyrogennete parted with her close ones in tears, but her emotions were quite different from Maria's conflicting feelings[2].

Interestingly, none of the extant sources mention Peter's view of Maria and the marriage arranged by George Sursuvul. In other words: how prestigious, honorable and politically advantageous was it for the young Bulgarian tsar to tie the knot with a woman from the Lekapenos family, who did not carry the title of *porphyrogennete* and was not even a daughter of the emperor (who, incidentally, was neither 'born in the purple' nor the sole ruler)?

---

  [2] *Russian Primary Chronicle*, AM 6496, p. 111–112: ѡна же не хотѧше ити. ꙗко в полонъ реⷱ҇ иду. лучи бы ми сде оумрети. и рѣста еи братья. еда како ѡбратить Бъ тобою рускую землю в покаꙗнье. а гречьскую землю избавишь ѿ лютыꙗ рати. видиши ли колько зла створиша Русь Грекомъ. и нынѣ аще не идеши то же имуть створити намъ. и ѡдва ю принудиша. ѡна же сѣдъши в кубару. цѣловавши оужики своꙗ. съ плачемъ поиде чресъ море. и приде къ Корсуню (*Anna, however, departed with reluctance. 'It is as if I were setting out into captivity,' she lamented; 'better were it for me to die at home.' But her brothers protested, 'Through your agency God turns the land of Rus' to repentance, and you will relieve Greece from the danger of grievous war. Do you not see how much harm the Russes have already brought upon the Greeks? If you do not set out, they may bring on us the same misfortunes.' It was thus that they overcame her hesitation only with great difficulty. The Princess embarked upon a ship, and after tearfully embracing her kinfolk, she set forth across the sea and arrived at Kherson* – transl. S. H. C r o s s, O. P. S h e r b o w i t z - W e t z o r, p. 112–113).

The chroniclers from the so-called circle of Symeon Logothete, who had personal ties to the court of Romanos I, and other writers well-disposed towards this ruler (e.g. Arethas of Caesarea or Theodore Daphnopates, considered the author of *On the Treaty with the Bulgarians*) present the agreement of 927 – whose stability was, after all, guaranteed by the marriage of Maria and Peter – as a substantial diplomatic achievement of the Lekapenos emperor, ensuring the long-desired peace on the north-ern border of Byzantium and neutralizing the Bulgarian threat for a long time[3]. Traces of this approach – no doubt propagandist to some extent – are also visible in the account of Constantine VII, although he was fully open about his aversion towards the Lekapenoi and their policies[4]. Even in the Bulgarian *Tale of the Prophet Isaiah*, we find the statement that Peter lived in cordial friendship with the Byzantine emperor, ensuring prosperity for his subjects for many years[5].

---

[3] J. S h e p a r d, *A marriage too far? Maria Lekapena and Peter of Bulgaria*, [in:] *The Empress Theophano. Byzantium and the West at the turn of the first millennium*, ed. A. D a v i d s, Cambridge 1995, p. 130–131; А. Н и к о л о в, *Политическа мисъл в ранносредновековна България (средата на IX-края на X в.)*, София 2006, p. 237–238; A. B r z ó s t k o w s k a, *Kroniki z kręgu Symeona Logotety*, [in:] *Testimonia najdawniej-szych dziejów Słowian. Seria grecka*, vol. V, *Pisarze z X wieku*, ed. A. B r z ó s t k o w s k a, Warszawa 2009, p. 64; K. M a r i n o w, *In the Shackles of the Evil One. The Portrayal of Tsar Symeon I the Great (893–927) in the Oration On the treaty with the Bulgarians*, "Studia Ceranea. Journal of the Waldemar Ceran Research Centre for the History and Culture of the Mediterranean Area and South-East Europe" 1, 2011, p. 157–190; i d e m, *Peace in the House of Jacob. A Few Remarks on the Ideology of Two Biblical Themes in the Oration On the Treaty with the Bulgarians*, "Bulgaria Mediaevalis" 3, 2012, p. 85–93; M.J. L e s z k a, K. M a r i n o w, *Carstwo bułgarskie. Polityka – społeczeństwo – gospodarka – kultura. 866–971*, Warszawa 2015, p. 160–162.

[4] C o n s t a n t i n e V I I P o r p h y r o g e n n e t o s, *On the Governance of the Empire*, 13, p. 74. Cf. Т. Т о д о р о в, *Константин Багренородни и династичният брак между владетелските домове на Преслав и Константинопол от 927 г.*, "Преславска книжовна школа" 7, 2003, p. 395.

[5] *Tale of the Prophet Isaiah*, p. 17: тогⷣа ꙋбо въ дни и лѣтⷶ ѥтто Пеⷮра цⷬрѧ вльгарь-скаⷢⷪ быⷭ изьꙍбьылїа ꙍ всего. сирѣчь пшеница и масло и медⷶ жⷷ и млѣка и вина, и ꙍ всего дарованїа Бжїа връше и кипѣше. и не вѣ ꙍсвⷹдⷮѣнїе ни ꙍ цюⷨь. Нь вѣ ситостъ изькꙍбильⷭ ꙍ всего до изволенїа Бжїа (*In the days and years of St. Peter, the tsar of the Bulgarians, there was plenty of everything, that is to say, of wheat and butter, honey, milk and wine, the land was overflowing with every gift of God, there was*

Liudprand of Cremona's remark on Maria's adopting her new name upon entering marriage should most likely be considered in the context of this 'pacifist' propaganda of the Byzantine court. After all, what we find in the *Antapodosis* is an exaggeration of the idea expressed in all of the above-mentioned texts: that Romanos I achieved the neutralization of Symeon's expansionist, anti-Byzantine plans, as well as the creation of a firm association between the Bulgarians and the empire, through signing a peace treaty advantageous for Constantinople. The originality of Liudprand's approach lies in his particular underscoring of Maria's role in this process: her marriage, according to the bishop of Cremona, became the foundation of a long-lasting friendship between Byzantium and Bulgaria. Therefore, according to the western diplomat, naming young Maria with an appellation meaning 'peace' was dictated by the desire to underline her special status as a *custodes pacis*[6].

It is worth noting that the ideological meaning of names of empress-es was occasionally used by them for propaganda purposes. Irene, for instance, masterfully used this aspect of her name by establishing an iconographic program of coins bearing her image, or by changing the name of Veria (a border town located in a previously troubled area) to Eirenopolis ('City of Irene' / 'City of Peace') in 784[7]. On the other hand, it should be borne in mind that no source except for Liudprand's account contains the information about Maria Lekapene changing her name to Irene. If such an act indeed took place, it ought to be treated as strictly

no dearth of anything but by the will of God everything was in abundance and to satiety). Cf. M.J. L e s z k a, K. M a r i n o w, *Carstwo bułgarskie...*, p. 162.

[6] L i u d p r a n d   o f   C r e m o n a, *Retribution*, III, 38, p. 86. Cf. S. G e o r g i e v a, *The Byzantine Princesses in Bulgaria*, "Byzantinobulgarica" 9, 1995, p. 166; J. S h e p a r d, *A marriage...*, p. 126; В. Г ю з е л е в, *Значението на брака на цар Петър (927–969) с ромейката Мария-Ирина Лакапина (911–962)*, [in:] *Културните текстове на миналото – носители, символи, идеи*, vol. I, *Текстовете на историята, история на текстовете. Материали от Юбилейната международна конференция в чест на 60-годишнината на проф. д.и.н. Казимир Попконстантинов, Велико Търново, 29–31 октомври 2003 г.*, София 2005, p. 30; А. Н и к о л о в, *Политическа мисъл...*, p. 234.

[7] J. H e r r i n, *Women in Purple. Rulers of Medieval Byzantium*, London 2002, p. 81; K. K o t s i s, *Defining Female Authority in Eighth-Century Byzantium: the Numismatic Images of the Empress Irene (797–802)*, "Journal of Late Antiquity" 5.1, 2012, p. 199–200.

symbolic. Had Peter's wife decided to formally change her name, the official *sigilla* used in Bulgaria in the years 927–945 would have borne the name of Irene, whereas, on surviving artifacts of this kind, we invariably find the name Maria[8].

However, let us return to the issue of what political benefits and prestige Peter may have gained through marrying a representative of the Lekapenos family. The consequences of the peace treaty of 927, including the unquestionable elevation of the Slavic ruler's status in the international arena (associated with Byzantium's recognition of his right to the title of emperor/tsar of the Bulgarians), are discussed elsewhere in this monograph. Here, on the other hand, we shall deal with a few questions of another kind, such as: Did Peter consider the opportunity to marry Maria an honor? Was this view shared by those around him, as well as by other contemporary European rulers?

Both of the above questions should, in fact, be answered in the positive. There can be no doubt that Maria and Peter's marriage was an unprecedented event – never before had such a high-ranking Byzantine woman, daughter and granddaughter of emperors, been married to a foreign monarch, ruling a people that had only become Christian some sixty years earlier. The momentousness of this act was hardly diminished by the fact that the young tsar's fiancée was not 'born in the purple[9].' The Byzantine-Bulgarian marriage was likely the talk of European courts,

---

[8] J. S h e p a r d, *A marriage...*, p. 141–143; Г. А т а н а с о в, *Инсигниите на средновековните български владетели. Корони, скиптри, сфери, оръжия, костюми, накити*, Плевен 1999, p. 98–99; И. Й о р д а н о в, *Корпус на печатите на Средновековна България*, София 2001, p. 58–60; В. Г ю з е л е в, *Значението на брака...*, p. 27; И. Б о ж и л о в, В. Г ю з е л е в, *История на средновековна България. VII–XIV в.*, София 2006, p. 275–276; Т. Т о д о р о в, *България през втората и третата четвърт на X век: политическа история*, София 2006 [unpublished PhD thesis], p. 156–159; i d e m, *Владетелският статут и титла на цар Петър I след октомври 927 г.: писмени сведения и сфрагистични данни (сравнителен анализ)*, [in:] *Юбилеен сборник. Сто години от рождението на д-р Васил Хараланов (1907–2007)*, Шумен 2008, p. 99–101; С. Г е о р г и е в а, *Жената в българското средновековие*, Пловдив 2011, p. 313–315; M.J. L e s z k a, K. M a r i n o w, *Carstwo bułgarskie...*, p. 159–160.

[9] S. G e o r g i e v a, *The Byzantine Princesses...*, p. 167; В. Г ю з е л е в, *Значението на брака...*, p. 30; M.J. L e s z k a, K. M a r i n o w, *Carstwo bułgarskie...*, p. 158.

becoming a source of inspiration for rulers of other countries to aim for similar arrangements.

This assertion is confirmed by two sources: chapter 13 of the treatise *On the Governance of the Empire* by Constantine VII and the account by Liudprand of Cremona. The former work, written before 952, includes a series of specific arguments with which a *basileus* – Romanos II, to whom the work is dedicated, and his successors – should reject claims of foreign rulers who, referring to what happened in 927, should wish to arrange a marriage with a woman from the imperial family (either for themselves or for one of their sons). The Porphyrogennetos advised that, during such negotiations, Romanos I should be presented as a simpleton, who not only lacked the knowledge about the most basic customs of the empire, but in fact knowingly disregarded them. Moreover, he ignored the law of the Church and the prohibition of Constantine I the Great, who supposedly strictly forbade his sons to enter into marriage with representatives of any of the foreign peoples, to the exception of the Franks. Constantine VII also advised emphasizing the low position of Christopher Lekapenos, who was – according to him – merely the third in the hierarchy of the rulers, thus lacking any actual power[10].

---

[10] Constantine VII Porphyrogennetos, *On the Governance of the Empire*, 13, p. 70–74. Cf. Г. Литаврин, *Константин Багрянородный о Болгарии и Болгарах*, [in:] *Сборник в чест на акад. Димитър Ангелов*, ed. В. Велков, София 1994, p. 30–37; J. Herrin, *Theophano. Considerations on the Education of a Byzantine Princess*, [in:] *The Empress Theophano. Byzantium and the West at the turn of the first millennium*, ed. A. Davids, Cambridge 1995, p. 68 [=J. Herrin, *Unrivalled Influence. Women and Empire in Byzantium*, Princeton 2013, p. 242]; S. Georgieva, *The Byzantine Princesses…*, p. 167; Т. Тодоров, *Константин Багренородни…*, p. 391–397; В. Гюзелев, *Значението на брака…*, p. 30–31; A. Paroń, *"Trzeba, abyś tymi oto słowami odparł i to niedorzeczne żądanie" – wokół De administrando imperio Konstantyna VII*, [in:] *Causa creandi. O pragmatyce źródła historycznego*, eds. S. Rosik, P. Wiszewski, Wrocław 2005, p. 345–361; M.J. Leszka, K. Marinow, *Carstwo bułgarskie…*, p. 158; П. Павлов, *Години на мир и "ратни беди" (927–1018)*, [in:] Г. Атанасов, В. Вачкова, П. Павлов, *Българска национална история*, vol. III, *Първо българско царство (680–1018)*, Велико Търново 2015, p. 411; С. Звездов, *Договорът от 927 година между България и Византия*, "History. Bulgarian Journal of Historical Education" 23.3, 2015, p. 268; idem, *Българо-византийските отношения при цар Петър I*, София 2016, p. 17–18.

In this part of the narrative, Porphyrogennetos undoubtedly vented his personal antipathy and resentment[11]. On the other hand, it is also clear from his reasoning that, during his reign, the tendency among foreign rulers to seek dynastic marriages with Constantinople had indeed increased; the 927 arrangement served as a pivotal precedent here. Reading chapter 13 of the treatise *On the Governance of the Empire*, one might even conclude that the rulers of the northern peoples, among them the Rus' and the Khazars, sought concessions on three specific points from the emperors: they wished to be sent imperial regalia, have the Byzantines disclose the secret formula for 'Greek fire,' and have them agree to a marriage between a Byzantine woman of high status with a representative of their own house[12].

Having died in 959, Constantine VII Porphyrogennetos did not live to see further such marriages, which he considered so abominable: Theophano only married Otto II in 972[13], while Constantine's own granddaughter Anna married Vladimir I in 988/989[14]. Some scholars are of

---

[11] Д.И. П о л ы в я н н ы й, *Царь Петр в исторической памяти болгарского средневековья*, [in:] *Средновековният българин и "другите". Сборник в чест на 60-годишнината на проф. дин Петър Ангелов*, eds. А. Н и к о л о в, Г.Н. Н и к о л о в, София 2013, p. 139.

[12] C o n s t a n t i n e V I I P o r p h y r o g e n n e t o s, *On the Governance of the Empire*, 13, p. 68–74.

[13] On the political and cultural consequences of this marriage see: I. Š e v č e n k o, *Byzanz und der Westen im 10. Jahrhundert*, [in:] *Kunst im Zeitalter der Kaiserin Theophanu. Akten des Internationalen Colloquiums veranstaltet vom Schnütgen-Museum*, eds. A. v o n E u w, P. S c h r e i n e r, Köln 1993, p. 5–30; H.K. S c h u l z e, *Die Heiratsurkunde der Kaiserin Theophanu. Die griechische Kaiserin und das römisch-deutsche Reich 972–991*, Hannover 2007; M. S m o r ą g - R ó ż y c k a, *Cesarzowa Teofano i królowa Gertruda. Uwagi o wizerunkach władczyń w sztuce średniowiecznej na marginesie rozważań o miniaturach w Kodeksie Gertrudy*, [in:] *Gertruda Mieszkówna i jej rękopis*, ed. A. A n d r z e j u k, Radzymin 2013, p. 129–133.

[14] A. P o p p e, *Państwo i Kościół na Rusi w XI w.*, Warszawa 1968, p. 20, 33; i d e m, *The Political Background to the Baptism of Rus': Byzantine-Russian Relations between 986–989*, "Dumbarton Oaks Papers" 30, 1976, p. 195–244; D. P o p p e, A. P o p p e, *Dziewosłęby o Porfirogenetkę Annę*, [in:] *Cultus et cognitio. Studia z dziejów średniowiecznej kultury*, eds. S.K. K u c z y ń s k i et al., Warszawa 1976, p. 451–468; A. P o p p e, *Ruś i Bizancjum w latach 986–989*, "Kwartalnik Historyczny" 85.1, 1978, p. 3–23; А.Ю. К а р п о в, *Владимир Святой*, Москва 2004, p. 198–216; A. K i j a s, *Chrzest Rusi*, Poznań 2006,

the opinion that, in his last years, the 'purple-born' emperor had to counter the ambitions of another Rus' ruler – princess Olga, who sought to marry her son Svyatoslav to one of the emperor's descendants (either daughter or granddaughter). Seeking consent for such a marriage may have been one of the goals of her visit to Constantinople (most likely in 957). The Kievan ruler's plan was not well received by Constantine VII, however. The fiasco of the marriage negotiations likely deepened Olga's dissatisfaction with the results of her diplomatic mission, stressed by the author of the *Russian Primary Chronicle*. The memory of her far-reaching intentions did, however, survive in the Old Rus' historiographical tradition. According to experts on the matter, it may be reflected in the above-mentioned oldest Kievan chronicle, whose extant form dates back to the early years of the 12th century: it includes a seemingly completely improbable story of Constantine VII Porphyrogennetos proposing to marry Olga[15].

---

p. 13–15; C.J. H i l s d a l e, *Byzantine Art and Diplomacy in an Age of Decline*, Cambridge 2014, p. 317.

     [15] *Russian Primary Chronicle*, AM 6463, p. 61–64: оудививъся црь разуму єя. бесѣдова к неи и рекъ єи. подобна єси цртѣти въ градⁱ с нами. она же разумѣвши реⁱ ко црю. азъ погана єсмь. да аще ма хощеши крⁱти. то крⁱт ма самъ. аще ли то не крⁱщюса. и крⁱти ю црь съ птⁱархмъ [...] и по крⁱщньи возва ю црь и рече єи хощю та поати собѣ женѣ. она же реⁱ како хочеши ма поати крⁱт ма самъ. и нарекъ ма тъщерью. а [въ] хⁱеянехъ того нѣⁱ закона а ты самъ вѣⁱ. и реⁱ црь прⁱеклюкала ма єси Шльга. и дасть єи дары многи злато и сребро. паволоки и съсуды различныа. и ѿпусти ю нарекъ ю дъщерью собѣ [...] Си же Шльга приде Киеву и присла к неи црь Гречьскии глⁱа. якⁱ много дарихъ та. ты бо глⁱще ко мнѣ. яко аще возъвращюса в Русь. многи дары прⁱслю ти челадь. воскъ. и съкру. и вои въ помощь. Ѿвѣщавши Шльга. и реⁱ къ сломъ. аще ты рьци такоже постоиши оу мене в Почаинѣ якоже азъ в Сюду то тогда ти дамь. и ѿпусти слы съ рекъши (*the Emperor wondered at her intellect. He conversed with her and remarked that she was worthy to reign with him in his city. When Olga heard his words, she replied that she was still a pagan, and that if he desired to baptize her, he should perform this function himself; otherwise, she was unwilling to accept baptism. The Emperor, with the assistance of the Patriarch, accordingly baptized her [...] After her baptism, the Emperor summoned Olga and made known to her that he wished her to become his wife. But she replied, 'How can you marry me, after yourself baptizing me and calling me your daughter? For among Christians that is unlawful, as you yourself must know.' Then the Emperor said, 'Olga, you have outwitted me.' He gave her many gifts of gold, silver, silks, and various vases, and dismissed her, still calling her his daughter [...] Thus Olga arrived in Kiev, and the Greek*

Neither Romanos II nor his successors heeded the advice laid out in the treatise *On the Governance of the Empire*, as can be seen from Liudprand of Cremona's account of his diplomatic mission to Constantinople in 968: his objective was to win Nikephoros II Phokas's approval for the marriage between the son of emperor Otto I with a member of the Byzantine imperial family. The diplomat admitted that, during the negotiations, he brought up the marriage between the daughter of Christopher Lekapenos and Bulgarian tsar Peter. The argument, however, was rejected by the Greek side, as Liudprand was told that Maria's father was not a *porphyrogennetos* – a remark that could almost have been taken directly from Constantine VII's work[16].

To sum up, Peter could be confident that he was obtaining an honor that many other monarchs had sought in vain. It was most likely the desire to boast of his Byzantine wife that led him to consistently include her image (and in some cases – also her name) on official Bulgarian seals during the period 927–945. Notably, this was a wholly new practice in the self-presentation of the Preslav court – none of the female

---

Emperor sent a message to her, saying, 'Inasmuch as I bestowed many gifts upon you, you promised me that on your return to Rus' you would send me many presents of slaves, wax, and furs, and despatch soldiery to aid me.' Olga made answer to the envoys that if the Emperor would spend as long a time with her in the Pochayna as she had remained on the Bosporus, she would grant his request. With these words, she dismissed the envoys – transl. S.H. C r o s s, O.P. S h e r b o w i t z-W e t z o r, p. 82–83). Cf. J.P. A r r i g n o n, *Les relations internationales de la Russie Kiévienne au milieu du Xe siècle et le baptême de la princesse Olga*, [in:] *Actes des congrès de la Société des historiens médiévistes de l'enseignement supérieur public. 9e congrès*, Dijon 1978, p. 172–173; Н.Ф. К о т л я р, *Древняя Русь и Киев в летописных преданиях и легендах*, Киев 1986, p. 105–108; Н.Л. П у ш к а р е в а, *Женщины Древней Руси*, Москва 1989, p. 18; Г. Л и т а в р и н, *Византия, Болгария, Древняя Русь (IX–начало XII в.)*, Санкт-Петербург 2000, p. 198, 211; А.В. Н а з а р е н к о, *Древняя Русь на международных путях. Междисциплинарные очерки культурных, торговых, политических связей IX–XII вв.*, Москва 2001, p. 302; М.Б. С в е р д л о в, *Домонгольская Русь. Князь и княжеская власть на Руси VI–первой трети XIII вв.*, Санкт-Петербург 2003, p. 204–205; F. T i n n e f e l d, *Zum Stand der Olga–Diskussion*, [in:] *Zwischen Polis, Provinz und Peripherie. Beiträge zur byzantinischen Geschichte und Kultur*, eds. L.M. H o f f m a n n, A. M o n c h i z a d e h, Wiesbaden 2005, p. 557; А.Ю. К а р п о в, *Княгиня Ольга*, Москва 2012, p. 180, 197.

[16] L i u d p r a n d o f C r e m o n a, *Embassy*, 16, p. 194. Cf. J. S h e p a r d, *A marriage...*, p. 122; В. Г ю з е л е в, *Значението на брака...*, p. 31.

Bulgarian rulers before Maria (and none after her) were honored in this manner[17].

What is more, the marriage was not only a source of splendor for Peter, but also brought tangible political benefits with it. By marrying Maria in 927, Symeon's son entered the family that produced four of the five Roman emperors ruling at the time: Romanos I and his sons Christopher, Stephen and Constantine. Through his marriage to Maria, Peter also became closely tied to Constantine VII Porphyrogennetos. In 933, the list of his politically influential connections was further extended by Theophylaktos, the new patriarch of Constantinople. Thus, the alliance with the ambitious 'Lekapenos clan' may have appeared to the young Bulgarian ruler as having a considerable political potential.

Consequently, we should probably agree with those scholars who view the previously mentioned seals (depicting Peter and Maria) as artifacts of a commemorative and propagandist nature. The *sigilla* were created to commemorate the peace treaty of 927 as well as to highlight the significance of this event for the Bulgarian state and its ruler[18]. It is also possible that Symeon's son wanted to use them to show how much he valued the family connection with Romanos I. One more thing is worth noting in this connection – the name and depiction of Maria disappear from Peter's seals after 945 (at the time when the Lekapenos family was removed from power and when Constantine VII Porphyrogennetos

---

[17] S. G e o r g i e v a, *The Byzantine Princesses...*, p. 167, 201; В. Г ю з е л е в, *Значението на брака...*, p. 27. Only a few of the later Bulgarian royal women could boast such a distinction. Irene Palaiologina, wife of John Asen III (1279–1280) used her own seal. Among women depicted on coins were e.g. Irene Komnene, regent for her son Michael I Asen (1246–1256); Theodora Palaiologina, wife of two consecutive tsars – Theodore Svetoslav (1300–1321) and Michael III Shishman (1323–1330); Theodora, second wife of John Alexander (1331–1371) and Anna, married to John Stratsimir (1356–1396). Г. А т а н а с о в, *Инсигниите...*, p. 190–192; В. И г н а т о в, *Българските царици. Владетелките на България от VII до XIV в.*, София 2008, p. 85–87, 89–90; С. Г е о р г и е в а, *Жената...*, p. 320–323, 348, 352–354.

[18] И. Б о ж и л о в, В. Г ю з е л е в, *История...*, p. 276; M.J. L e s z k a, K. M a r i n o w, *Carstwo bułgarskie...*, p. 159; И. Й о р д а н о в, *Корпус на средновековните български печати*, София 2016, p. 89.

began his sole rule)[19]. One may, therefore, get the impression that both Maria's inclusion into the self-presentation scheme of the Bulgarian ruler in 927 as well as her removal in 945 were dictated by diplomacy and foreign policy: in both cases, it was a bow to the reigning *basileus*[20].

[19] S. R u n c i m a n, *The Emperor Romanus Lecapenus and His Reign. A Study of Tenth-Century Byzantium*, Cambridge 1969, p. 229–237; Г. А т а н а с о в, *Инсигниите...*, p. 100; Т. Т о д о р о в, *Константин Багренородни...*, p. 396–397; А. Н и к о л о в, *Политическа мисъл...*, p. 269–278; Т. Т о д о р о в, *България...*, p. 159; Г. А т а н а с о в, *Печатите на българските владетели от IX–X в. в Дръстър (Силистра)*, [in:] *От тука започва България. Материали от втората национална конференция по история, археология и културен туризъм "Пътуване към България", Шумен 14–16.05.2010 година*, ed. И. Й о р д а н о в, Шумен 2011, p. 289.

[20] И. Й о р д а н о в, *Корпус на печатите...*, p. 63; M.J. L e s z k a, K. M a r i n o w, *Carstwo bułgarskie...*, p. 160.

V

Zofia A. Brzozowska

Maria Lekapene as a Mother

There is no doubt that Maria fulfilled what medieval people considered the basic duty of a wife and empress consort – she gave Peter male offspring, providing him with an heir. Relating the events that occurred at the close of the 10th century, Byzantine chroniclers (among them John Skylitzes and John Zonaras) mention two of Maria and her husband's sons, who reigned in Bulgaria in succession: first Boris II, then Romanos[1]. The couple had at least one more child, however. This is clear from the information included in the *Continuation of George the Monk*, as well as in the *Chronicle of Symeon Logothete*, and repeated in the *Continuation of Theophanes*: after the death of her father, Maria embarked on her final journey to Constantinople, taking her three children with her. Interestingly, while the phrasing in the original Greek versions of these works does not specify the sex of the tsaritsa's children (μετὰ παίδων τριῶν)[2], the 14th-century

---

[1] John Skylitzes, p. 255, 288, 297, 310, 328, 329, 346; John Zonaras, XVI, 23, p. 495; XVII, 1, p. 522; XVII, 2, p. 529; XVII, 4, p. 536; XVII, 6, p. 547; XVII, 8, p. 560.

[2] Continuator of George the Monk, p. 913; Symeon Logothete, 136, 67, p. 334; Continuator of Theophanes, VI, 35, p. 422. A similar wording is found in the oldest translation of the *Continuation of George the Monk* into Slavic

author of the Slavic translation of the *Chronicle of Symeon Logothete* altered the source's information, stating that she arrived in the city on the Bosporos with her three sons (съ трими сꙑнови)[3].

Thus, in the literature on the subject we occasionally encounter the view that Maria and Peter had a third son aside from the male offspring noted by the Byzantine sources. He would have been Plenimir, whose name appears in the laudatory part of the *Synodikon of Tsar Boril*, directly after the mention of Peter and before that of Boris and Romanos[4]. It cannot be ruled out that Plenimir was the first child of the imperial couple, who – because of a premature death or poor health – did not play any significant role in the history of the Bulgarian state. Consequently, he would not have been noted by the Byzantine chroniclers[5].

Ivan Duychev, in an article devoted to this character, drew attention to another interesting question: while both of Peter and Maria's sons present in the Byzantine chronicles bore the names of their great-grandfathers (Bulgarian prince Boris-Michael and emperor Romanos I Lekapenos), the couple's hypothetical firstborn child would have been given the exceedingly rare Slavic name Plenimir[6]. It may be useful to examine the etymology of this anthroponym here. Excluding the possibility of an error on the part of the scribe who completed the late, 16th-century copy of the *Synodikon of Tsar Boril* in which we find the laudation, we could assume that the name had the shape Плѣнимиръ[7]. This is a compound consisting of two Old Church Slavic nouns: плѣнъ ('captivity, prize of war') and

---

(as well as in the Old Rus' *Hellenic and Roman Chronicle* of the second redaction, based on the latter): с троими дѣти. C o n t i n u a t o r   o f   G e o r g e   t h e   M o n k (Slavic), 10, p. 566; *Hellenic and Roman Chronicle*, p. 501.

[3] S y m e o n   L o g o t h e t e (Slavic), p. 140.

[4] *Synodikon of Tsar Boril*, p. 149–150; В. И г н а т о в, *Българските царици. Владетелките на България от VII до XIV в.*, София 2008, p. 14; M.J. L e s z k a, K. M a r i n o w, *Carstwo bułgarskie. Polityka – społeczeństwo – gospodarka – kultura. 866–971*, Warszawa 2015, p. 187.

[5] И. Д у й ч е в, *Българският княз Пленимир*, "Македонски преглед" 13.1, 1942, p. 19–20; S. G e o r g i e v a, *The Byzantine Princesses in Bulgaria*, "Byzantinobulgarica" 9, 1995, p. 168–169.

[6] И. Д у й ч е в, *Българският княз...*, p. 20. J o h n   S k y l i t z e s (p. 346) adds that Romanos was also called Symeon, in honor of his grandfather.

[7] *Synodikon of Tsar Boril*, p. 149–150.

миръ ('peace'). As we saw earlier, Constantine VII Porphyrogennetos and the author of *On the Treaty with the Bulgarians* claim that one of the consequences of the peace of 927 was the exchange of prisoners, owing to which many Byzantine soldiers held in Bulgarian captivity could return to their homeland[8]. Perhaps this took place at the time (928) during which the Bulgarian imperial couple's firstborn entered the world? Maria Lekapene, aware of the propaganda significance of rulers' names (according to Liudprand of Cremona, she became known as Irene in 927), may have arranged for her eldest child to receive a symbolic name – one referring to the peace treaty concluded a few months earlier, and to the accompanying exchange of prisoners of war.

Maria and Peter may also have had one or several daughters. In the historiography, the two girls from the Bulgarian 'royal family' (βασιλικὸν γένος) who – according to Leo the Deacon – were sent to Constantinople in 969 as the spouses-to-be of Basil II and Constantine VIII have occasionally been considered to have been Maria and her husband's children[9]. Similar views have been expressed concerning the anonymous Bulgarian woman who became one of the wives of Vladimir I, prince of Rus', and who bore him two sons (the elder received the rather telling name of Boris-Romanos[10]).

---

[8] Constantine VII Porphyrogennetos, *On the Governance of the Empire*, 13, p. 74; *On the Treaty with the Bulgarians*, 5, p. 260. Cf. Т. Тодоров, *Константин Багренородни и династичният брак между владетелските домове на Преслав и Константинопол от 927 г.*, "Преславска книжовна школа" 7, 2003, p. 395–396; K. Marinow, *In the Shackles of the Evil One. The Portrayal of Tsar Symeon I the Great (893–927) in the Oration On the treaty with the Bulgarians*, "Studia Ceranea. Journal of the Waldemar Ceran Research Centre for the History and Culture of the Mediterranean Area and South-East Europe" 1, 2011, p. 178; idem, *Peace in the House of Jacob. A Few Remarks on the Ideology of Two Biblical Themes in the Oration On the Treaty with the Bulgarians*, "Bulgaria Mediaevalis" 3, 2012, p. 85; M.J. Leszka, K. Marinow, *Carstwo bułgarskie...*, p. 156; С. Звездов, *Договорът от 927 година между България и Византия*, "History. Bulgarian Journal of Historical Education" 23.3, 2015, p. 267; idem, *Българо-византийските отношения при цар Петър I*, София 2016, p. 13–14.

[9] Leo the Deacon, V, 3, p. 79; И. Дуйчев, *Българският княз...*, p. 18; В. Игнатов, *Българските царици...*, p. 14.

[10] *Russian Primary Chronicle*, AM 6488, p. 81: ѿ Болгарыни Бориса и Глѣба (*by a Bulgarian woman, Boris and Gleb* – transl. S.H. Cross, O.P. Sherbowitz-Wetzor, p. 94). А.А. Молчанов, *Владимир Мономах и его имена. К изучению*

Both of these hypotheses, however, have to be rejected for chronological reasons. Rather, the princesses mentioned above may have been Maria's granddaughters and Boris II's daughters: born ca. 960, they may have been considered of appropriate age to become the fiancées of the sons of Romanos II and Theophano[11]. Similarly, even if we were to assume that Vladimir's Bulgarian wife was a very late child of Maria, it would be difficult to accept that she was the mother of prince Gleb-David, most likely still a teenager in the year of his death (1015). The woman in question – if we were to acknowledge the hypothesis of her Preslav origin in the first place – may have been a granddaughter of the Bulgarian tsaritsa (e.g. a child of Boris II, or of one of her daughters)[12].

княжеского именника Рюриковичей X–XII вв., "Славяноведение" 2004, 2, p. 81–83; А.Ф. Л и т в и н а, Ф.Б. У с п е н с к и й, *Выбор имени у русских князей в X–XVI вв. Династическая история сквозь призму антропонимики*, Москва 2006, p. 477–478.

[11] S. G e o r g i e v a, *The Byzantine Princesses...*, p. 169; G. A t a n a s o v, *On the Origin, Function and the Owner of the Adornments of the Preslav Treasure from the 10th century*, "Archaeologia Bulgarica" 3.3, 1999, p. 91; i d e m, *Инсигниите на средновековните български владетели. Корони, скиптри, сфери, оръжия, костюми, накити*, Плевен 1999, p. 234–235; M.J. L e s z k a, K. M a r i n o w, *Carstwo bułgarskie...*, p. 190.

[12] Based on anthroponomical material, certain contemporary Russian historians are inclined to consider the mother of Boris-Romanos and Gleb-David to have been a descendant of the Bulgarian royal family, albeit without specifying their exact relation to Maria Lekapene and Peter (А.А. М о л ч а н о в, *Владимир Мономах...*, p. 81–83; А.Ф. Л и т в и н а, Ф.Б. У с п е н с к и й, *Выбор имени...*, p. 477–488). The literature on the subject, however, features several other views on her origins. Among other things, it has been assumed that she came from Volga Bulgaria (Е.В. П ч е л о в, *Генеалогия древнерусских князей IX–начала XI в.*, Москва 2001, p. 202–204; В. И г н а т о в, *Българските царици...*, p. 109). An interesting point of view has also been put forth by Polish scholar Andrzej Poppe. He argues that the Bulgarian woman mentioned in the *Russian Primary Chronicle* is in fact the Byzantine Anna, and that the term used there should be considered not so much an ethnonym as a sobriquet. It would have been given to the 'purple-born' imperial daughter in Constantinople or in Rus' due to her connections to the court in Preslav – after all, tsaritsa Maria Lekapene was her aunt (A. P o p p e, *La naissance du culte de Boris et Gleb*, "Cahiers de civilisation médiévale" 24, 1981, p. 29; i d e m, *Walka o spuściznę po Włodzimierzu Wielkim 1015–1019*, "Kwartalnik Historyczny" 102.3/4, 1995, p. 6–10). This view is shared by Ukrainian researcher Nadezhda Nikitenko (Н.Н. Н и к и т е н к о, *София Киевская и ее создатели. Тайны истории*, Каменец-Подольский 2014, p. 106–107). A different opinion is presented e.g. by Aleksandr Nazarenko (А.В. Н а з а р е н к о, *Древняя Русь на международных путях. Междисциплинарные очерки культурных, торговых, политических связей*

Georgi Atanasov theorizes that the small diadem found in the so-called 'Preslav treasure' (which contained the imperial family's jewelry, hidden during the war of 969–971) may have belonged to one of the daughters of Maria Lekapene. The Bulgarian scholar is of the opinion that the girl accompanied her mother on one of her journeys to Constantinople, and that the diadem was an exquisite gift from her Byzantine relatives[13] – one of the many treasures that the tsaritsa, according to the aforementioned chroniclers, received from Romanos I Lekapenos[14].

In the literature on the subject, there have been occasional attempts to establish the time at which Maria's two sons (as well as the third, unnamed child) were born, based on the above-mentioned accounts in the Byzantine sources. After all, the anonymous Continuator of George the Monk and the authors dependent on him state that when the Bulgarian tsaritsa arrived in Constantinople for the final time, her father was no longer among the living[15]. Considering that Christopher Lekapenos died in August 931, one should assume that Maria's visit took place in the autumn of that year at the earliest. Numerous scholars tend to use this date to argue that the relations between the empire and Bulgaria became cooler in the later period, so that Maria stopped visiting her relatives[16].

IX–XII вв., Москва 2001, p. 449). Finally, one should mention the rather controversial suppositions of certain Bulgarian historians that Boris-Romanos and Gleb-David were Vladimir and Anna's children, but that Anna, contrary to the testimony of Byzantine and Old Rus' chroniclers, was the daughter or perhaps granddaughter of Maria Lekapene and Peter (in the latter case, she would have been Boris II's daughter); И. Д о б р е в, *Българите за руския народ, държава и култура*, София 2011, p. 562–576.

[13] G. A t a n a s o v, *On the Origin...*, p. 91–92; i d e m, *Инсигниите...*, p. 235.

[14] C o n t i n u a t o r o f G e o r g e t h e M o n k, p. 913; S y m e o n L o g o t h e t e, 136, 67, p. 334; C o n t i n u a t o r o f T h e o p h a n e s, VI, 35, p. 422.

[15] C o n t i n u a t o r o f G e o r g e t h e M o n k, p. 913; S y m e o n L o g o t h e t e, 136, 67, p. 334; C o n t i n u a t o r o f T h e o p h a n e s, VI, 35, p. 422.

[16] И. Д у й ч е в, *Българският княз...*, p. 19; Г. А т а н а с о в, *Инсигниите...*, p. 99; А. Н и к о л о в, *Политическа мисъл в ранносредновековна България (средата на IX– края на X в.)*, София 2006, p. 244; Т. Т о д о р о в, *България през втората и третата четвърт на X век: политическа история*, София 2006 [unpublished PhD thesis], p. 159; i d e m, *Владетелският статут и титла на цар Петър I след октомври 927 г.: писмени сведения и сфрагистични данни (сравнителен анализ)*, [in:] *Юбилеен сбор- ник. Сто години от рождението на д-р Васил Хараланов (1907–2007)*, Шумен 2008, p. 101; Г. А т а н а с о в, *Печатите на българските владетели от IX–X в. в Дръстър*

Fig. 5. Diadem and jewelry that belonged to a Bulgarian tsarevna (daughter of Maria Lekapene?) from the so-called 'Preslav treasure', Byzantium, mid-10th century. Drawing (after G. Atanasov & G. Zhekov): E. Myślińska-Brzozowska

It should be pointed out, however, that the relevant sources do not suggest that Maria's final visit to the Byzantine capital took place immediately after her father's death. According to the chroniclers, the official reason for the Bulgarian tsaritsa's journey was the wish to visit her grandfather – therefore, all that we can conclude is that it took place prior to 944, when Romanos I Lekapenos was deposed[17]. Accordingly, the imperial couple's three children could have been born at any time between 928 and 944.

(*Силистра*), [in:] *От тука започва България. Материали от втората национална конференция по история, археология и културен туризъм "Пътуване към България", Шумен 14–16.05. 2010 година*, ed. И. Й о р д а н о в, Шумен 2011, p. 289.

[17] И. Д у й ч е в, *Българският княз...*, p. 19; S. G e o r g i e v a, *The Byzantine Princesses...*, p. 168.

Maria, like many other medieval royal consorts, most likely wanted to fulfil her duty as soon as possible. At the time of Christopher's death, therefore, she could easily have been a mother of three already. It is difficult to say, however, whether she would have decided to take them on the rather long and exhausting journey as early as 931. They would have been between one and three years old at the time; it is doubtful that a responsible mother would have exposed an infant to hardships that could result in serious health issues. Rather, we should assume that Maria's final visit to Constantinople took place in 933/934, when her children were at the ages of three to six[18].

On the other hand, it cannot be completely ruled out that Boris and Romanos were born considerably later than is commonly thought[19]. It should be borne in mind that Leo the Deacon, relating the events of 971, clearly mentions that Boris was a father of two infant children at the time[20]. Had he been born soon after his parents' wedding in 927, one would expect that in the 970s his children would have been fully grown.

In summary, the existing source material does not unequivocally settle the question of how many children Peter and Maria had; the exact time of their birth likewise remains uncertain. In all likelihood, the imperial couple had three sons (Plenimir, Boris and Romanos) and several daughters, whose names we do not know.

---

[18] The remark about Maria's visits to Constantinople was placed by the Continuator of George the Monk (and, following him, by Symeon Logothete and the Continuator of Theophanes) between the information on Theophylaktos Lekapenos's elevation to the patriarchal see of Constantinople (February 933) and the note on the marriage of his brother Stephen as well as on the first raid by the Hungarians (April 934). Continuator of George the Monk, p. 913; Symeon Logothete, 136, 67, p. 334; Continuator of Theophanes, VI, 35, p. 422.

[19] It is possible that they were not among the children taken by Maria to Constantinople in 933/934 at all. Conversely, she may have been accompanied by her daughters, the prematurely deceased Plenimir, or another son who died before reaching adulthood.

[20] Leo the Deacon, VIII, 6, p. 136.

VI

Zofia A. Brzozowska
Mirosław J. Leszka

On the Bulgarian Throne
at Peter's Side

Maria Lekapene was Bulgarian tsaritsa from October 927 until her death, most likely in the early 960s. Thus, she would have been on the Preslav throne for about thirty-five years. In order to gain a better understanding of the circumstances in which Maria came to rule Bulgaria, it is necessary to devote some space to a discussion of her husband's political activity. Shortly after signing the peace treaty with Byzantium and arriving in Preslav with Maria, Peter found himself confronted with a plot led by his brother John. However, the conspiracy, which probably developed in 928[1], never reached the stage of actually removing the tsar from power – the intrigue was uncovered, while the leader as well as those who joined

---

[1] It is not possible to date this event precisely based on the sources at our disposal. The Byzantine authors place it in their narratives between the conclusion of peace with Byzantium (October 927) and Michael's rebellion. John's plot has been traditionally dated to 928, on the assumption that it was a rapid reaction to the conclusion of peace with the empire. It cannot be ruled out, however, that the plot happened later, in 929 or even in 930. It must have taken place before Michael's insurgency, which, however is only vaguely dated to 930 (without indicating even the time of year). Assuming that the rebellion was a consequence of the discovery of John's plot, it is possible that it broke out shortly after the latter event.

him in plotting against Peter were punished². The ruler treated his brother John mercifully (he was flogged, imprisoned and probably forced to become a monk), but he dealt more harshly with his supporters³.

Sometime after the plot had been thwarted, John⁴ left Bulgaria for Constantinople. According to Byzantine sources, he was supposedly evacuated by Byzantine envoy John the Rhaiktor without Peter's knowledge⁵. In the empire's capital, John broke his monastic vows, marrying a certain Armenian, and received considerable wealth from the emperor. Romanos I Lekapenos imparted exceptional significance to the wedding of Symeon's son, as it was witnessed by Christopher (son and co-emperor of Romanos I and Peter's father-in-law) as well as by the aforementioned John the Rhaiktor⁶.

It is, however, hardly credible that John, until recently a pretender to the throne, left for Constantinople without Peter's approval⁷. Perhaps, in fact, the latter did not want him in Bulgaria, where he would have posed a potential threat to his rule. On the other hand, his potential execution, blinding or long-term imprisonment in Bulgaria would have

---

² The plot seems to have had no repercussions outside of the capital. Else, the Byzantine authors would have probably mentioned it, just as they wrote about Michael, who started his revolt against Peter outside of the capital (C o n t i n u a t o r o f   T h e o p h a n e s, p. 420; J o h n   S k y l i t z e s, p. 226).

³ C o n t i n u a t o r   o f   T h e o p h a n e s, p. 419. Cf. S y m e o n   L o g o t h e t e, 136.60; J o h n   S k y l i t z e s, p. 225.

⁴ It is possible that until that time, he had been imprisoned in Preslav in one of the towers located by the eastern part of the inner walls. К. П о п к о н с т а н т и н о в, *Епиграфски бележки за Иван, Цар Симеоновият син*, "Българите в Северното Причерноморие" 3, 1994, p. 75.

⁵ S y m e o n   L o g o t h e t e, 136.60; C o n t i n u a t o r   o f   T h e o p h a n e s, p. 419; J o h n   S k y l i t z e s, p. 225.

⁶ S y m e o n   L o g o t h e t e, 136.60; C o n t i n u a t o r   o f   T h e o p h a n e s, p. 419; J o h n   S k y l i t z e s, p. 225.

⁷ Similarly П. П а в л о в, *Братята на цар Петър и техните загавори*, "История" 7.4/5, 1999, p. 4; Л. С и м е о н о в а, *Щрихи към историята на тайната дипломация, разузнаването и контраразузнаването в средновековния свят*, [in:] *Тангра. Сборник в чест на 70. годишнината на Акад. Васил Гюзелев*, eds. М. К а й м а к а в о в а et al., София 2006, p. 504–506; П. П а в л о в, *Векът на цар Самуил*, София 2014, p. 21; M.J. L e s z k a, *Spisek Jana przeciw carowi Piotrowi (928) – raz jeszcze*, "Balcanica Posnaniensia" 23, 2016, p. 11.

created the risk of a new rebellion by his supporters. Abroad, without the support of Bulgarian dignitaries, John was far less dangerous. Besides, his inclusion into the Byzantine aristocracy may have compromised the erstwhile pretender to the Bulgarian crown in the eyes of his support-ers, assuming that he had indeed championed anti-Byzantine policies. Romanos I Lekapenos's attitude towards him may be explained by the fact that John was, after all, the brother of Christopher's son-in-law, which would also be a likely reason for the co-emperor's presence at John's wed-ding. Additionally, the emperor was thus able to secure the stability of the freshly concluded peace with his northern neighbor[8]. Some scholars, however, take the Byzantine authors' account at face value; according-ly, John would have become a kind of a specter, a menace haunting the Bulgarian ruler[9]. Even if this were so, John was never actively used in this role; in fact, we know nothing about his later fate. One could say that dispatching John to Byzantium removed him from the picture.

It is possible that the failure of John's plot spurred Michael, Symeon I the Great's firstborn son (who had remained in a monas-tery at the beginning of Peter's reign), into action. He probably moved against Peter in 930[10]. Our information about this event comes from two

---

[8] M.J. L e s z k a, K. M a r i n o w, *Carstwo bułgarskie. Polityka – społeczeństwo – gospo-darka – kultura. 866–971*, Warszawa 2015, p. 153.

[9] E.g. J.V.A. F i n e, *The Early Medieval Balkans: a Critical Survey from the Sixth to the Late Twelfth Century*, Ann Arbor 1983, p. 162; И. Б о ж и л о в, В. Г ю з е л е в, *История на средновековна България. VII–XIV в.*, София 2006, p. 278. Cf. M.J. L e s z k a, K. M a r i n o w, *Carstwo bułgarskie. Polityka – społeczeństwo – gospodarka – kultu-ra. 866–971*, Warszawa 2015, p. 153; П. П а в л о в, *Братята...*, p. 5. This hypothesis, however, cannot be verified. It is often forgotten in this context that Peter's wife was Christopher's daughter: it is difficult to imagine that her father, potentially Romanos's heir, would have wanted to move against her husband. Still, needless to say, one cannot rule out the possibility entirely.

[10] The date is approximate: neither of the sources informs us when it happened. Since both in the *Continuation of Theophanes* and in the *Chronicle of John Skylitzes* it precedes events from March 931 (the misfortunes that befell Constantinople – C o n t i n u a t o r o f T h e o p h a n e s, VI, 30, p. 420; S y m e o n L o g o t h e t e, 136, 61. Cf. J o h n S k y l i t z e s, p. 226, where the same episode is related without a specified date), it is commonly accepted that it happened in 930 (В.И. З л а т а р с к и, *История на българската държава през средните векове*, vol. 1/2, *Първо българско Царство. От славянизацията на държавата до падането на Първото царство*

Byzantine sources – the *Continuation of Theophanes* and John Skylitzes[11], generally in agreement as regards their account of the course of the rebellion. They only differ in some details, primarily concerning the terms used to refer to Michael's supporters and the initial territory they passed through during their flight after Michael's death. In the *Continuation of Theophanes*, his supporters are referred to as Scythians, whereas John Skylitzes calls them Bulgarians[12]. The *Continuation of Theophanes* indicates Μακέτιδος as the first Byzantine territory they crossed, while the land mentioned in this context by John Skylitzes is Μακηδονίας[13].

(852–1018), София 1927, p. 840). Regarding the *terminus post quem*, the problem is more serious, since we only have the information that Michael's rebellion followed John's plot; the latter, as mentioned previously, can only be dated approximately (most commonly to 928).

[11] C o n t i n u a t o r   o f   T h e o p h a n e s, VI, 29, p. 420: *However also the monk Michael, brother of Peter, attempting with all strength to gain power over the Bulgarians, started a rebellion in a certain Bulgarian fortress. To him flocked Scythians, who refused to obey Peter's rule. After his [Michael's] death, they attacked Roman territories, that is they went from Maketidos through Strymon to Hellas, entered Nikopolis and there plundered everything.* J o h n   S k y l i t z e s, p. 226 (transl. J. W o r t l e y, p. 248 – including the change in the translation of the word σαββατίσαντες): *Now Michael, Peter's other brother, aspired to become ruler of the Bulgars. He occupied a powerful fortress and greatly agited the Bulgars lands. Many flocked to his banner but, when he died shortly after, these people, for fear of Peter's wrath, entered Roman territory. They reached Nikopolis by way of Macedonia, Strymon and Helladikon theme, laying waste everything that came to hand, and there, finally, settled* (καὶ τέλος ἐν αὐτῇ σαββατίσαντες). *In due course and after a number of reverse, they became Roman subjects.*

[12] This issue has been dealt with in the scholarship. It seems advisable to agree with the assumption that the author of the fourth book of the *Continuation of Theophanes* used the name 'Scythians' to refer to Bulgarians; the source shows a tendency to use archaic names. Cf. M.J. L e s z k a, *Bunt Michała przeciw carowi Piotrowi (?930)*, "Slavia Antiqua" 58, 2017 (in press).

[13] V.I. Zlatarski (В.И. З л а т а р с к и, *История...*, p. 838) thought that Maketidos referred to the territories of historical Macedonia (most likely between the Strymon/Struma and the Nestos/Mesta), while Michael's rebellion took place in the region of Struma (*Струмската область*). This idea found relatively wide acceptance in the later scholarly literature; nowadays it is thought, albeit sometimes with a degree of caution, that the areas where Michael's insurgency broke out were in what is now south-western Bulgaria (П. М у т а ф ч и е в, *История на българския народ (681–1323)*, София 1986, p. 201; J.A.V. F i n e, *Early...*, p. 162; П. П а в л о в, *Братята...*, p. 5). On the other hand, those scholars who rely on John Skylitzes (Byzantine Macedonia) in dealing

It would seem that, based on the available sources, one may formulate a general hypothesis that Michael's revolt had a local character, and that its supporters mostly included the inhabitants of the captured fortress as well as the nearby populace. Contrary to the opinion of certain scholars[14], no large-scale military activity (if any at all) took place during the insurgency. It cannot be ruled out that the only fortress captured by Michael fell into his hands not as a result of fighting, but due to a betrayal arranged through some earlier agreements. Furthermore, Michael's supporters left Bulgarian territory not as a result of action on the part of Peter's army but, as the sources inform us[15], out of fear of it.

One might wonder whether Michael's uprising really did constitute a more serious threat to Peter's reign than John's plot, as some scholars contend[16]. Considering specific actions (the taking of a fortress), this was indeed the case. Nonetheless, it would seem that if John's plot – involving the Bulgarian elites and active in the very heart of the country – had ever entered its active phase, it would have had a better chance of success than Michael's local rebellion, which would have likely been quelled by forces loyal to Peter without much difficulty.

It does not appear that Michael's revolt was inspired by the Byzantines, working to destabilize the situation in Bulgaria and thus weaken its position relative to their own. The clearest indication that this was not the case lies in the fact that while Michael's supporters sought refuge within

---

with the issue of where Michael started his rebellion against Peter claim that the area in question was the Bulgarian part of Thrace or the vicinity of Bulgaria's main cities: Preslav and Pliska (Т. Т о д о р о в, *Вътрешнодинастичният проблем в България от края на 20-те–началото на 30-те години на X в.*, "Историкии" 3, 2008, p. 275. Cf. П. К о л е д а р о в, *Цар Петър I*, "Военно-исторически сборник" 51, 1982, p. 199; Х. Д и м и т р о в, *История на Македония*, София 2004, p. 60). On the Byzantines' view of the territorial extent of Macedonia cf.: П. К о л е д а р о в, *Македония*, [in:] *Кирило-методиевска енциклопедия*, vol. II, ed. П. Д и н е к о в, София 1995, p. 592–593; T.E. G r e g o r y, *Macedonia*, [in:] *Oxford Dictionary of Byzantium*, ed. A.P. K a z h d a n, New York–Oxford 1991, p. 1261–1262). Based on the sources at our disposal, the issue of where Michael initiated the rebellion cannot be resolved definitively.

[14] Т. Т о д о р о в, *Вътрешнодинастичният...*, p. 274.

[15] C o n t i n u a t o r of T h e o p h a n e s, VI, 29, p. 420; J o h n S k y l i t z e s, p. 226.

[16] Т. Т о д о р о в, *Вътрешнодинастичният...*, p. 274.

the empire, they were hardly welcomed there with open arms; as a matter of fact, their march towards Nikopolis resembled a looting raid. The Byzantines were only able to enforce their dominion over them with the use of military might. Had the rebels been in prior communication with the empire, one might expect that they would have been supported during their flight by the Byzantines, who would have peacefully settled them in the indicated territory.

Thus, Michael's rebellion ended in failure; his sudden death[17] made it pointless for his supporters to continue the action against Peter. This clearly indicates that the initiative undertaken by Symeon's oldest son reflected the struggle (strictly speaking, the last manifestation thereof) for power within the ruling house. Peter emerged victorious from this rivalry; from that moment onwards, his position in the Bulgarian state remained unthreatened.

Again, it is worth noting that Romanos I Lekapenos did not side with Peter's opponents. He remained loyal to his granddaughter's husband, thus making it more difficult for her to adjust to the life at the Bulgarian court, which – at least at the beginning – was quite foreign to her.

It is quite remarkable that once Michael's attempt failed, Peter virtually disappeared from the Byzantine sources for a period of over thirty years. As a consequence, our knowledge of his rule at the time when Maria was by his side is very limited (which, in fact, also holds true for the later period); what we do know mainly concerns religious issues, the Bogomil heresy being regarded as the most important among them[18]. Although the

----

[17] The fact that this happened at a moment advantageous from Peter's perspective, and that Michael was still a relatively young man, does raise suspicion. However, in view of the fact that the Byzantine authors – for whom it must have been just as evident that Michael's death was a boon for Peter – cast no aspersions regarding this matter, we shall refrain from any speculations here.

[18] On Bogomilism see e.g.: D. O b o l e n s k y, *The Bogomils*, Cambridge 1948; Д. А н г е л о в, *Богомилството в България*, София 1961; S. R u n c i m a n, *The Medieval Manichee. A Study of the Dualist Heresy*, Cambridge 1982; S. B y l i n a, *Bogomilizm w średniowiecznej Bułgarii. Uwarunkowania społeczne, polityczne i kulturalne*, "Balcanica Posnaniensia" 2, 1985, p. 133–145; Д. А н г е л о в, *Богомилство*, София 1993; Y. S t o y a n o v, *The Other God. Dualist Religions from Antiquity to the Cathar Heresy*, New Haven 2000, p. 125–166; G. M i n c z e w, *Remarks on the Letter of the Patriarch*

heresy unquestionably deserves attention, its significance has been blown out of proportion by scholars. Its emergence is usually linked with Peter's reign, although in fact it can be traced back to Symeon's times. We are able to determine neither its social base nor the measures which were taken against it, inspired by both secular and church authorities. The fact that Peter turned to Theophylaktos Lekapenos, patriarch of Constantinople and Maria's uncle[19], for help and counsel, indicates that he took note of it and considered it a threat. Nevertheless, it must be noted that this deeply religious ruler, driven by the commitment to the idea of the purity of the religion adhered to by his subjects, may have dealt with the movement in a manner incommensurate with its actual strength and size[20]. It should also be kept in mind that Bogomil views – those regarding theology as well as those expressing criticism of the existing social order – must have been an issue of concern for the ruler even if they were not shared and perpetrated by a significant number of people.

Theophylact to Tsar Peter in the Context of Certain Byzantine and Slavic Anti-heretic Texts, "Studia Ceranea. Journal of the Waldemar Ceran Research Centre for the History and Culture of the Mediterranean Area and South-East Europe" 3, 2013, p. 113–130; i d e m, *Słowiańskie teksty antyheretyckie jako źródło do poznania herezji dualistycznych na Bałkanach*, [in:] *Średniowieczne herezje dualistyczne na Bałkanach. Źródła słowiańskie*, eds. G. M i n c z e w, M. S k o w r o n e k, J.M. W o l s k i, Łódź 2015, p. 13–57.

[19] *Letter of the Patriarch Theophylact to Tsar Peter*. The letter was recently analyzed by: G. M i n c z e w, *Remarks on the Letter…* (the work includes a bibliography of this issue).

[20] It must not be forgotten that according to the Byzantine doctrine of power, the ruler was obliged to ensure the purity of his subjects' faith as fundamental to their salvation. This principle became instilled in Bulgaria right after its conversion to Christianity. Interestingly, Peter was reminded of it in a letter that he received from the patriarch of Constantinople: *A faithful and God-loving soul is such a great treasure – our spiritual son, the best and the most notable of our relatives – especially if it is the soul of the ruler and leader which, as Yours, can love and worship what is good and beneficial. By leading a prudent life and by behaving well, it not only secures good for itself but, surrounding everyone under its authority with great care, gives them everything that is important and that concerns their salvation. Can there be anything more important and more beneficial than the uncorrupted and sincere faith and the healthy concept of divinity thanks to which we worship one God, the purest and holiest God, with clear consciousness? And that is the most important element of our salvation* (*Letter of the Patriarch Theophylact to Tsar Peter*, p. 311). See also: А. Н и к о л о в, *Политическа мисъл в ранносредновековна България (средата на IX–края на X в.)*, София 2006, p. 245–269.

The need to return to the ideals of the first Christians and to establish an intimate relationship with God was reflected in the development of the monastic movement, especially in its eremitic version[21]. Although one could hardly claim any detailed knowledge of the issue, Peter's ties to monasticism were clearly very strong. Bearing witness to this is his acceptance of the Little Schema shortly before his death, as well as the fact that his cult as a saint flourished mainly in connection with his monastic activity[22]. Peter is known to have held monks in high regard, especially John of Rila, Bulgaria's most famous saint, an anchorite and the founder of the monastic community that gave rise to the celebrated Rila Monastery[23]. Thoroughly impressed by John's holiness[24], the ruler – according to his

---

[21] For more on Bulgarian monasticism in the century in question see: Б. Н и к о-
л о в а, *Монашество, манастири и манастирски живот в средновековна България*,
vol. I, *Манастирите*, София 2010, p. 41–270.

[22] On this issue see: И. Б и л я р с к и, *Покровители на Царство. Св. Цар Петър
и св. Параскева-Петка*, София 2004, p. 21–24; i d e m, М. Й о в ч е в а, *За датата
на успението на цар Петър и за култа към него*, [in:] *Тангра. Сборник в чест на
70-годишнината на акад. Васил Гюзелев*, eds. М. К а й м а к а в о в а et al., София
2006, p. 543–557; Д. Ч е ш м е д ж и е в, *Култът към български цар Петър I (927–969):
монашески или държавен?*, [in:] *5. International Hilandar Conference, 8–14 September
2001, Raska, Jugoslavija. Love of learning and devotion to God in orthodox monasteries*,
Beograd–Columbus 2006, p. 245–257; Б. Н и к о л о в а, *Цар Петър и характерът
на неговия култ*, "Palaeobulgarica" 33.2, 2009, p. 63–77; e a d e m, *Монашество...*,
vol. II, *Монасите*, София 2010, p. 826–843; М. К а й м а к а м о в а, *Култът към
цар Петър (927–969) и движещите идеи на българските освободителни въстания
срещу византийската власт през XI–XII в.*, "Bulgaria Mediaevalis" 4/5, 2013/2014,
p. 417–438; Д. Ч е ш м е д ж и е в, *Култовете на българските светци през IX–XII в.
Автореферат*, Пловдив 2016, p. 13–15.

[23] John was born around 876. We have no certain information about his origin
and the reasons for which he decided to settle in the Rila Mountains to live the life
of a hermit – one that gave him the fame and reputation which he did not seek.
In any case, he founded the community and became its first hegumen. He died as
a hermit; in all probability, his life came to an end in 946. For more on John of Rila's life
see: И. Д у й ч е в, *Рилският светец и неговата обител*, София 1947; I. D o b r e v,
Sv. Ivan Rilski, vol. I, Linz 2007; Б. Н и к о л о в а, *Монашество...*, p. 790–815;
Й. А н д р е е в, *Иван Рилски*, [in:] i d e m, И. Л а з а р о в, П. П а в л о в, *Кой кой
е в средновековна България*, София 2012, p. 270–275.

[24] И. Д у й ч е в, *Рилският...*, p. 123sqq; *Ziemscy aniołowie, niebiańscy ludzie.
Anachoreci w bułgarskiej literaturze i kulturze*, ed. G. M i n c z e w, Białystok 2002,
p. 19. Cf. Б. Н и к о л о в а, *Монашество...*, p. 274–285; 626–628, 790–815.

hagiographers – went to a lot of trouble trying, unsuccessfully, to secure a meeting with the holy hermit; after the latter's death, he saw to it that his remains were transferred from his hermitage in Rila to Sofia[25].

There is no doubt that Peter took care of the Church and provided material support to it. However, we are not able to adduce any details regarding this aspect of his activity. It cannot be ruled out that scholars such as Plamen Pavlov[26] are right in claiming that Peter was not easily influenced by the clergy, as well as that his policy towards the Church was rational and consistent with the interests of his state. He sought, for example, to hinder the Church from excessively increasing its holdings – an approach modeled on the policy used by Byzantine emperors.

Peter's reign is often described as a period of a deteriorating economy and a resulting impoverishment of the masses of the Bulgarian society, especially the peasants. However, the picture is based not on reliable sources but on arbitrary assumptions, arising from the interpretation of the growth of the Bogomil movement as a reaction to the material deprivation of the Bulgarian society. Without engaging in a detailed polemic with this view, it is worth noting that there is historical evidence to suggest that Bulgaria's economic situation was not as poor as usually described. This is borne out by the fact that the Bulgarian lands became a tasty morsel for Svyatoslav I, prince of Kievan Rus', who not only displayed much zeal in plundering them but, as some scholars believe, was even going to settle there. We may point to the well-known description of Pereyaslavets on the Danube, reportedly uttered by the prince – a picture quite at odds with the notion of Bulgaria's economic decline:

не любо ми есть в Киевѣ быти. хочю жити с Переяславци в Дунаи. яко то есть середа в земли моеи. яко ту вся блгая сходатса.

---

[25] Naturally, detailed information to be found in hagiographic accounts must be treated with caution. Then again, there seems to be nothing surprising about the notion of a pious ruler willing to meet a hermit. Doubts have been raised as to whether Peter had a hand in transferring John's remains to Sofia; the problem has been analyzed by: И. Дуйчев, *Рилският...*, passim. Cf. Д. Чешмеджиев, *За времето на пренасяне на мощите на св. Иоанн Рилски от Рила в Средец*, "Bulgaria Mediaevalis" 6, 2015, p. 79–89.

[26] П. Павлов, *Векът...*, p. 55–57.

ѿ Грекъ злато паволоки. вина [и] ѡвощеве розноличныꙗ. и-Щехъ
же из Урогъ сребро и комони. из Руси же скора и воскъ медъ.
и челѧд.

I do not care to remain in Kiev, but should prefer to live in Pereyaslavets
on the Danube, since that is the centre of my realm, where all riches
are concentrated; gold, silks, wine, and various fruits from Greece, silver and horses from Hungary and Bohemia, and from Rus' furs, wax,
honey, and slaves[27].

This description, not to move too far away from the letter of the source,
can be treated at least as evidence proving that trade in the Bulgarian
territories was not in decline. The problem is, however, that scholars
analyzing the source recently raised doubts as to the account's reliability.
In their opinion, as far as Svyatoslav's expeditions are concerned, the
account confuses Pereyaslavets with Veliki Preslav. In reality, the source
needs to be regarded as reflecting the role of the first city as a trading
center in the 11th and 12th centuries; the description of the emporium's
central location and the goods that flowed into it from all directions
is based on biblical accounts regarding the significance and wealth of
Tyre and Jerusalem[28].

---

[27] *Russian Primary Chronicle*, AM 6477, p. 68 (transl. S.H. C r o s s, O.P. S h e r -
b o w i t z-W e t z o r, p. 86). Cf. A. K i j a s, *Stosunki rusko-bułgarskie do XV w. ze
szczególnym uwzględnieniem stosunków kulturalnych*, "Balcanica Posnaniensia" 2, 1985,
p. 115; М. Р а е в, *Преслав или Переяславец на Дунае? (Предварительные замечания
об одном из возможных источников ПВЛ и его трансформации)*, "Наукові запис-
ки з української історії: Збірник наукових статей" 20, 2008, p. 37–40. See also:
J. B a n a s z k i e w i c z, *Jedność porządku przestrzennego, społecznego i tradycji początków ludu. (Uwagi o urządzeniu wspólnoty plemienno-państwowej u Słowian)*, "Przegląd
Historyczny" 77, 1986, p. 448–449.
[28] И. Д а н и л е в с к и й, *Повесть временных лет: герменевтические основы изучения летописных тестов*, Москва 2004, p. 163–167; В. Р ы ч к а, *Чью славу переял
Переяслав?*, "Наукові записки з української історії: Збірник наукових статей" 16,
2005, p. 129–134; М. Р а е в, *Переяславец на Дунав – мит и действителност в речта
на княз Святослав в Повесть временных лет*, "Годишник на Софийския Университет.

The account found in the *Tale of the Prophet Isaiah* testifies to the fact that, despite the skeptical remarks regarding the previous passage, Peter's reign was indeed remembered as a period of prosperity – or at least that people chose to remember it that way. In the *Tale*, we read:

тогⷣа ꙋбо въ дни и лѣтⷶ сⷮго Пеⷮра цⷬя бльгарьскагⷪ быⷭ изьꙍбьιлïа ꙍ всего. сирⷺчь пшеница и масло и меда жⷷ и млⷪка и вина, и ꙍ всего дарованïа бжïа врⷺше и кипⷺше. и не бⷺ ꙍскꙋдⷺнïе ни ꙍ цⷫоⷨ. нь бⷺ ситость изьꙍбильⷭтво ꙍ всего до изволенïа бжïа

In the days and years of St. Peter, the tsar of the Bulgarians, there was plenty of everything, that is to say, of wheat and butter, honey, milk and wine, the land was overflowing with every gift of God, there was no dearth of anything but by the will of God everything was in abundance and to satiety[29].

* * *

It is worth asking what role Maria came to play in Bulgaria, and what position she occupied as the wife of tsar Peter in the contemporary power structures. Significantly, none of the surviving written sources mention Maria's activity in public affairs. We find no traces of the tsaritsa's independent actions even in the sphere traditionally assigned to a Christian empress consort: charitable or foundation activities, or propagating Christianity (such evidence exists in relation to the Rus' princesses Olga[30]

Научен център за славяно-византийски проучвания 'Иван Дуйчев'" 95.14, 2006, p. 193–203; M.J. L e s z k a, K. M a r i n o w, *Carstwo bułgarskie...*, p. 166.

[29] *Tale of the Prophet Isaiah*, p. 17.

[30] In the pages of the *Russian Primary Chronicle*, we primarily find the description of princess Olga's efforts at converting her son Svyatoslav. Nonetheless, neither in this source nor in any other of the Old Rus' chronicles do we come across any information concerning her personal initiatives related to Christianization. The liturgy book from 1307 (*Apostolos*), however, mentions the construction of the first, most likely wooden, church of St. Sophia (Divine Wisdom) in Kiev during the reign of Olga: въ тъ же день [11 мая] священïе святыя Софья Кыеве въ лето 6460 [952] – *On this day*

[11ᵗʰ of May] the dedication of Saint Sophia in Kiev, in year 6460 [952]. Even though
the text of this source still causes some doubts among scholars, some of them are certainly
ready to accept the hypothesis that the wooden church dedicated to Divine Wisdom may
have existed in Kiev long before the princess's successors initiated the work on the stone
church that exists to this day. A. P o p p e, *Państwo i Kościół na Rusi w XI w.*, Warszawa
1968, p. 43; М.Ю. Б р а й ч е в с к и й, *Утверждение Христианства на Руси*, Киев
1989, p. 112; J.S. G a j e k, *U początków świętości Rusi Kijowskiej*, [in:] *Chrystus zwyciężył.
Wokół chrztu Rusi Kijowskiej*, eds. J.S. G a j e k, W. H r y n i e w i c z, Warszawa 1989, p. 96;
Г. К о л п а к о в а, *Искусство Древней Руси. Домонгольский период*, Санкт-Петербург
2007, p. 20; А.Ю. К а р п о в, *Княгиня Ольга*, Москва 2012, p. 223.

   The later church tradition also sees Olga as the founder of the original church
of the Divine Wisdom in Kiev, which rather naturally elevated the topic of her efforts
in spreading Christianity throughout Rus' to a much higher status than in medieval
historiography. Indeed, the preserved hagiographies devoted to her inform us not only
about her attempts to convince Svyatoslav I of the worth of the new faith, but also
of Olga's forceful fight against paganism as well as her promoting Christianity within
the Rus' society. The author of the *Praise of Olga* (a part of the *Remembrance and Praise
of Prince of Rus' Vladimir* by Jacob the Monk, from the 11ᵗʰ century) states that upon
her return from Constantinople, the ruler destroyed places of pagan worship (тревнца
въсовьскаа съкрѹшн). Similar information can also be found in several of the versions
of her vita: *Prologue Life of St. Olga* (Rus' redaction, 12ᵗʰ–13ᵗʰ centuries), *Prologue Life
of St. Olga* (Bulgarian redaction, 12ᵗʰ–13ᵗʰ centuries), *Life of St. Olga* (so-called 'Pskov'
version, 1560s) as well as *Life of St. Olga* included in the *Book of Degrees of the Royal
Genealogy* (ca. 1560); М.Ю. Б р а й ч е в с к и й, *Утверждение...*, p. 110; M. Ł a b u ń k a,
*Od Olgi do Włodzimierza. Sytuacja religijna na Rusi Kijowskiej w okresie poprzedzającym
oficjalną chrystianizację*, [in:] *Teologia i kultura duchowa Starej Rusi*, eds. J.S. G a j e k,
W. H r y n i e w i c z, Lublin 1993, p. 44; Z.A. B r z o z o w s k a, *Święta księżna kijowska
Olga. Wybór tekstów źródłowych*, Łódź 2014, p. 46–47, 58–59, 86–87, 96–97, 146–147.

   Moreover, the hagiographical accounts go one step further, crediting the Kievan
princess not only for an independent attempt at eradicating paganism in Rus', but also
for her foundation activity. Later versions of her life state that in each of the old pagan
cult sites, Olga ordered the raising of crosses, which – as the hagiographer claims – soon
became famous for numerous miracles. Were we to accept this account, we could conclude that the Christianization undertaken by the Kievan ruler was indeed a planned
and deeply thought-out enterprise, in which the attachment of the people of Rus' to
their old 'holy sites' was used for fortifying the new faith. Z.A. B r z o z o w s k a, *Święta
księżna...*, p. 86–89, 96–97, 146–147.

   The Church tradition also considers Olga to have been the initiator of the construction of several temples across Rus'. As was mentioned above, her name is sometimes associated with the oldest church of St. Sophia (Divine Wisdom) in Kiev. This

and Anna Porphyrogennete[31].

is not the only endeavor ascribed to her, however, for she is also very often linked with the Trinity Church in Pskov (М.Ю. Б р а й ч е в с к и й, *Утверждение*..., p. 112–113; Г. К о л п а к о в а, *Искусство Древней Руси*..., p. 20; А.Ю. К а р п о в, *Княгиня Ольга*..., p. 223). Different versions of the life of St. Olga, written in the 16th century on the basis of (among other things) north Russian oral tradition, include an interesting prophetic element related to this church: the Kievan princess, standing at the confluence of the rivers Velikaya and Pskova, supposedly had a vision in which she saw a great and wealthy city as well as a church of the Holy Trinity in the place of her birth. Interestingly, her words seem to be a direct reference to the prophecy of St. Andrew, uttered in the place in which Kiev – the 'Mother of Rus' cities' – was to be built after many centuries: **На мѣстѣ сем бꙋдет церкви Свѧтыꙗ и нераздѣлимыꙗ Троица, и град бꙋдетъ велик и славен зѣло и всем изобилен бꙋдет** – *In this place there shall be a church of the holy and undivided Trinity, the city shall be great and very famous, and shall abound in everything.* Z.A. B r z o z o w s k a, *Święta księżna*..., p. 88–89, 96–97, 146–147.

[31] Princess Anna Porphyrogennete's contribution to the Christianization of Kievan Rus', i.e. the founding of many churches, is mentioned in the *Chronicle of Yahyā of Antioch* (ca. 975–1066); the writer was a Christian (Melkite) writing in Arabic (Y a h y ā o f A n t i o c h, p. 423; A. P o p p e, *Państwo i Kościół*..., p. 33–36; А.В. Н а з а р е н к о, *Древняя Русь на международных путях. Междисциплинарные очерки культурных, торговых, политических связей IX–XII вв.*, Москва 2001, p. 445; А.Ю. К а р п о в, *Владимир Святой*, Москва 2004, p. 283, 402). According to Arab historian Abū Shudjā al-Rūdhrāwarī (1045–1095), princess Anna played a key role in Vladimir's conversion – her refusal to marry an infidel supposedly persuaded the prince to accept baptism (R ū d h r ā w a r ī, p. 118–119; A. P o p p e, *Przyjęcie chrześcijaństwa na Rusi w opiniach XI w.*, [in:] *Teologia i kultura duchowa Starej Rusi*, eds. J.S. G a j e k, W. H r y n i e w i c z, Lublin 1993, p. 94; А.Ю. К а р п о в, *Владимир Святой*..., p. 219).

Anna Porphyrogennete's influence on Vladimir's conversion and the Christianization of Rus' is also mentioned by East Slavic authors (e.g. in the *Russian Primary Chronicle*). The role of the *mulier suadens*, however, is filled in Old Rus' literature not by her, but by Vladimir's grandmother – Olga (M. H o m z a, *The Role of Saint Ludmila, Doubravka, Saint Olga and Adelaide in the Conversions of their Countries (The Problem of Mulieres Suadentes, Persuading Women)*, [in:] *Early Christianity in Central and East Europe*, ed. P. U r b a ń c z y k, Warszawa 1997, p. 194–196; i d e m, *St. Ol'ga. The Mother of All Princes and Tsars of Rus'*, "Byzantinoslavica" 63, 2005, p. 131–141; i d e m, *The Role of the Imitatio Helenae in the Hagiography of Female Rulers until the Late Thirteenth Centures*, [in:] *България, Българите и Европа – мит, история, съвремие*, vol. III, Велико Търново 2009, p. 138–140; i d e m, *Mulieres suadentes – Persuasive Women. Female Royal Saints in Medieval East Central and Eastern Europe*, Leiden 2017, p. 143–168). Ukrainian scholar Nadezhda Nikitenko notes that the princess's contribution

Thus, the common view in older Bulgarian historiography according-ing to which the tsaritsa enjoyed an exceptionally high position at the Preslav court – including real political power and the ensuing possibility of influencing Peter's decisions[32] – could only find confirmation in the sphragistic material. The latter includes, for example, the aforementioned lead *sigilla* from 927–945, on the reverse of which we find the depiction of the royal couple (based on the Byzantine model).

The creation of such artifacts can hardly be considered the result of Maria's personal ambition and independent efforts, not consulted with her husband and his advisers. The seal images in question were certainly not a reflection of the status of Peter's spouse as an actual co-ruler, as some researchers think[33]. As previously mentioned, such items served primarily

---

to the transplantation of the new religion onto East Slavic ground – along with elements of Byzantine culture – may have been far greater than currently accepted in the historiog-raphy. In her publications, Nikitenko examines mechanisms that led to princess Anna being 'ousted' from the Old Rus' historiographical tradition, while the status of the propagator of Christianity was transferred to princess Olga (Н.Н. Никитенко, *Русь и Византия в монументальном комплексе Софии Киевской. Историческая проблематика*, Киев 2004, p. 36–88, 341–352; e a d e m, *Крещение Руси в свете данных Софии Киевской*, "Софія Київська: Візантія. Русь. Україна" 3, 2013, p. 415–441; e a d e m, *София Киевская и ее создатели*, Каменец-Подольский 2014, p. 229–241). The subject of Anna as the *mulier suadens* in the Old Rus' tradition was recently taken up by: G. P a c, *Kobiety w dynastii Piastów. Rola społeczna piastowskich żon i córek do połowy XII w. – studium porównawcze*, Toruń 2013, p. 42–61.

[32] В.И. Златарски, *История...*, p. 535–536; П. Мутафчиев, *История...*, p. 201. Cf. Г. Бакалов, *Средновековният български владетел. Титулатура и инсиг-нии*, [2]София 1995, p. 183; В. Гюзелев, *Значението на брака на цар Петър (927–969) с ромейката Мария-Ирина Лакапина (911–962)*, [in:] *Културните текстове на миналото – носители, символи, идеи*, vol. I, *Текстовете на историята, история на текстовете. Материали от Юбилейната международна конференция в чест на 60-годишнината на проф. д.и.н. Казимир Попконстантинов, Велико Търново, 29–31 октомври 2003 г.*, София 2005, p. 27; В. Игнатов, *Българските царици. Владетелките на България от VII до XIV в.*, София 2008, p. 14.

[33] S. Georgieva, *The Byzantine Princesses in Bulgaria*, "Byzantinobulgarica" 9, 1995, p. 168; И. Йорданов, *Корпус на печатите на Средновековна България*, София 2001, p. 59; С. Георгиева, *Жената в българското средновековие*, Пловдив 2011, p. 313–314; Д.И. Полывянный, *Царь Петр в исторической памяти болгарского средневековья*, [in:] *Средновековният българин и "другите". Сборник*

to commemorate the events of 927. They were also a convenient means of propaganda, through which the Bulgarian ruler was able to express his attachment to the Lekapenoi family; finally, they served to legitimize Peter's title. In this context, Maria – granddaughter of the Byzantine emperor – was merely a rather passive vehicle of imperial status; it was thanks to marrying her that the Bulgarian monarch gained the formal right to use the title of tsar/emperor[34].

It is worth noting that in the social realities of the 10th century, the expression of appreciation for the spouse's lineage – and the desire to flaunt it to one's subjects, as well as other courts – was by no means equivalent to granting her even the slightest degree of tangible political power. In fact, it did not even guarantee fulfilling elementary obligations and being respectful towards her. Let us refer once again to the relationship between the prince of Rus' and Anna Porphyrogennete, described in the sources in much more detail than that of the Bulgarian royal couple.

в чест на 60-годишнината на проф. дин Петър Ангелов, eds. А. Н и к о л о в, Г.Н. Н и к о л о в, София 2013, p. 138; П. П а в л о в, *Години на мир и "ратни беди" (927–1018)*, [in:] Г. А т а н а с о в, В. В а ч к о в а, П. П а в л о в, *Българска национална история*, vol. III, *Първо българско царство (680–1018)*, Велико Търново 2015, p. 413; И. Й о р д а н о в, *Корпус на средновековните български печати*, София 2016, p. 89.

[34] Г. Б а к а л о в, *Царската промулгация на Петър и неговите приемници в светлината на българо-византийските дипломатически отношения след договора от 927 г.*, "Исторически преглед" 39.6, 1983, p. 36; F. T i n n e f e l d, *Byzantinische auswärtige Heiratspolitik vom 9. zum 12 Jahrhundert*, "Byzantinoslavica" 54.1, 1993, p. 23; Г. Б а к а л о в, *Средновековният български владетел...*, p. 170; Г. А т а н а с о в, *Инсигниите на средновековните български владетели. Корони, скиптри, сфери, оръжия, костюми, накити*, Плевен 1999, p. 96–98; И. Й о р д а н о в, *Корпус на печатите...*, p. 59; И. Б о ж и л о в, В. Г ю з е л е в, *История...*, p. 276; А. Н и к о л о в, *Политическа мисъл...*, p. 239; Т. Т о д о р о в, *България през втората и третата четвърт на Х век: политическа история*, София 2006 [unpublished PhD thesis], p. 163; P. B o r o ń, *Kniaziowie, królowie, carowie... Tytuły i nazwy władców słowiańskich we wczesnym średniowieczu*, Katowice 2010, p. 40; С. Г е о р г и е в а, *Жената...*, p. 314; M.J. L e s z k a, K. M a r i n o w, *Carstwo bułgarskie...*, p. 159–160; С. З в е з д о в, *Договорът от 927 година между България и Византия*, "History. Bulgarian Journal of Historical Education" 23.3, 2015, p. 267–268; i d e m, *Българо-византийските отношения при цар Петър I*, София 2016, p. 14; Z.A. B r z o z o w s k a, *Rola carycy Marii-Ireny Lekapeny w recepcji elementów bizantyńskiego modelu władzy w pierwszym państwie bułgarskim*, "Vox Patrum" 66, 2016, p. 452.

Fig. 6. Anna Porphyrogennete accompanied by a *zoste patrikia*. Wall painting from the interior of the Church of St. Sophia (Divine Wisdom) in Kiev, first half of 11th century. Drawing (after F.G. Solncev): E. Myślińska-Brzozowska

Much like Peter, Vladimir I put his wife in the limelight of public life, making it clear that she was 'born in the purple' – daughter and sister of Constantinopolitan emperors. While no seals of this ruler survive, whereas the golden and silver coins minted by this him only show the enthroned prince himself[35], it is nonetheless known that princess Anna's name was mentioned in official documents (e.g. in the short redaction of the so-called *Church Statute of Prince Vladimir*: и сгадав аз со своею княгинею Анною)[36]; besides, her painted image adorned the Church

[35] М.П. Сотникова, И.Г. Спасский, *Тысячелетие древнейших монет России. Сводный каталог русских монет X–XI вв.*, Ленинград 1983, p. 60–81, 115–180.
[36] Я.Н. Щапов, *Княжеские уставы и церковь в Древней Руси XI–XIV вв.*, Москва 1972, p. 115–127; i d e m, *Древнерусские княжеские уставы XI–XV вв.*, Москва 1976,

of Divine Wisdom in Kiev[37], and the memory of her imperial origins survived in later Rus' historiography.

On the other hand, the ambiguous chronology of the birth of Vladimir's sons has allowed certain researchers to speculate that the Rus' prince may have moved away from Anna due to her infertility. Such opinions might be considered exaggerated, although one other issue is clear – even if the Porphyrogennete remained the sole official spouse of Vladimir I until her death in 1011/1012, it did not hinder her husband from pursuing erotic relationships with (numerous) other women[38].

There is also no evidence in the source material to support the claim, advanced by certain Bulgarian scholars, that Maria served as a 'Byzantine spy' at the Preslav court[39]. Such views are based wholly on the aforementioned enigmatic remark by the Continuator of George the Monk (further repeated by Symeon Logothete and the author of the *Continuation of Theophanes*) on how the tsaritsa traveled to Constantinople several times, accompanied by her children, to visit her father and grandfather – the latter being emperor Romanos I Lekapenos[40]. It goes without saying that, during such visits, Maria might have provided her Byzantine relatives with information about the plans and doings of her husband; however, we do not have sufficient source material to determine what was discussed during her sojourns in the Byzantine capital. It should be emphasized that Maria and her children's journeys to Constantinople could not have taken place without Peter's knowledge and consent. It would have

---

p. 66. For a summary of the discussion of the authenticity of the *Church Statute of Prince Vladimir* and selected works on the subject cf.: G. P o d s k a l s k y, *Chrześcijaństwo i literatura teologiczna na Rusi Kijowskiej (988–1237)*, transl. J. Z y c h o w i c z, Kraków 2000, p. 270–272.

[37] Н.Н. Н и к и т е н к о, *Русь и Византия*..., p. 36–88; e a d e m, *София Киевская*..., p. 75–117; e a d e m, *Крещение Руси*..., p. 415–441.

[38] А.Ю. К а р п о в, *Владимир Святой*..., p. 287–288.

[39] В.И. З л а т а р с к и, *История*..., p. 535–536; П. М у т а ф ч и е в, *История*..., p. 201; В. И г н а т о в, *Българските царици*..., p. 14.

[40] C o n t i n u a t o r o f G e o r g e t h e M o n k, p. 913; S y m e o n L o g o-t h e t e, 136, 67, p. 334; C o n t i n u a t o r o f T h e o p h a n e s, VI, 35, p. 422.

been unlikely for the tsar to be amenable to such undertakings – and to allow them – had they been detrimental to the Bulgarian reason of state.

Unfortunately, the paucity of source material renders it impossible to prove another hypothesis. As we mentioned before, the Byzantine historians agree that Maria, both in 927 and during her later visits to the empire's capital, received innumerable riches from her relatives[41]. One is led to wonder whether these goods were not offered for a specific purpose: after all, with their aid, coupled with a modicum of diplomatic skills, Maria could have won over many of the people surrounding Peter, thus gaining some influence over his policies.

A view that needs to be debunked as a historiographical myth concerns the alleged far-reaching Byzantinization of Old Bulgarian culture during Maria Lekapene's presence at the court. As correctly pointed out by Jonathan Shepard, Bulgaria had been drawn into the sphere of Byzantine civilization much earlier, while the reception of the elements of Byzantine traditions was a long-lasting process. Thus, in 927, our heroine arrived in a country whose political and intellectual elites were already quite familiar with the culture of Eastern Christianity, as well as with the views on monarchy prevalent in Constantinople[42]. Suffice it to say that during the reign of Peter's father Symeon I the Great – a ruler educated in Constantinople and undoubtedly fascinated with the Eastern Roman ideals of imperial power[43] – several Greek legal compilations had already been adapted in Bulgaria. These included fragments of the

---

[41] Continuator of George the Monk, p. 907, 913; Symeon Logothete, 136, 51, 67, p. 329, 334; Continuator of Theophanes, VI, 23, 35, p. 415, 422.

[42] J. S h e p a r d, *A marriage too far? Maria Lekapena and Peter of Bulgaria*, [in:] *The Empress Theophano. Byzantium and the West at the turn of the first millennium*, ed. A. D a v i d s, Cambridge 1995, p. 140.

[43] M.J. L e s z k a, *The Monk versus the Philosopher. From the History of the Bulgarian-Byzantine War 894–896*, "Studia Ceranea. Journal of the Waldemar Ceran Research Centre for the History and Culture of the Mediterranean Area and South-East Europe" 1, 2011, p. 55–57; i d e m, *Symeon I Wielki a Bizancjum. Z dziejów stosunków bułgarsko--bizantyńskich w latach 893–927*, Łódź 2013, p. 29–34.

Ekloga, *Nomokanon of Fifty Titles* and *Nomokanon of Fourteen Titles*[44], as well as deacon Agapetos's *Ekthesis*, 72 chapters of advice to emperor Justinian I the Great (a brief treatise providing a synthetic exposition of Byzantine 'imperial theology'), translated into Slavic[45].

The fact that, by the year 927, the Preslav court was well-acquainted with the accomplishments of Byzantine civilization does not, however, exclude the possibility of Maria's personal impact on her new milieu. The tsaritsa most likely attempted to embed in the Bulgarian capital the customs and elements of court ceremonial that she knew from the Constantinople palace[46]; nevertheless, due to insufficient source material, we are unable to determine the scope of her influence. Most likely, it did not extend beyond the walls of the tsar's seat and the narrow circle of people directly surrounding her[47]. The archaeological material (e.g. the aforementioned 'Preslav treasure' as well as the most recent discoveries of Bulgarian researchers) allows us to conclude that during Maria's time, Byzantine models of female fashion became commonplace in Preslav; in that period, jewelry produced in the workshops of Constantinople came to be greatly desired by ladies from the highest social circles[48].

---

[44] Г. Б а к а л о в, *Средновековният български владетел...*, p. 136; K. M a k s i-m o v i c h, *Byzantine Law in Old Slavonic Translations and the Nomocanon of Methodius*, "Byzantinoslavica" 65, 2007, p. 10; Т. С л а в о в а, *Юридическа литература*, [in:] *История на българската средновековна литература*, ed. A. М и л т е н о в а, София 2008, p. 195–197.

[45] А. Н и к о л о в, *Старобългарският превод на "Изложение на поучителни глави към император Юстиниан" от дякон Агапит и развитието на идеята за достойнството на българския владетел в края на IX–началото на X в.*, "Palaeobulgarica" 24.3, 2000, p. 77–85; i d e m, *Политическа мисъл...*, p. 214–230, 250–268.

[46] J. S h e p a r d, *A marriage...*, p. 140–141; M.J. L e s z k a, *Wizerunek władców pierwszego państwa bułgarskiego w bizantyńskich źródłach pisanych (VIII–pierwsza połowa XII w.)*, Łódź 2003, p. 124–125; i d e m, *Obrazът na българския цар Борис II във византийските извори*, "Studia Balcanica" 25, 2006, p. 146.

[47] П. П а в л о в, *Години на мир...*, p. 416.

[48] G. A t a n a s o v, *On the Origin, Function and the Owner of the Adornments of the Preslav Treasure from the 10ᵗʰ century*, "Archaeologia Bulgarica" 3.3, 1999, p. 85–92; i d e m, *Инсигниите...*, p. 193, 230–235; С. Т о д о р о в а - Ч а н е в а, *Женският накит от епохата на Първото българско царство. VII–XI в.*, София 2009, p. 26–28.

VII

Zofia A. Brzozowska
Mirosław J. Leszka

Maria Lekapene and the Transfer of the Idea of the *Imperial Feminine* in Medieval Bulgaria

In spite of what has been said in the previous chapter, Maria and Peter's reign did see a fundamental shift in the manner in which medieval Bulgarians perceived their tsaritsa and her role within the state. Until 927, women occupying the throne in Preslav – unlike contemporary Byzantine empresses – had been almost invisible in the public sphere: they were not mentioned in official diplomatic correspondence, nor were their images included on coins or seals. The sole predecessor of our protagonist whose name survived in historical texts is another Maria, wife of Boris-Michael; meanwhile, both of Symeon I the Great's spouses (including Peter's mother) will forever remain anonymous[1]. One may, therefore, suppose that prior to 927, the position of Bulgarian royal consorts had been similar to the status of wives of kings in the Germanic states of the West during the 5th–8th centuries. No tradition of crowning women existed there, and some

---

[1] Г. Атанасов, *Инсигниите на средновековните български владетели. Корони, скиптри, сфери, оръжия, костюми, накити*, Плевен 1999, p. 182, 184; В. Игнатов, *Българските царици. Владетелките на България от VII до XIV в.*, София 2008, p. 9–12.

political systems (e.g. that of the Vandals) did not recognize the function of a queen[2]. As Magda Hristodulova and Sashka Georgieva rightly observe, Maria Lekapene should be considered the first medieval Bulgarian female royal to enter the public sphere[3]. It is difficult to give an unequivocal reply to the question of whether this was accomplished thanks to the tsaritsa's strength of character and personal determination, or rather through the efforts of the people accompanying her – the Byzantines who arrived in Preslav in Maria's retinue. Peter's attitude also played a role here, since he would be expected to care about underlining the high status of his wife: after all, marrying her gave him the right to use the title of emperor/tsar[4].

Whatever the case may be, Maria, unlike her predecessors, was not only a companion of the Bulgarian tsar at the table and in the bedchamber, but also a true ruler of the Bulgarians. This elevation in the status of the Preslav tsaritsa during this era can be associated with the introduction of the Byzantine view regarding the role of the empress within the state (the *imperial feminine*, to use the term introduced into the historiographical discourse by Judith Herrin) to Old Bulgarian culture[5].

---

[2] J. H e r r i n, *Women in Purple. Rulers of Medieval Byzantium*, London 2002, p. 246–247.

[3] М. Х р и с т о д у л о в а, *Титул и регалии болгарской владетельницы в эпоху средневековья (VII–XIV вв.)*, "Études Balkaniques" 1978, 3, p. 142; С. Г е о р г и е в а, *Жената в българското средновековие*, Пловдив 2011, p. 312, 352.

[4] Г. Б а к а л о в, *Царската промулгация на Петър и неговите приемници в светлината на българо-византийските дипломатически отношения след договора от 927 г.*, "Исторически преглед" 39.6, 1983, p. 36; F. T i n n e f e l d, *Byzantinische auswärtige Heiratspolitik vom 9. zum 12 Jahrhundert*, "Byzantinoslavica" 54.1, 1993, p. 23; Г. Б а к а л о в, *Средновековният български владетел. Титулатура и инсигнии*, София 1995, p. 170; Г. А т а н а с о в, *Инсигниите...*, p. 96–98; И. Б о ж и л о в, В. Г ю з е л е в, *История на средновековна България. VII–XIV в.*, София 2006, p. 276; А. Н и к о л о в, *Политическа мисъл в ранносредновековна България (средата на IX-края на X в.)*, София 2006, p. 239; Т. Т о д о р о в, *България през втората и третата четвърт на X век: политическа история*, София 2006 [unpublished PhD thesis], p. 163; M.J. L e s z k a, K. M a r i n o w, *Carstwo bułgarskie. Polityka – społeczeństwo – gospodarka – kultura. 866–971*, Warszawa 2015, p. 159–160; С. З в е з д о в, *Договорът от 927 година между България и Византия*, "History. Bulgarian Journal of Historical Education" 23.3, 2015, p. 267–268.

[5] J. H e r r i n, *The Imperial Feminine in Byzantium*, "Past and Present" 169, 2000, p. 5–35 [=J. H e r r i n, *Unrivalled Influence: Women and Empire in Byzantium*, Princeton 2013, p. 161–193].

1. Female Authority in Byzantium

1.1. The Byzantine Model of the Empress

According to the English Byzantinologist, the concept of the *imperial feminine* comprises three fundamental elements:

> The first lies in the Late Antique transition from a Roman to a Christian society, marked by significant visual changes, which witnesses the introduction of the Virgin as a novel symbol of maternal value into an environment dominated visually by pagan monuments. It develops in symbiosis with imperial and civic rites into a powerful new cult. The second strand springs from the process of adapting Roman imperial structures to accommodate the needs of dynasty and claims to rule by inheritance, necessarily transmitted by women. The third, and perhaps most crucial, element lies in the development of New Rome, Constantinople, where imperial and public space, court structures and rituals – not least [...] the existence of a third sex of eunuchs, whom they could command – allowed ruling women to elaborate new roles[6].

Two of the three elements mentioned by Judith Herrin – namely the reproductive and ceremonial functions – were of decisive value for the status of empresses and the role they played. The empress was, if one may say so, an indispensable factor without which the functioning of the imperial court was difficult, if possible at all. This thought was expressed laconically (though quite categorically) in the *Continuation of Theophanes*, in the fragment describing Michael II's quandary following the death of his wife, during his contemplation of another marriage. It is articulated as follows: *For it is impossible [...], to live as emperor without a wife, and to deprive our spouses of a mistress and empress[7].*

---

[6] J. H e r r i n, *Women in Purple...*, p. 241–242; see also: e a d e m, *The Imperial Feminine...*, p. 3–25.

[7] C o n t i n u a t o r o f T h e o p h a n e s, II, 24, p. 114 (transl. M. F e a t h e r s t o n e, J. S i g n e s C o d o ñ e r, p. 115).

It should be noted that rulers did, by and large, abide by this rule. As might be expected, it is possible to point out some who did not adhere to it (e.g. Basil II); still, even those would customarily ensure the presence of a woman with an imperial title (mother, sister or daughter) at their court. Especially instructive in this context is the case of Leo VI, who crowned his daughter Anna so that the court would not remain without an empress[8].

* * *

The highest title that could be bestowed on an empress was that of *augusta*[9], harking back to the times of pagan Rome. Empress consorts did not obtain it obligatorily during the wedding; the decision to grant it fell within the ruler's competence. Notably, the honorific was not restricted exclusively for emperors' wives, although the latter did constitute the vast majority of women who received it. Thus, for instance, in 325 Constantine I the Great conferred the title of *augusta* on Helena, his mother, and Theodosios II – on his sister, Pulcheria (in 414)[10]. Tiberios II Constantine gave the title to his daughter – Constantina (?582)[11]; finally, Leo VI granted it to his young daughter Anna, as mentioned above. Empress consorts would receive the honorific at different moments of their relationship with the ruler. Beside the very beginning of the marriage, which was

---

[8] S. T o u g h e r, *The Reign of Leo VI (886–912). Politics and People*, Leiden–New York–Köln 1997, p. 147; L. G a r l a n d, *Byzantine Empresses. Women and Power in Byzantium, AD 527–1204*, London–New York 1999, p. 114.

[9] For more on this issue cf. E. B e n s a m m a r, *La titulature de l'impératrice et sa signification. Recherches sur les sources byzantines de la fin du VIIIe siècle à la fin du XIIe siècle*, "Byzantion" 46, 1976, p. 270, 286–287 ; B. H i l l, *Imperial Women in Byzantium 1025–1204. Power, Patronage and Ideology*, New York 1999, p. 102–108; L. J a m e s, *Empresses and Power in Early Byzantium*, Leicester 2001, p. 118–125.

[10] Helena – A.H.M J o n e s, J.R. M a r t i n d a l e, J. M o r r i s, *The Prosopography of Later Roman Empire* [cetera: *PLRE*], vol. I, Cambridge 1971, p. 410, s.v. *Fl. Iulia Helena 3*; Pulcheria – J. M a r t i n d a l e, *PLRE*, vol. II, Cambridge 1980, p. 929, s.v. *Aelia Pulcheria*.

[11] J. M a r t i n d a l e, *PLRE*, vol. III, Cambridge 1992, p. 338, s.v. *Augusta quae et Constantina (Aelia Constantina) 1*; cf. M.J. L e s z k a, *Konstantyna, żona cesarza Maurycjusza*, "Przegląd Nauk Historycznych" 1.1, 2002, p. 22–23.

the most common case, a typical moment of earning this token of dignity in the early Byzantine period was giving birth to a child (not necessarily of the male sex)[12]. However, it could also happen that an empress consort would never receive the title. This was the case with Maria of Amnia, wife of Constantine VI[13]. It is commonly thought that this state of affairs was orchestrated by Irene, the emperor's mother, who wanted to be the only woman holding the title. This may well be accurate to a certain degree; nevertheless, it should be noted that such a situation would not have been possible without the consent of Constantine VI himself. As is well-known, he happened not to be particularly fond of his empress consort and was consequently reluctant to strengthen her position[14].

The fact that it was the emperor who bestowed the title of *augusta* unequivocally confirms his superordinate position in relation to the woman receiving the honor. This observation is also reflected in legal regulations. In Justinian I's *Digest*, we read that *[t]he emperor is not bound by statutes. And though the empress is bound by them, nevertheless, emperors give the empress the same privileges as they have themselves*[15]. Several hundred years later, the tenet was reiterated in the 9th–century collection of laws known as the *Basilika*: *The emperor is not subject to the law. The empress is subject to the law until the emperor passes his rights/prerogatives to her*[16].

In early Byzantium, the name of the empress was often accompanied by the element *Aelia*. This phenomenon is observed not only among empresses from the times of the Theodosian dynasty, but also later, up

---

[12] L. G a r l a n d, *Byzantine Empresses...*, p. 2–3; L. J a m e s, *Empresses...*, p. 119–122; cf. D. M i s s i o u, *Über die Institutionele Rolle der Byzantinischen Kaiserin*, "Jahrbuch der Österreichischen Byzantinistik" 32, 1982, p. 489–498.

[13] *Prosopographie der mittelbyzantinischen Zeit. Erste Abteilung (641–867)* [cetera: *PMB I*], vol. III, ed. F. W i n k e l m a n n et al., Berlin–New York 2000, p. 147–149, s.v. *Maria (4127)*.

[14] On this subject see e.g.: L. G a r l a n d, *Byzantine Empresses...*, p. 81, 84; J. H e r r i n, *Women in Purple...*, p. 91–96.

[15] *Digest of Justinian*, I, 3, 31: *Princeps legibus solutus est: Augusta autem licet legibus soluta non est, princeps tamen eadem illi privilegia tribuunt, quae ipsi habent* (transl. A. W a t s o n, p. 13). Cf. L. J a m e s, *Empresses...*, p. 72.

[16] *Basilika*, II, 6, 1.

until Fabia, first wife of Herakleios. The term was derived from the family of the Aelii, from which Flaccilla, first wife of Theodosios I, happened to be descended. It was not a title, but rather a form of showing honor in the form of a connection with previous empresses[17].

According to some scholars, the title of *augusta* functioned roughly until the end of the 13th century; its marginal use, however, is attested until the end of Byzantium's existence[18]. From the 9th century onwards, the term *basilissa* comes to be used with reference to empresses, while other denominations (such as *anassa* or *despoina*) start appearing in the sources as well. These were not titles, however. Rather, they were mere terms used when speaking of empresses; moreover, they did not necessarily denote them exclusively[19]. Female rulers who reigned autonomously, such as e.g. Irene, presumably employed the title of *basileus* (emperor)[20].

Empresses possessed certain insignia connected with their position. They would wear crowns (*stemma*), often adorned with gemstone pendants (*pendilia*), and had their own scepters[21]. They sat on the throne at the emperor's side, had a dedicated place in Constantinople's most distinguished church – Hagia Sophia, and enjoyed the right to wear imperial (purple) attire as well as shoes. Empresses' insignia and clothing can be seen in the Byzantine mosaics in the Church of San Vitale in Ravenna, which feature a portrayal of Theodora, wife of Justinian I, along with her court[22]. The dress worn by empresses as seen in their official depictions was of a solemn, ceremonial character. In all likelihood, they would dress differently on an everyday basis; however, as far as the period under discussion is concerned, no relevant source material is available.

---

[17] L. J a m e s, *Empresses...*, p. 127–128.

[18] B. H i l l, *Imperial Women...*, p. 102–104.

[19] *Ibidem*, p. 108–117; L. J a m e s, *Empresses...*, p. 125–127.

[20] L. G a r l a n d, *Byzantine Empresses...*, p. 87, 260. Cf. R.-J. L i l i e, *Byzanz unter Eirene und Konstantin VI (780–802). Mit einem Kapitel über Leon IV (775–780)*, Frankfurt am Main 1996, p. 277–279; J. H e r r i n, *Women in Purple...*, p. 101–102.

[21] L. G a r l a n d, *Byzantine Empresses...*, p. 2.

[22] A. M c C l a n a n, *Ritual and Representation of the Byzantine Empress' Court at San Vitale, Ravenna*, [in:] *Acta XIII Congressus Internationalis Archaelogiae Christianae*, eds. M. C a m b i, E. M a r t i n, vol. II, Citta del Vaticano–Split 1998, p. 11–20.

1.2. The Empress's Court

The empress had at her disposal a part of the Great Palace (*gynaiko-nitis*, *gynaeceum*), and subsequently – of the Palace of Blachernai. We do not know precisely which fragments of the palace were her domain. The latter certainly included the so-called Porphyry (Purple) Chamber, where imperial children were born, and some of the other chambers were clearly under full control of empresses and their trusted associates as well[23]. This is evident e.g. from the case of Justinian's wife Theodora, who reportedly used her part of the palace to shelter Anthimos (bishop of Trebizond, patriarch of Constantinople, 535–536) for an extended period of time[24]; she is also said to have imprisoned her enemies there[25]. We may leave aside the question of whether Justinian was genuinely unaware of this; but if the authors of the sources depict the matter in this way, then it must have seemed a credible state of affairs to their audience. Another example confirming the existence of palace space under complete authority of the empress is the situation from December 969: the conspirators preparing to overthrow Nikephoros II Phokas were hidden in empress Theophano's rooms, from where they proceeded to the emperor's bedroom[26].

The empress had at her disposal her own court (*sekreton ton gynaikon*, women's court)[27] and separate financial means. Our knowledge about the latter is rather scanty. It has been surmised that empresses' wealth may have come from several sources. These certainly included property inherited from their parents – naturally, as long as they were affluent enough (which also determined the value of the dowry obtained by the bride). Finally,

---

[23] J. H e r r i n, *Unrivalled Influence*..., p. 223–225.

[24] W.H.C. F r e n d, *The Rise of the Monophysite Movement. Chapters in the History of Church in Fifth and Sixth Centuries*, Cambridge 1972, p. 272; C. F o s s, *The Empress Theodora*, "Byzantion" 72, 2002, p. 144; V. M e n z e, *Justinian and the Making of the Syriac Orthodox Church*, Oxford 2008, p. 207.

[25] P r o k o p i o s, *Secret History*, 3.

[26] L e o t h e D e a c o n, V, 6–7; J o h n Z o n a r a s, p. 517–518. Cf. L. G a r l a n d, *Byzantine Empresses*..., p. 132; M.J. L e s z k a, *Rola cesarzowej Teofano w uzurpacjach Nicefora Fokasa (963) i Jana Tzymiskesa (969)*, [in:] *Zamach stanu w dawnych społecznościach*, ed. A. S o ł t y s i k, Warszawa 2004, p. 233.

[27] J. H e r r i n, *Unrivalled Influence*..., p. 225–233.

one should mention wedding gifts received by empresses from their husbands. Even at further stages of the marriage, the *basilissa* sometimes
continued receiving presents from the emperor, be it in the form of money,
valuables or real estate[28]. Although a rare case, empresses apparently did
at times make active attempts to enlarge their wealth. Theodora, wife
of Theophilos, is reported to have possessed a fleet of merchant ships,
from which she drew considerable income. Her husband, upon discov-
ering this, decided that such activity was not worthy of an empress and
ordered the ships to be destroyed along with the cargo. Whether or not
these events are authentic is not crucial here; the account clearly reflects
the conviction that it did not befit the *basilissa* to undertake economic
and commercial endeavors[29].

   The immediate surrounding of the empress consisted of various ladies
of the court arranged in a hierarchy of social rank, beginning with the
zoste patrikia. Women's titles were derived from those of their husbands:
patrikia, protospatharia, spatharia, kandidatissa; they also wore appropriate attire, corresponding to their rank. The title of *zoste patrikia* was
often granted to the empress's mother; the first woman to receive it
was the mother of empress Theodora, wife of Theophilos[30]. It may be
added that empresses who hailed from the provinces of the empire would
bring their families to the imperial court. The female part of the family,
most prominently the mother, would enter the most intimate group
of people surrounding the new empress. The latter had the authority
to shape her own court, although she would largely inherit it from her
predecessor. That enabled her to acquire experienced female courtiers
– *koubikoulariai*, who could introduce her into the convoluted world
of court ceremonies (which the empress was obliged to attend) and the
general intricacies of courtly life.

---

[28] L. J a m e s, *Empresses...*, p. 70.

[29] Cf. J. H e r r i n, *Women in Purple...*, p. 192.

[30] L. G a r l a n d, *Byzantine Empresses...*, p. 5; J. H e r r i n, *Unrivalled Influence...*
p. 228; cf. Н. К ъ н е в, *Византийската титла патрикия-зости (IX–XI в.).
Приносът на сфрагистиката за попълване на листата на носителките на титлата,* "Историкии" 4, 2011, p. 191–198.

Empresses who came from outside the borders of the Byzantine Empire would arrive in Constantinople with female companions. Some of the latter would remain at the imperial court permanently, alleviating the feeling of estrangement that must have haunted the empress at least in the initial stages of her residence in Byzantium.

The role of the *koubikoulariai* was not limited to accompanying the empress in her daily palace life. They were also present at her side when she left the premises of the Great Palace and participated in various ceremonies that took place in the urban spaces of Constantinople, or when she visited places outside of the palace for other reasons. *Koubikoulariai* were no strangers to emperors: sometimes their relationships became rather close, even intimate. Theodote, second wife of Constantine VI[31], had been a lady-in-waiting of Maria of Amnia, the emperor's first wife. Likewise, Zoe Zaoutzaina had been a *koubikoularia* before she became the wife of Leo VI[32].

It is worth noting that the imperial court was often home not only to the wife of the reigning emperor, but also to other empresses, usually widows. Oftentimes, this led to rivalries and clashes. We may adduce the example of Helena Lekapene (a relative of the protagonist of the book – tsaritsa Maria), mother of Romanos II, and her relationship with Theophano, his wife. According to some sources, Theophano would pressure Romanos to expel his mother from the palace along with his five sisters. The emperor did not yield to the demand and the mother remained in the palace, although she did not live for much longer. It may be that Theophano's harsh position was less of a product of her grand ambitions and evil-minded character than an aftereffect of the ill treatment she received at the hands of Helena while Constantine VII Porphyrogennetos was still alive[33]. Many more situations of this sort could be cited, and it was not universally true that the current wife of the reigning emperor would emerge victorious form them.

---

[31] J. H e r r i n, *Unrivalled Influence...*, p. 227.

[32] S. T o u g h e r, *The Reign of Leo VI...*, p. 56–57; M.J. L e s z k a, *Zoe, o oczach czarnych jak węgiel, czwarta żona Leona VI Filozofa*, [in:] *Kobiety i władza w czasach dawnych*, eds. B. C z w o j d r a k, A. K l u c z e k, Katowice 2015, p. 96–97.

[33] For more on this cf. M.B. L e s z k a, M.J. L e s z k a, *Bazylisa. Świat bizantyńskich cesarzowych IV–XV w.*, Łódź 2017, p. 336–337.

The court of an empress usually also housed girls or women from other countries, coming to Constantinople as hostages, guests or candidates for imperial brides. Women of this latter category received particularly devout care and thorough preparation for their prospective role.

An empress's environment certainly also included nannies, wet-nurses and caregivers of the imperial children. Their existence is directly confirmed through the tragic incident that cost the life of Constantine, son of Theophilos and Theodora: he fell into the palace cistern and drowned, which resulted in the punishment of his caregivers[34]. When Theophano, wife of Romanos II, was in labor giving birth to a daughter in 963, and was subsequently banished from the palace for some time by Nikephoros II Phokas, her sons Basil II and Constantine VIII were being taken care of by female custodians[35].

Empresses had at their disposal various kinds of female servants – dressers, bath attendants, hairdressers, tailors, cooks, and the like; some of them were slaves. These personnel guaranteed the empress a high standard of living.

Another group that formed an important part of an empress's staff were eunuchs. Representatives of this 'third sex' were close to both the empress and the emperor and they played a salient role by their side. Not infrequently, they enjoyed a particularly high degree of trust and were assigned important state functions[36]. A prime example is that of Theoktistos, who held the position of *logothetes tou dromou*[37], or of Manuel, a *magistros*[38], both of whom were appointed by Theophilos as regents of Michael III. They were to support Theodora, the minor emperor's mother. In the 10th century, Basil, a relative of the protagonist of the book – tsaritsa Maria, emerged as a remarkably powerful figure. An illegitimate son

---

[34] J. H e r r i n, *Women in Purple...*, p. 192.

[35] J. H e r r i n, *Unrivalled Influence...*, p. 225–226.

[36] Recent literature on the role of eunuchs at the imperial court and in Byzantine society includes: K. R i n g r o s e, *The Perfect Servant. Eunuchs and Social Construction of Gender in Byzantium*, Chicago 2003; S. To u g h e r, *The Eunuch in Byzantine History and Society*, London 2008.

[37] *PMB I*, vol. IV, ed. F. W i n k e l m a n n et al., Berlin–New York 2001, p. 578–581, s.v. *Theoktistos (8050)*.

[38] *PMB I*, vol. III, p. 136–141, s.v. *Manuel (4707)*.

of Romanos I Lekapenos, he was made a eunuch and achieved the rank of *parakoimomenos*[39]. The apogee of his career came during the first decade of the reign of Basil II, during which the *parakoimomenos* practically ruled the state. Eunuchs helped manage the empress's court, playing an influential part in organizing her daily life and overseeing her possessions; however, it should be emphasized that they remained her clear subordinates.

How many people in total did the empress's court number? Answering this question is by no means easy, if at all possible. The figure would have been different for each particular stage of the history of Byzantium. In order to save their readers from a state of complete vagueness, scholars have tried to produce at least a rough estimate. We know, for example, that empress Theodora (wife of Justinian I) was accompanied by 4000 people when attending the spa in Python[40]. Nevertheless, it should be borne in mind that not all of them belonged to the empress's court; some were members of the court of the emperor himself. Based on Constantine Porphyrogennetos's *Book of Ceremonies*, it has been conjectured that the court may have totaled around 1000 people in the 10th century[41].

1.3. Coronations of Empresses

Before being wed to the emperor, the prospective empress consort was first crowned. The one to coronate her was the emperor himself, a fact that clearly marked her new position as the outcome of his decision (as opposed to divine will, the source of his own status). The crowning of the

---

[39] W.G. B r o k a a r, *Basil Lecapenus*, "Studia bizantina et neohellenica Neerlandica" 3, 1972, p. 199–234; И. Й о р д а н о в, *Печати на Василий Лакапин от България*, [in:] *Средновековният българин и "другите". Сборник в чест на 60-годишнината на проф. дин Петър Ангелов*, eds. А. Н и к о л о в, Г.Н. Н и к о л о в, София 2013, p. 159–166; *Prosopographie der mittelbyzantinischen Zeit. Zweite Abteilung (867–1025)*, vol. I, ed. F. W i n k e l m a n n et al., Berlin–Boston 2013, p. 588–598, s.v. *Basileios Lakapenos (20925)*;

[40] J o h n   M a l a l a s, XVIII, 25. Cf. L. G a r l a n d, *Byzantine Empresses...*, p. 5; J. H e r r i n, *Unrivalled Influence...*, p. 222, 234.

[41] C o n s t a n t i n e   V I I   P o r p h y r o g e n n e t o s, *The Book of Ceremonies*, I, 49 (40); L. G a r l a n d, *Byzantine Empresses...*, p. 5; cf. J. H e r r i n, *Unrivalled Influence...*, p. 221–222.

empress took place in the palace, not in a church, which is thought to echo the above-mentioned concept as well[42].

The relevant procedures are described in the *Book of Ceremonies*; in particular, chapters 40 and 41 of this work are devoted to the coronation of the empress as well as the wedding ceremony[43]. Although no names are mentioned, it is commonly assumed that the actual event described is the coronation and wedding of Irene, wife of Leo IV[44]. This is not overly significant, since other ceremonies of this kind presumably followed a similar pattern.

Both events took place in the Great Palace complex. The emperor(s) entered the Augusteus hall, where state officials and senators would gather arranged by groups, from the *magistroi* to the *stratelatai*. At that time, the patriarch of Constantinople would cross the Palace of Daphne towards the Church of St. Stephen, where he awaited being summoned by the emperor. As soon as the signal arrived, he proceeded into the Augusteus, accompanied by clergy. At that point, the prospective empress was led into the hall, escorted by her suite and wearing an imperial robe (*sticharion*) as well as veil (*maphorion*). The patriarch commenced the prayer over the empress's chlamys, while she held candles, which she handed to the *primikerios* or the *ostiarios* when the prayer was concluded. Next, the emperor(s) took off her veil, which was spread around her by the *koubikoularioi*. The patriarch took the chlamys and passed it to the ruler(s), who put it on the *augusta*. The hierarch proceeded to pray over the crown; after that, he handed it to the emperor, who placed it on the *augusta*'s head. The patriarch produced the *prependoulia*, which the emperor attached to the crown. Following this act, the patriarch, bishops and other clergy withdrew to the Church of St. Stephen, while the emperor(s) and the *augusta* assumed position on their thrones to receive *proskynesis* and acclamations from state dignitaries. The latter subsequently left the Augusteus: the *patrikioi* went to the Onopous, the consuls to the Triklinos of the 19 Couches, and the remaining ones to the Tribunal. Meanwhile, female representatives

---

[42] B. Hill, *Imperial Women...*, p. 107.

[43] Constantine VII Porphyrogennetos, *The Book of Ceremonies*, I, 40–41.

[44] L. James, *Empresses...*, p. 52; cf. J. Herrin, *Women in Purple...*, p. 60.

of the state elite would enter the Augusteus, divided into II groups. They would likewise perform *proskynesis* three times and acclaim the newly crowned empress. Afterwards, they would proceed to the Golden Hand Room, where the *augusta* herself arrived as well; from there, she continued to the Onopous, where she received bows and acclamation (*for many good years!*)[45] from the *patrikioi* gathered there. Subsequently, the empress moved to the Dikionion in order to accept further bows and acclamations from the senators and the *patrikioi*. Finally, the procession reached the terrace of the Tribunal. The senators would gather on both sides of the stairs descending towards the terrace, while the commanders of palace guard units (*tagmata*) gathered on the terrace itself. A cross, scepters, labara and other insignia were placed there. Commanders, factions and other participants of the ceremony stood in front of the insignia on display. At that point, the empress emerged accompanied by two dignitaries (the *praipositos* and the *primikerios*) and stationed herself in the middle of the terrace. The exclamations began: *Holy, holy, holy! Glory to God in the highest and peace on earth!*[46]. The factions would recite coronation formulae, each of which was to be repeated three times. Their content was as follows:

> Goodwill to Christian people... For God has had mercy on his people... This is the great day of the Lord. This is the day of salvation for the Romans. This day is the joy and glory of the world... On which the crown of the imperial power has righty been placed on your head. Glory to God, the ruler of all. Glory to God who has proclaimed you empress. Glory to God who has crowned your head. Glory to God who has thus determined... Having crowned you, so-and-so, with his own hand. May he guard you for a great number of years in the purple... To the glory and exaltation of the Romans. May God listen to your people[47].

---

[45] Constantine VII Porphyrogennetos, *The Book of Ceremonies*, I, 41 (transl. p. 210).

[46] Constantine VII Porphyrogennetos, *The Book of Ceremonies*, I, 41 (transl. p. 211).

[47] Constantine VII Porphyrogennetos, *The Book of Ceremonies*, I, 40 (transl. p. 205–206).

The empress took two candles and bowed down in front of the cross, while the commanders would bow down to her. The labara, scepters and all other insignia placed at the terrace were lowered in front of the empress. This stage – which was also a key part of the emperor's own coronation procedure – was the pinnacle of the ceremony. Afterwards, the dignitaries would begin to withdraw, while the empress, having bowed down to the factions (whose members cheered: *may God preserve the augusta!*[48]), advanced deeper into the palace, receiving further acclamations from *patrikioi* and consuls on her path. In the Augusteus hall, she was greeted by cries in Latin: *welcome, welcome, augusta, welcome, augusta!*[49]. She moved to the Octagon, where the emperor – her future husband – awaited her. Together, they continued to the Church of St. Stephen, where the wedding ceremony took place.

1.4. Imperial Wedding Ceremonies and Festivities

The coronation was followed by the wedding. Before we proceed to discuss the marriage ceremony as portrayed in the above-mentioned *Book of Ceremonies*, we shall present another example – the wedding of Maurice and Constantina. It was arranged through the efforts of Tiberios II Constantine, the bride's father, who nevertheless did not live to see his plans materialize – he died on August 14th, 582. The wedding ceremony must have taken place shortly after (but not directly following) his funeral[50]. In view of the status of the bride and groom, the one in charge of the procedure was John the Faster, patriarch of Constantinople. The ceremony and the ensuing festivities, all of which took place in the Church of St. Stephen in the imperial palace, were conducted in an impressive setting. Church historian Evagrios Scholastikos left the following account:

---

[48] Constantine VII Porphyrogennetos, *The Book of Ceremonies*, I, 41 (transl. p. 212).

[49] Constantine VII Porphyrogennetos, *The Book of Ceremonies*, I, 41 (transl. p. 212).

[50] The problem of dating Constantina and Maurice's wedding is discussed in: M.J. L e s z k a, *Konstantyna...*, p. 23–24.

The other presented a robe shot with gold, decorated with purple and
Indian stones, and crowns most precious with their abundance of gold
and the varied splendor of the jewels, and all those numbered among the
offices at court and the armies, who lit the marital candles, magnificently
dressed and with the insignia of their rank, celebrating in song the festival
of the bringing of the bride[51].

Participation in the event was not restricted for the bride and groom's
families and dignitaries – residents of the capital city also joined widely.
Feasts, artistic performances and horse races were organized for them.
The festivities are reported to have lasted seven days[52].

The *Book of Ceremonies* offers more details, at least as far as certain
stages of the wedding and the ensuing reception are concerned[53]. The
work confirms that the ceremony took place in the Church of St. Stephen,
celebrated by the patriarch of the imperial capital. Following the festive
service, he put wedding crowns (*stephanoi*) on the bride and groom's
heads. No further specifics concerning the ceremony are provided in this
source. It is presumed that the patriarch blessed the young couple and
joined their right hands, as well as that the exchange of wedding rings took
place. Following the conclusion of this part of the ceremony, the emperor
and empress proceeded to the marital chamber in the Magnaura Palace.
This was accompanied by acclamations from dignitaries and factions as
well as by what we might nowadays call a wedding music service. After
depositing their imperial crowns in the chamber, the newlyweds made
their way to the Triklinos of the 19 Couches. A festive wedding reception
was held there, with the participation of guests chosen from among the
state elite by the emperor himself.

On the third day after the wedding, a ritual bath took place. Faction
representatives were positioned along the empress's way to the bath
of St. Christina, which was situated within the Great Palace. Organ sounds
could be heard. First, linen towels, scents and toiletries were brought to

---

[51] Evagrios Scholastikos, VI, 1 (transl. p. 290).
[52] Theophylaktos Simokattes, I, 10. 10–12.
[53] Constantine VII Porphyrogennetos, *The Book of Ceremonies*, I, 41.

the bath; next, the empress herself arrived, receiving acclamations on her way. Her return to the marital chamber was organized in an analogous fashion. Our source notes that the empress was assisted by three female members of her suite, carrying pomegranates made of porphyry; the latter were presumably meant to symbolize fertility[54].

The glamorous wedding ceremony, no doubt a major attraction for both court members and regular citizens of Constantinople, marked the beginning of the imperial couple's married life. Besides, it was no doubt designed to win the subjects' favor.

1.5. Participation in Secular and Religious Ceremonies

One of the important tasks of an empress was to take part in assorted court ceremonies and religious processions[55]. Empresses participated in festivities organized at the Hippodrome, audiences for foreign diplomats as well as receptions for military leaders and dignitaries. The 'catalogue' of events of this sort in which a Byzantine empress was expected to engage in evolved over time. This process is not easy to detect in the sources, all the more so because the most crucial of them – the *Book of Ceremonies* – rarely makes explicit mention of the empress's involvement in the proceedings described (coronation, wedding, baptism of children). Although they generally fail to enhance this picture significantly, other sources sometimes allow us to get a glimpse of empresses in certain situations as they appear at their husbands' sides.

For instance, we have sources with interesting references to the participation of Theodora (wife of Theophilos) in a number of court ceremonies. We know that she took part in the solemn welcome of her husband upon his return from the victorious expedition against the Arabs (831, 837)[56]. When news arrived that the emperor was nearing Constantinople, the

---

[54] J. H e r r i n, *Women in Purple...*, p. 268, fn. 20.

[55] L. J a m e s, *Empresses...*, p. 50–58; E. M a l a m u t, *L'impératrice byzantine et le cérémonial (VIIIe–XIIe siècle)*, [in:] *Le saint, le moine et le paysan: Mélanges d'histoire byzantine offerts à Michel Kaplan*, eds. O. D e l o u i s, S. M e t i v i e r, P. P a g e s, Paris 2016, p. 329–374.

[56] J. H e r r i n, *Women in Purple...*, p. 199–200.

whole senate led by the prefect made their way to greet him at the Palace of Hieria (the site, situated on the Asian bank of the Bosporos, was the traditional reception point for emperors' triumphal returns from campaigns in Asia). The meeting occurred near the palace. The senators fell to the ground, bowing to the emperor in the traditional fashion. Empress Theodora, however, only greeted him inside the palace. When he got off his horse, she paid homage to him and kissed him. The emperor remained in the palace for seven days, awaiting the arrival of Arab prisoners-of-war who were to be part of the triumph ceremony. He asked for senators' wives to be invited to the palace, so that they could accompany his wife. Presumably, the women (including the empress) participated in festive receptions organized for the emperor and his commanders. The emperor – in all likelihood accompanied by his wife – left Hieria for the Palace of St. Mamas, where he tarried for three days, before moving forward to Blachernai.

The triumph ceremony was organized on a truly grand scale. Entering the city through the Golden Gate, the emperor proceeded by the Mese, reaching the Hagia Sophia and the Chalke – the gate of the Great Palace. Along the way, he received homage from the military and ordinary citizens gathered nearby. Captives and spoils of war preceded the emperor in the procession. The ruler would make pauses and deliver speeches; money was distributed. What apparently distinguished this ceremony from similar events of this kind is the fact that – as noted in the sources – the emperor was greeted by the children of Constantinople, who were wearing wreaths made of flowers. Also included in the festivities was a racing event at the Hippodrome; Theodora accompanied Theophilos in the imperial box (*kathisma*), a fact mentioned in Arab sources[57]. Conceivably, the eager emperor participated in the races himself. His feat was greeted by supporters of the factions of the Blues and the Greens with the cry ἀσύγκρι-τος φακτιονάρης (*welcome, peerless champion!*)[58] – normally restricted for outstanding victors of chariot racing competitions, such as Porphyrios,

---

[57] *Ibidem*, p. 200, 288.
[58] George the Monk, p. 707; J. Herrin, *Women in Purple...*, p. 199; cf. Al. Cameron, *Circus Factions. Blues and Grens at Rome and Byzantium*, Oxford 1976, p. 11–12.

the hero of Hippodrome races at the turn of the 5th and 6th centuries[59]. It is uncertain whether the empress presented a prize to her victorious husband, but this cannot be excluded.

Arab sources mention that the empress was present at meetings with diplomats. Yahyā al-Ghazal, a member of the caliph of Cordoba's mission to the Byzantine court in the years 839–840, recalls that he would see Theodora participate in official meetings with Arab emissaries alongside the emperor, state officials and interpreters. Yahyā took notice of the *basilissa*'s beauty, even the color of her eyes, purportedly black and beguiling; he also drew attention to her remarkable attire, which, as argued by one scholar, may have been designed by Theophilos himself[60].

It may be presumed that other empress consorts participated in the same ceremonies as Theodora. Sources confirm, for example, the involvement of Helena Lekapene, wife of Constantine VII, in meetings with princess Olga of Kiev, likely in the year 957. First, the empress, accompanied by her daughter-in-law and a number of ladies-in-waiting, met with Olga and her suite. Helena sat on the imperial throne, and her daughter-in-law on a seat positioned at its side. The talks were carried out through the mediation of the *praipositos*. Later, a meeting of the emperor with Olga took place[61]; Helena accompanied Constantine in this session as well,

---

[59] For more on Porphyrios cf.: Al. C a m e r o n, *Porphyrius the Charioteer*, London 1973.

[60] M a q q a r i, IV, 4.

[61] C o n s t a n t i n e   V I I   P o r p h y r o g e n n e t o s, *The Book of Ceremonies*, II, 15. On Olga's visit in Constantinopole see e.g.: Г.Г. Л и т а в р и н, *Путешествие русской княгини Ольги в Константинополь. Проблема источников*, "Византийский Временник" 42, 1981, p. 35–48; O. P r i t s a k, *When and Where was Ol'ga Baptized?*, "Harvard Ukrainian Studies" 9, 1985, p. 5–24; F. T i n n e f e l d, *Die Russische Fürstin Olga bei Konstantin VII. und das Problem der "Purpurgeborenen Kinder"*, "Russia mediaevalis" 6, 1987, p. 30–37; А.В. Н а з а р е н к о, *Когда же княгиня Ольга ездила в Константинополь?*, "Византийский Временник" 50, 1989, p. 66–84; J. F e a t h e r s t o n e, *Ol'ga's Visit to Constantinople*, "Harvard Ukrainian Studies" 14, 1990, p. 293–312; A. P o p p e, *Once Again Concerning the Baptism of Olga, Archontissa of Rus'*, "Dumbarton Oaks Papers" 46, 1992, p. 271–277; J. F e a t h e r s t o n e, *Olga's Visit to Constantinople in De Cerimoniis*, "Revue des études byzantines" 61, 2003, p. 241–251; F. T i n n e f e l d, *Zum Stand der Olga–Diskussion*, [in:] *Zwischen Polis, Provinz und Peripherie. Beiträge zur byzantinischen Geschichte und Kultur*, eds. L.M. H o f f m a n n,

along with their children. Similarly, they attended the reception held in Olga's honor together[62].

Naturally, it must be borne in mind that empresses acted as leaders of their own (female) part of the court and it was in this capacity that they shaped and took part in numerous activities: receptions for wives and daughters of state dignitaries, audiences for female monarchs (e.g. Helena Lekapene's meeting with Olga), wives of foreign envoys, as well as the envoys themselves. They would receive important figures of the state and the church who, for various reasons, sought their help and support.

As regards the set of religious ceremonies attended by empresses, it reflected the rhythm of the liturgical year. For example, the *Book of Ceremonies* gives an account of how the empress would – just like the emperor – meet church dignitaries on Palm Sunday, beginning from the *sakellarios* of Hagia Sophia, and receive crosses from them[63]. On Easter Monday, we see empress Irene leaving the Church of the Holy Apostles (presumably at the last stage of a procession visiting various churches of Constantinople) and entering a golden carriage pulled by four white horses, led by four *patrikioi*, including two commanders. The empress is throwing coins to the crowd gathered at the scene[64]. In this case, Irene enters the role of the emperor, who on that day participated in a procession beginning at the Great Palace and terminating at the very same Church of the Holy Apostles. On his path, the ruler visited many other temples[65]. We may also mention the Pentecost, when the empress, situated in the gallery of Hagia Sophia, sends a kiss to the *patrikiai*, while the emperor sends the same greeting to the *patrikioi* in the main nave of the church[66].

A. M o n c h i z a d e h, Wiesbaden 2005, p. 531–567; Z.A. B r z o z o w s k a, *Święta księżna kijowska Olga. Wybór źródeł*, Łódź 2014, p. 19–27.

[62] C o n s t a n t i n e V I I P o r p h y r o g e n n e t o s, *The Book of Ceremonies*, II, 15.

[63] C o n s t a n t i n e V I I P o r p h y r o g e n n e t o s, *The Book of Ceremonies*, I, 10, 65–77.

[64] T h e o p h a n e s, AM 6291.

[65] C o n s t a n t i n e V I I P o r p h y r o g e n n e t o s, *The Book of Ceremonies*, I, 5; I, 10; L. J a m e s, *Empresses...*, p. 55; J. H e r r i n, *Women in Purple...*, p. 114–115.

[66] C o n s t a n t i n e V I I P o r p h y r o g e n n e t o s, *The Book of Ceremonies*, I, 9.

1.6. Philanthropy and Donation Activities

Philanthropy and donations were among the basic duties of an empress. Building new churches or monasteries was seen as an expression of her piety, as signifying particularly close ties with the patrons of the foundations, and as a confirmation of the exceptional status of the ruling family. Supporting the poor, the underprivileged, the old and the sick helped empresses win popularity, which, in turn, must have affected the way the society viewed their husbands.

With considerable financial assets at their disposal, Byzantine empresses were able to engage in foundation activities. The list of their achievements in this area is impressively long. Below, we shall outline the foundation-related enterprises of several empresses.

It seems fitting to begin the survey with empress Helena, since we are dealing with yet another sphere in which she became a model for her successors. She is reported to have developed her foundation work – needless to say, based on the financial support of her son – primarily in Palestine, which she visited following the tragic family events of the year 326 (the death of her grandson Crispus and her daughter-in-law Fausta). The foundation of several churches is ascribed to her, including the Church of the Nativity in Bethlehem as well as the Church of the Holy Sepulcher and the Chapel of the Ascension in Jerusalem. It appears, however, that the true figure behind these acts of foundation was her son[67]. During her stay in Palestine, the *augusta* merely inspected the progress in the construction; but she also made generous donations at that occasion. In the later tradition, the role of Constantine as the founder was forgotten, with his mother replacing him in this position.

Pulcheria, sister of Theodosios II and wife of Marcian, was the foundress of a number of temples associated with the cult of the Theotokos in Constantinople. The churches of St. Mary of Blachernai, of the Hodegetria, and of the Theotokos of Chalkoprateia are all attributed

---

[67] J. D r i j v e r s, *Helena Augusta, the Mother of Constantine the Great and the Legend of Her Finding of the Cross*, Leiden–New York–Kobenhavn–Köln 1992, p. 55–72; H.A. P o h l s a n d e r, *Helena. Empress and Saint*, Chicago 1995, p. 84sqq.

to her. She is also said to have contributed to the construction of other temples, namely the churches of St. Lawrence and of Isaiah the Prophet as well as the chapel of St. Stephen in the Great Palace[68].

Theodora was active in this field as well. Besides initiating the building of the Church of St. Panteleemon in Constantinople and the reconstruction of the Church of the Holy Apostles, she would institute alms-houses, hospitals and inns[69]. She contributed greatly to the rebuilding of Antioch following the earthquake of 528[70].

Another empress to join the ranks of great foundresses was Irene, wife of Leo IV[71]. Her flagship foundation was the Eleutherios Palace, situated in the part of Constantinople descending towards the Harbor of Theodosios. The palace was associated with workshops in which silk was woven; a number of other artisan shops as well as bakeries were located there too. The palace was the empress's favorite place of residence. Other important foundations were the Monastery of the Theotokos on the Prince Islands (in the Marmara Sea) as well as the one later known as the Monastery of St. Euphrosyne. Besides, she is reported to have rebuilt the Church of St. Euphemia as well as the church in the Monastery of the Holy Mother of the Life-Giving Spring. We shall close this recital here. Irene was also very active in the sphere of philanthropy, supporting the sick, the old, and foreigners.

Euphrosyne, second wife of Michael II, is connected in the sources with two monasteries in Constantinople[72]. The first one, situated under the walls of the capital, was called *ta Libadeia* before being taken over by Euphrosyne. It had been founded by her grandmother Irene (cf. above),

[68] For more on Pulcheria's foundations cf.: K.G. H o l u m, *The Theodosian Empresses. Women and Imperial Dominion in Late Antiquity*, Los Angeles 1981, p. 196; Ch. A n g e l i d i, *Pulcheria. La castità al potere (399–c. 455)*, Milano 1998, p. 120–121; L. J a m e s, *Empresses...*, p. 153–154; S. B r a l e w s k i, *Konstantynopolitańskie kościoły*, [in:] *Konstantynopol–Nowy Rzym. Miasto i ludzie w okresie wczesnobizantyńskim*, eds. M.J. L e s z k a, T. W o l i ń s k a, Warszawa 2011, p. 140, 142.
[69] L. J a m e s, *Empresses...*, p. 150; C. F o s s, *Empress...*, p. 148.
[70] J. H e r r i n, *Women in Purple...*, p. 158–159.
[71] On Irene's foundations and philanthropy cf.: J. H e r r i n, *Women in Purple...*, p. 115; M.B. L e s z k a, M.J. L e s z k a, *Bazylisa...*, p. 305.
[72] J. H e r r i n, *Women in Purple...*, p. 158–161.

but it had since fallen into ruin and was rebuilt by none other than Euphrosyne, from whom it took its later designation. The other object in question was located within the limits of Constantinople, although not in the city center. It is reported to have been bought from Niketas, a *patrikios*, and converted into a female monastery called *ta Gastria*.

1.7. Political Influence of Byzantine Empresses

Women sitting at the side of Byzantine emperors were not formally entitled to co-rule the state in their own name[73]. They were able to realize their potential ambitions in this area – we cannot stipulate that all of them necessarily had such aspirations – through influencing their husbands. Again, it should be borne in mind that the empress was subordinate to her husband from the formal point of view. The effectiveness of any influence attempt depended on the personalities of the parties involved as well as on the particularities of their relationship. As long as the wife could count on her husband's feelings and trust, as well as his appreciating her skills (as e.g. in the case of Theodora and Justinian I), the impact may, of course, have been more substantial. The same was probably true if the woman was the one with the more independent personality in the relationship (as e.g. in the case of Eudoxia and Arkadios). These are, needless to say, mere educated guesses: finding their confirmation in the extant sources would be a daunting task. The claim that a given decision of the emperor was made due to the counsel or inspiration of his wife remains pure speculation.

The position of the empress was entirely different when, for one reason or another, the emperor was not able to rule personally (as was the case with Sophia during the illness of Justin II)[74]. Even in such cases, however, it is challenging to assess whether the empress's decisions were her own – administered autonomously – or whether she remained under the

---

[73] Cf. e.g.: S. R u n c i m a n, *Some Notes on the Role of the Empress*, "Eastern Churches Review" 4, 1972, p. 119–124; L. G a r l a n d, *Byzantine Empresses...*, p. 1.

[74] Av. C a m e r o n, *The Empress Sophia*, "Byzantion" 45, 1975, p. 8–15 (esp. 15); L. G a r l a n d, *Byzantine Empresses...*, p. 50–52.

influence of state dignitaries who, under normal circumstances, supported the reign of her husband.

It would seem that the situation was altered completely when an empress became the regent of her minor son(s) after the death of her husband. It may be suspected that she did have the final say in such cases, at least if she enjoyed sufficient personal authority and could count on adequate political support at the court. Nevertheless, it must be pointed out that her decisions were still issued in the name of the minor *basileus*, not in her own. It is only in those cases in which the woman assumed the role of the *basileus* that we are entitled to speak of fully independent, direct reign. In the times preceding the life of our protagonist Maria Lekapene, such a situation had occurred all but once: Irene, the widow of Leo IV and mother of Constantine VI, ruled autonomously from 797 to 802[75].

Wholly different cases of empresses influencing the course of the empire's history arose from situations in which they exercised their right to participate in the election of a new ruler. This would happen when the choice of the new emperor was tantamount to selecting a husband for the empress. It is thought that she had the right to make this decision[76]. This was the case with Pulcheria, sister of Theodosios II: following the latter's death in 450, she supported the choice of Marcian and subsequently became his wife[77]. Ariadne acted in a similar fashion after the death of Zeno. She was granted the right to recommend a candidate for the succession (although, truth be told, this did not happen outright)[78]. It might be expected that an empress's involvement in securing the throne for her husband would strengthen her position *vis-à-vis* the new emperor and give her hope that he would be susceptible to her influence. Whether

---

[75] On Irene's independent reign cf. e.g.: L. G a r l a n d, *Byzantine Empresses...*, p. 87–92; J. H e r r i n, *Women in Purple...*, p. 112–128.

[76] S. R u n c i m a n, *Notes...*, p. 123; M.J. L e s z k a, *Uzurpacje w cesarstwie bizantyńskim w okresie od IV do połowy IX w.*, Łódź 1999, p. 117–118.

[77] On the circumstances of Marcian's rise to the throne cf.: R.W. B u r g e s s, *The Accession of Marcian in the Light of Chalcedonian Apologetic and Monophysite Polemic*, "Byzantinische Zeitschrift" 86/87, 1993/1994, p. 47–68.

[78] K. T w a r d o w s k a, *Cesarzowe bizantyńskie 2 poł. V w. Kobiety a władza*, Kraków 2009, p. 209–217.

this was indeed the case is a different question. Be that as it may, the foremost beneficiary of the empress's actions was her new husband: not only did he ascend the throne, but he was also able to fortify his position outright by forging a link with his predecessor's family.

1.8. Rule from Behind the Throne

One of the areas in which empresses' influence on their husbands manifested itself the most clearly was filling posts in state administration. By distributing positions to relatives or other people dear to them, they obtained an instrument of manipulating state matters. If they had no such ambitions, they were at least able to reinforce the influence of their family and to buy the gratitude of her other protégés.

One of the earliest Byzantine empresses whose doings indicate a high level of care for her relatives was Athenais-Eudokia, wife of Theodosios II. It must have been due to her protection that her brothers, Gessios and Valerios, obtained their important posts[79] (the former became praetorian prefect of Illyricum and the latter *magister officiorum*). Apart from Athenais-Eudokia's brothers, a prestigious function was also entrusted to her uncle Asklepiodotos[80], appointed praetorian prefect of the East.

It was apparently owing to empress Ariadne's efforts that Anthemios (the brother-in-law of Leontia, Ariadne's sister) became consul under Anastasios I in 515. Earlier still, the empress requested for him to be appointed praetorian prefect, but at that time the emperor declined on 'professional grounds,' as we might say today: in his view, Anthemios did not have the qualifications necessary for this office. The change of opinion must have been either due to Ariadne's increasingly effective urges or – which seems more probable – to the fact that the position of the consul did not require any extraordinary skills[81].

---

[79] For basic information on Gessios and Valerios cf.: *PLRE*, vol. II, p. 510, s.v. *Gessius 2*; p. 1145, s.v. *Valerianus 6*.

[80] On Asklepiodotos cf.: *PLRE*, vol. II, p. 160, s.v. *Ascepiodotus 1*.

[81] On Anthemios cf.: *PLRE*, vol. II, p. 99, s.v. *Procopius Anthemius 9*; M.J. L e s z k a, *Cesarzowa Ariadna*, "Meander" 54, 1999, p. 277–278.

Another empress to pursue an active personnel policy was Theodora, who both bolstered people she trusted and combatted those she feared or disdained for some reason[82]. To the former group belonged e.g. Narses[83], Peter Barsymes and Peter the Patrikios, of whom the first one is particularly noteworthy. This eunuch, stemming from Armenia, attained the position of *praepositus sacri cubiculi*, which was the highest rank available to those of his standing. It was assigned to the most trusted individuals, exclusively eunuchs, who in view of their mutilation could not aspire to the imperial purple. The position offered Narses immediate access to the emperor at any hour of the day or night. While enjoying the confidence of Justinian I, he was at the same time a close associate of Theodora's, sharing her religious sympathies. When it turned out that he displayed military leadership skills, he was utilized as a counterbalance for Belisarios and appointed commander in the war against the Goths. Peter the Patrikios was likewise an eminent figure – imperial ambassador, *magister officiorum*, responsible for foreign policy. As regards the empress's other allies, we do not know their names; their number must have been impressive, however, judging by the fact that she was both able to organize assistance for her protégés and capable of using the palace dungeons to imprison her enemies. Even the most powerful among the latter had to be on their guard at all times. One of those to learn it the hard way was John the Cappadocian[84], one of Justinian's most trusted counsellors. The empress hatched a most sophisticated intrigue against John[85], as a result of which his career lay in ruins.

---

[82] On Theodora's personnel policy cf.: T. W o l i ń s k a, *Justynian Wielki*, Kraków 2003, p. 30–31; D. P o t t e r, *Theodora. Actress, Empress, Saint*, Oxford 2015, p. 121sqq.

[83] On Narses's career cf.: *PLRE*, vol. III, p. 912–928, s.v. *Narses 1*; T. W o l i ń s k a, *Armeńscy współpracownicy Justyniana Wielkiego*, II, *Wielka kariera eunucha Narsesa*, "Przegląd Nauk Historycznych" 4.1, 2005, p. 29–50.

[84] For basic information on John the Cappadocian cf.: *PLRE*, vol. III, p. 627–635, s.v. *Ioannes 11*.

[85] On Theodora's relation with John the Cappadocian, as well as her role in his deposition, cf.: J.A.S. E v a n s, *The Age of Justinian. The circumstances of Imperial power*, London–New York 1996, p. 196–197; T. W o l i ń s k a, *Justynian Wielki, cesarzowa Teodora i upadek Jana z Kapadocji*, "Piotrkowskie Zeszyty Historyczne" 1, 1998, p. 5–29.

The promotion of family members did not always turn out for the best, which became a bitter lesson for another Theodora, wife of Theophilos. Her brother Bardas[86], who became a *patrikios* and held high military posts during the life of his imperial brother-in-law, contributed (much later, after the emperor's death) to the termination of Theodora's regency[87]. All the same, it appears that the empress was not wholly without blame in this situation: she had been actively minimizing her brother's influence in favor of Theoktistos, one of her closest counsellors. She also viewed her other brother, Petronas[88] – whom Theophilos made *patrikios* – with mistrust.

Empresses would get involved in the sphere of foreign policy. This was the case e.g. with Theodora, wife of Justinian I. Particularly interesting in this context is her participation in the plot that culminated in the death of Amalasuntha, queen of the Ostrogoths[89].

Sophia, Theodora's successor, would take over the responsibility of ruling the empire during the times when her husband Justin II became incapacitated by his condition. This included the sphere of international

---

[86] On Bardas cf.: *PMB I*, vol. I, ed. F. Winkelmann et al., Berlin–New York 1999, p. 261–267, s.v. *Bardas (791)*.

[87] On Bardas's role in dismissing Theodora from the regency cf.: J. Herrin, *Women in Purple...*, p. 226–228.

[88] On Theodora's relations with Petronas cf.: J. Herrin, *Women in Purple...*, p. 215–216; on Petronas's career cf.: *PMB I*, vol. III, p. 564–566., s.v. *Petronas (5929)*.

[89] Prokopios (*On the Wars*, V, 4; cf. *Secret History*, 16) suggests that when she was imprisoned on the orders of her husband Theodahad, a diplomatic mission from Constantinople led by Peter the Patrikios was dispatched to him. Peter carried an official letter from Justinian I, in which the emperor warned the Gothic king that he would avenge the injustice done to Amalasuntha; but the envoy also received unofficial instructions from Theodora. The chronicle has the empress tacitly encourage the murder out of fear of the beautiful and educated competitor, hailing from the royal house of the Amali. Nevertheless, it is worth remembering that the assassination of Amalasuntha was in fact beneficial to Justinian I, who intended to reconquer the Italian peninsula from the Ostrogoths and was short of an excuse to attack their kingdom. He was now free to step into the role of an avenger of the slain queen, daughter of Theodoric the Great, who had occupied Italy in accordance with the agreement with Zeno – Justinian's predecessor on the imperial throne. On the circumstances of Amalasuntha's death cf.: J.A.S. Evans, *The Age of Justinian...*, p. 137–138; A. Daniel Frankforter, *Amalasuntha, Procopius and a Woman's Place*, "Journal of Women's History" 8.2, 1996, p. 49–54.

relations; notably, the empress managed to bring about a halt to hostilities on the Persian front. She sent a letter to the Persian ruler Chosroes,
in which she pleaded as follows:

> (...) bewailing her husband's misfortunes and the state's lack of a leader,
> and saying that he ought not to trample upon a widowed woman, a pros-
> trate emperor and a deserted state; for indeed when he had been sick
> not only had he obtained comparable treatment, but the best doctors
> of all had also been sent to him by the Roman state, and they in fact
> dispelled his sickness[90].

In all likelihood, what convinced Chosroes was not so much the above
argumentation as the concomitant promise to pay 45 000 gold coins.
Whatever the case may be, Sophia did secure a three-year armistice in the
struggle with Persia[91].

The presence of empresses' influence is visible in religious policy. Often
quite pious themselves, and with ardent religious convictions of their own,
empresses sought to advise their husbands in this sphere – sometimes
reinforcing the emperors' existing persuasions and sometimes striving to
force through their own divergent sentiments. For instance, empresses
Dominica[92] and Zenonis[93] have been considered responsible for their

---

[90] Evagrios Scholastikos, V, 12 (transl. p. 271). Cf. L. Garland, *Byzantine Empresses...*, p. 51.

[91] On Byzantine-Persian relations during the reign of Justin II cf.: M. Whitby, *The Successors of Justinian*, [in:] *The Cambridge Ancient History*, vol. XIV, *Late Antiquity. Empire and Successors AD 425–600*, eds. Av. Cameron, B. Ward-Perkins, M. Whitby, Cambridge 2000, p. 91–94.

[92] On the allegations against Dominica (wife of Valens) for supporting Arianism cf.: N. Lenski, *Failure of Empire. Valens and the Roman State in the Fourth Century AD*, Berkeley–Los Angeles–London 2002, p. 243–244.

[93] Theodore Anagnostes, a historian of the Church writing relatively soon after the events, claimed that it was Zenonis who spurred her husband Basiliskos's turning away from orthodoxy (Theodore Anagnostes, p. 112; Theophanes, AM 5967). The scholarly opinion on Zenonis's actual influence on her husband's religious policy is divided; cf.: W.H.C. Frend, *The Rise...*, p. 169–170; M.J. Leszka, *Aelia Zenonis, żona Bazyliskosa*, "Meander" 57, 2002, p. 89–90; K. Twardowska, *Cesarzowe...*, p. 145–152; R. Kosiński, *The Emperor Zeno. Religion and Politics*, Cracow 2006, p. 83.

husbands' fraternizing with adherents of heresies instead of upholding orthodox faith. In the former case, the heresy in question was Arianism, and in the latter – Monophysitism. Nevertheless, it must be emphasized that their husbands' decisions to associate themselves with these fractions of Christianity were primarily motivated by other considerations.

Empresses were viewed by clergy of various ranks, as well as by monks, as capable of persuading their husbands into reaching decisions favorable to them. Accordingly, clerics and monks tried to bring various issues to empresses' attention – be it personally, through intermediaries, or by writing letters. Predictably, whether or not their interventions would turn out successful varied from case to case.

As an example of an empress who exerted considerable influence on the religious policies of her husband, we may again refer to Theodora, wife of Justinian I. It is widely known that she supported Monophysitism, while Justinian embraced a pro-Chalcedonian attitude. The *basileus* was well aware of his responsibility to maintain the religious unity of the empire. He would undertake repressive actions against certain religious minorities, such as pagans and Nestorians, but at the same time he knew that a full-blown conflict with the Monophysites inhabiting the eastern provinces was out of the question, even if he could not – or did not want to – tolerate them completely. In 533, at the instigation of Theodora, he entrusted the office of patriarch of Constantinople to Anthimos, whose views were close to Monophysitism; he made a similar decision with regard to the patriarchate of Alexandria, for which position he nominated Theodosios. Softening the stance on Monophysitism hardly produced the expected results, however. Thus, in 536, Justinian I resolved to topple Anthimos and to adopt a harsher policy towards the community. The empress harbored Anthimos in her part of the palace for a number of years; she also tried to come to the succor of other Monophysite clergy, such as e.g. Severos of Antioch. Although some sources maintain that she did so unbeknownst to the emperor, this should be regarded as doubtful. More convincing is the view that the empress acted with the consent of Justinian, who was cautious not to fully alienate Monophysite circles. Furthermore, the empress had her say in the election of the bishop of Rome. She played a role in the deposition of Silverius and the appointment of Vigilius – even though, as eventually became evident, her protégé did not quite live up to the expectations[94].

Empresses arguably participated in what might today be called social policy. They engaged in activities aimed at aiding orphans, the old, the poor and the sick. This was the purpose of their philanthropic endeavors, as already described above. Some empresses worked towards improving the situation of those in debt. Empress Sophia, wife of Justin II, is reported to have procured a settlement between debtors and their creditors[95]. The debts in question were – it is generally assumed – to be repaid by the state. It is difficult to ascertain whether this was an initiative of hers, for which she recruited Justin II, or whether she merely acted on his behalf by participating in the negotiations with the creditors. Irrespective of the exact circumstances, she personally endorsed the operation.

From the formal point of view, empresses could not undertake legislative activities; legal acts never bore their names. This, of course, by no means excludes the possibility that they may have played a role in the process of developing certain legal regulations; admittedly, however, their influence may usually only be conjectured. Somewhat perversely, it may be said that such presence may be detectable both in acts of legislation and in acts of non-legislation. To illustrate this latter case, we shall use the example of Euphemia, reported to have opposed the marriage of Justinian I and Theodora relying on a law that barred actresses – even former ones – from marrying senators. Euphemia's resistance was successful: as long as she was alive, no new regulation was implemented in this regard[96]. While upon this subject, we may remark that Theodora was

---

[94] On Theodora's religious activity cf. e.g.: D. Potter, *Theodora*..., p. 157sqq.

[95] T h e o p h a n e s, AM 6060. Cf. Av. C a m e r o n, *Empress*..., p. 9–10; L. G a r l a n d, *Byzantine Empresses*..., p. 43.

[96] P r o k o p i o s, *Secret History*, 9. Cf. M.J. L e s z k a, *Lupicyna–Eufemia – żona Justyna I*, "Meander" 54, 1999, p. 559–562; D. D a u b e, *The marriage of Justinian and Theodora. Legal and Theological Reflections*, "Catholic University of America Law Review" 16, 1967, p. 380–399. Cf. E. L o s k a, *Sytuacja aktorów i aktorek w rzymskim prawie małżeńskim*, "Zeszyty Prawnicze UKSW" 12, 2012, p. 93–99.

ostensibly responsible for the all-out abolition of the ban on marriages between senators and women of low birth. We find such a resolution in one of the amendments (*Novellae*, 117.6) by emperor Justinian I[97].

1.9. Female Regents

An empress reigning as regent was a fairly common phenomenon in Byzantine history, arising when an emperor died leaving minor heirs. A regency led by the imperial mother was established in such situations. This practice, it was deemed, would enable the empresses to ensure their son or sons' legal right to the throne. A regency council was appointed to aid the empress; it included the most eminent state dignitaries as well as – apparently – the patriarch of Constantinople, who was the second in succession to preside over this body (following the empress). We know the composition of the regency council that held power in the name of Constantine VII Porphyrogennetos after the death of Alexander: led by patriarch Nicholas Mystikos, it also comprised *magistroi* Stephen and John Eladas, as well as John the Rhaiktor, Euthymios, Basilitzes and Gabrielopoulos[98]. In this case, as can be seen, the (seemingly) unwritten rule that the empress mother should preside over the regency was violated. The position of Zoe Karbonopsina, mother of Constantine VII and fourth wife of Leo VI, was markedly vulnerable, not least because she was not recognized as Leo's lawful spouse by all of the parties involved. In addition, Alexander, who seized both factual rule and the formal custody of Constantine VII immediately upon his brother Leo VI's death, was ill--disposed towards Zoe and deprived her of her son's guardianship. It was he who installed the above-mentioned regency council before his death. At the end of the day, however, Zoe did come to preside over the council; this happened in 914, following the deposition of the previous chair Nicholas Mystikos and other members inimical towards the empress[99].

---

[97] *Novellae*, 117.6.

[98] S. R u n c i m a n, *The Emperor Romanus Lecapenus and his Reign. A Study of Tenth-Century Byzantium*, Cambridge 1969, p. 47–48; M.J. L e s z k a, *Zoe...*, p. 102.

[99] On Zoe's path towards dominating the regency council cf.: S. R u n c i m a n, *The Emperor Romanus...*, p. 56; M.J. L e s z k a, *Zoe...*, p. 104–105.

Putting aside other reasons, such as animosities within the council, this act reflected the robustness of the principle that asserted the mother's right to lead the regency. Still, it was not always the empress mother or the patriarch who chaired the council; it was not uncommon for other figures (usually relatives of the minor heir) to fulfil this role. During the minority of Theodosios II, his sister Pulcheria took control of the regency[100]. What made this situation particularly exceptional was Pulcheria's young age at the time.

The empress mother's tenure as regent did not necessarily only come to an end once the young emperor reached the age of 16, legally allowing him to assume the throne and embark on autonomous rule. Aware of the fact that a regency furnished an auspicious setting for ambitious and popular army leaders to try to seize the throne, empress mothers sought for (or had others seek for) husbands who would warrant the retention of their position; this, in turn, would help safeguard their children's imperial right. In a sense, this was the case with Theophano, wife of Romanos II. It appears that she struck an agreement with Nikephoros, a celebrated commander hailing from the mighty Phokas family; in accordance with the deal, Nikephoros would marry Theophano and become the custodian of her sons Basil II and Constantine VIII. Her regency lasted no longer than five months[101].

In the times preceding the era of our protagonist Maria Lekapene, two empresses exercised regency powers for a particularly long time: Irene, widow of Leo IV, and Theodora, widow of Theophilos. The former ruled in the name of Constantine VI for seven years (780–787) and proceeded to co-rule with him (787–797); finally, after his deposition, she reigned independently in the years 797–802. The latter led the regency for thirteen years (842–855). It appears symbolic that both cases involved a conflict between mother and son, culminating in a bloodshed. In the former instance, it was the mother who ultimately unseated her son from

---

[100] On Pulcheria's role during the minority of Theodosios II cf.: K.G. H o l u m, *The Theodosian Empresses...*, p. 92sqq.

[101] On Theophano's regency and the circumstances surrounding her marriage with Nikephoros II Phokas cf.: L. G a r l a n d, *Byzantine Empresses...*, p. 128–130; M.J. L e s z k a, *Rola cesarzowej Teofano...*, p. 228–230.

power, orchestrating his mutilation and premature death[102]. In the latter case, the mother lost whatever influence she had had with her son and was ousted from her position, while Theoktistos, the cornerstone of her rule, was murdered.

In those cases where the regency lasted for an extended period of time, the empress mother could hold actual power (though – let us reiterate – in the name of her son or sons), as opposed to merely lending her name to decisions made by state dignitaries. This was certainly true of Irene, who did not limit herself to overseeing the regency and finally attained independent rule for a certain time.

The success of a regency was measured by whether it led to the imperial son(s) assuming single-handed rule. Most Byzantine empresses, we may add, did accomplish this goal. Even those who did not do so fought for their cause with full determination until the very end, knowing that their failure would mean condemning their sons to death or to a life in permanent jeopardy. This was the fate of empress Martina and her sons: stripped of their power, they were maimed and exiled to the island of Rhodes, left to die in obscurity[103].

Empresses had the means to influence state politics; however, they mostly exercised this power through their husbands or in the name of their sons. They were only able to assume direct, autonomous control by entering the role of the *basileus* themselves (Irene).

Hopefully, this brief review of the role of empresses in the Byzantine Empire will make it possible to understand what notion of the future role at her husband's court Maria Lekapene may have had when leaving for Preslav, where she was to confront a reality so profoundly different from the Byzantine model.

---

[102] On Irene's relations with Constantine VI cf.: P. S p e c k, *Kaiser Konstantin VI. Die Legitimation einer fremden und der Versuch einer eigenen Herrschaft. Quellenkritische Darstellung von 25 Jahren byzantinischer Geschichte nach dem ersten Ikonoklasmus*, Münich 1978, p. 251; R.-J. L i l i e, *Byzanz...*, p. 220–277, 305–308; L. G a r l a n d, *Byzantine Empresses...*, p. 80–87, 93; J. H e r r i n, *Women in Purple...*, p. 92–99.

[103] For more on Martina's tragic fate cf.: L. G a r l a n d, *Byzantine Empresses...*, p. 70; M.J. L e s z k a, *Cesarzowa Martyna, żona Herakliusza*, "Meander" 58, 2003, p. 456.

2. Maria Lekapene, Empress of the Bulgarians – Titulature, Seals, Insignia

There can be no doubt that Maria's titulature was modeled on the appellations used by Constantinopolitan empresses. On the official seals of the Bulgarian royal couple, produced soon after 927, we find a Greek inscription in which Maria and Peter are titled Emperors of the Bulgarians: Πέτρος καὶ Μαρίας βασιλεῖς τῶν Βουλγάρων[104]. During the 940s, the writing accompanying the images of the couple was modified somewhat; the most likely reconstruction is Πέτρος καὶ Μαρίας ἐν Χριστῷ αὔγουστοι βασιλεῖς or Πέτρος καὶ Μαρίας ἐν Χριστῷ αὐτοκράτορες βασιλεῖς Βουλγάρων[105]. Thus, the analysis of the sigillographic evidence allows us to state that Maria used the titles conventionally worn by women reigning in the Byzantine capital: *basilissa* and *augusta*[106].

---

[104] It should not be considered surprising that Maria and Peter are described here with the term βασιλεῖς. In Byzantine sphragistics and numismatics, this was the accepted form of referring to two co-rulers, regardless of their sex. For example, on the coins minted in the years 914–919, Zoe Karbonopsina and her minor son Constantine VII Porphyrogennetos were titled βασιλεῖς Ῥωμαίων (A.R. B e l l i n g e r, Ph. G r i e r s o n, *Catalogue of the Byzantine Coins in the Dumbarton Oaks Collection and in the Whittemore Collection*, vol. III, *Leo III to Nicephorus III. 717–1081*, Washington 1993, p. 12).

[105] J. S h e p a r d, *A marriage too far? Maria Lekapena and Peter of Bulgaria*, [in:] *The Empress Theophano. Byzantium and the West at the turn of the first millennium*, ed. A. D a v i d s, Cambridge 1995, p. 142; Г. А т а н а с о в, *Инсигниите...*, p. 98–99; И. Й о р д а н о в, *Корпус на печатите на Средновековна България*, София 2001, p. 58–60; В. Г ю з е л е в, *Значението на брака на цар Петър (927–969) с ромейка-та Мария-Ирина Лакапина (911–962)*, [in:] *Културните текстове на миналото – носители, символи, идеи*, vol. I, *Текстовете на историята, история на текстовете. Материали от Юбилейната международна конференция в чест на 60-годишнина-та на проф. д.и.н. Казимир Попконстантинов, Велико Търново, 29–31 октомври 2003 г.*, София 2005, p. 27; И. Б о ж и л о в, В. Г ю з е л е в, *История...*, p. 275–276; Т. Т о д о р о в, *България...*, p. 156–159; i d e m, *Владетелският статут и титла на цар Петър I след октомври 927 г.: писмени сведения и сфрагистични данни (сравнителен анализ)*, [in:] *Юбилеен сборник. Сто години от рождението на д-р Васил Хараланов (1907–2007)*, Шумен 2008, p. 99–101; С. Г е о р г и е в а, *Жената...*, p. 313; M.J. L e s z k a, K. M a r i n o w, *Carstwo bułgarskie...*, p. 159–160; И. Й о р д а н о в, *Корпус на средновековните български печати*, София 2016, p. 90–95.

[106] Z.A. B r z o z o w s k a, *Cesarzowa Bułgarów, Augusta i Bazylisa – Maria-Irena Lekapena i transfer bizantyńskiej idei kobiety-władczyni (imperial feminine) w średnio-wiecznej Bułgarii*, "Slavia Meridionalis" 17, 2017, p. 18.

We also find some interesting information in the works of Byzantine chroniclers. The anonymous Continuator of George the Monk, Symeon Logothete and – dependent on both of them – the Continuator of Theophanes noted a particularly significant detail: Maria Lekapene, just after her marriage with Peter, was proclaimed 'ruler of the Bulgarians' (δέσποινα Βουλγάρων) in Constantinople[107]. It is worth nothing that the term found here – *despoina* – was, according to numerous researchers, an appellation used by Byzantine empresses interchangeably with the titles of *augusta* and *basilissa*[108].

The sources mentioned above do not, however, allow us to provide a definitive answer to the question of how Maria's Slavic subjects addressed her. Given that the tsaritsa does not appear in a single original medieval Bulgarian text, a scholar studying the titulature of Peter's wife is forced to rely on the analysis of Slavic translations of Byzantine chronicles. The author of the oldest translation of the *Continuation of George the Monk*, writing – as mentioned before – at the close of the 10th century or during the first decades of the 11th century, translated the passage about the title granted to Maria in 927 with extreme fidelity. The Greek term *despoina* is – in accordance with its etymology – rendered as *vladyčica*, i.e. 'female ruler' (причетаса моүжю цр҃ю и владычица блъгаром наре́на)[109]. In another Slavic translation of this chronicle, completed in the Balkans in the 14th century, we find a notable semantic shift: the text states outright that Maria was called *carica* (tsaritsa, empress) of the Bulgarians (цр҃ю припрѧжеса мѫжѫ и царица Блъгаромь наречеса)[110]. One can suspect that the latter term was the most popular appellation used in Preslav when referring to Peter's wife. At that time, it most likely took the form

[107] Continuator of George the Monk, p.907; Symeon Logothete, 136, 51, p. 329; Continuator of Theophanes, VI, 23, p. 415.

[108] S. M a s l e v, *Die staatsrechtliche Stellung der byzantinischen Kaiserinnen*, "Byzantinoslavica" 27, 1966, p. 310; E. B e n s a m m a r, *La titulature...*, p. 270, 286–287; L. G a r l a n d, *Byzantine Empresses...*, p. 2; B. H i l l, *Imperial Women...*, p. 102–117; L. J a m e s, *Empresses...*, p. 118–127; Z.A. B r z o z o w s k a, *Cesarzowa Bułgarów...*, p. 5.

[109] Continuator of George the Monk (Slavic), 7, p.562; А. Н и к о л о в, *Политическа мисъл...*, p. 134, 236.

[110] Symeon Logothete (Slavic), p. 137; А. Н и к о л о в, *Политическа мисъл...*, p. 134, 236.

cěsarica. In the subsequent centuries, it went through several phonetic changes (*cěsarica* ≥ *cesarica* ≥ *cьsarica* ≥ *carica*), acquiring its final form known from later works: *carica*[111].

The *Book of Ceremonies* by Constantine VII Porphyrogennetos confirms that during the 10th century, the Bulgarian tsaritsa was listed in the official diplomatic protocol. The imperial author, who was one of the eyewitnesses of the ceremonies that accompanied the signing of the 927 peace treaty, admitted that the status of the Preslav monarch had changed during his reign: he had become a 'spiritual son' of the *basileus*. Notably, however, the 'purple-born' author does not mention any alteration in the Bulgarian tsaritsa's titulature that would have accompanied this – according to him, both before and after 927 she was to be addressed *by God archontissa of Bulgaria* (ἐκ Θεοῦ ἀρχόντισσα Βουλγαρίας)[112].

The placing of Maria's image on the lead seals from the years 927–945 should also be considered a result of transplanting Byzantine traditions onto Bulgarian soil. Scholars who claim that portraying the ruler's wife on an official *sigillum* was a phenomenon characteristic only of 10th-century Bulgaria, with no analogue in Byzantine sigillography or numismatics, are mistaken[113].

---

[111] G. M o r a v s c i k, *Zur Geschichte des Herrschertitels "caesar>царь"*, "Zbornik Radova Vizantološkog Instituta" 8, 1963, p. 234; L. M o s z y ń s k i, *Staro-cerkiewno-słowiańskie apelatywy określające osoby będące u władzy*, "Balcanica Poznaniensia" 2, 1985, p. 44; Г. Б а к а л о в, *Средновековният български владетел...*, p. 155–158; Z.A. B r z o z o w s k a, *Geneza tytułu "car" w świetle zabytków średniowiecznego piśmiennictwa słowiańskiego*, "Die Welt der Slaven" 46, 2012, p. 36–38; e a d e m, *Car i caryca czy cesarz i cesarzowa Bułgarów? Tytulatura Piotra i Marii-Ireny Lekapeny w średniowiecznych tekstach słowiańskich (Jak powinniśmy nazywać władców bułgarskich z X stulecia)*, "Die Welt der Slaven" 62, 2017, p. 17–26.

[112] C o n s t a n t i n e V I I P o r p h y r o g e n n e t o s, *The Book of Ceremonies*, II, 47, p. 681–682; М. Х р и с т о д у л о в а, *Титул...*, p. 142; Г. Б а к а л о в, *Царската промулгация...*, p. 37; i d e m, *Средновековният български владетел...*, p. 171–172; Т. То д о р о в, *България...*, p. 152; i d e m, *Владетелският статут...*, p. 95; P. B o r o ń, *Kniaziowie, królowie, carowie... Tytuły i nazwy władców słowiańskich we wczesnym średniowieczu*, Katowice 2010, p. 40–41; M.J. L e s z k a, K. M a r i n o w, *Carstwo bułgarskie...*, p. 206–207.

[113] Г. А т а н а с о в, *Инсигниите...*, p. 98, 184; Т. То д о р о в, *България...*, p. 162–163; i d e m, *Владетелският статут...*, p. 104.

The tradition of placing the image and name of female royals on coinage had been passed down from the *Imperium Romanum* to the Byzantine empire. As attested by Eusebios of Caesarea, after 324 Constantine I the Great ordered that coins be struck with the image of his mother, Helena, on the obverse[114]. This privilege was shared by his second wife, Fausta, as well as several other women from the imperial family[115].

After an interval of several decades, issues with the empress's likeness resurface in 383, during the reign of Flaccilla, wife of Theodosios I. Nearly all of her successors on the Byzantine throne from the Theodosian dynasty (Eudoxia, Pulcheria, Athenais-Eudokia) or from Leo I's family (Verina, Zenonis, Ariadne) could boast having their portrayals and names on gold, silver and bronze coins struck on the orders of their husbands or brothers. Moreover, analogous artifacts were produced in the 5th century in the western part of the empire – with images of e.g. Galla Placidia and Licinia Eudoxia. The majority of the extant artifacts from the 4th–5th centuries follow the same iconographic model: the empress's profile bust on the obverse coupled with an allegorical female figure on the reverse. Occasionally, we find a full-length depiction of the enthroned empress on the reverse (Eudoxia, Pulcheria, Athenais-Eudokia). The coins showing Licinia Eudoxia appear to be artistically unique in that they portray the empress *en face*[116]. Another detail is more striking, however: none

---

[114] Eusebios of Caesarea, III, 47, p. 97.

[115] K.G. Holum, *Theodosian Empresses...*, p. 32–35; L. Brubaker, *Memories of Helena: Patterns in Imperial Female Matronage in the 4th and 5th Centuries*, [in:] *Women, Men and Eunuchs*, ed. L. James, London–New York 1997, p. 57–59; L. Garland, *Byzantine Empresses...*, p. 51; L. Brubaker, H. Tobler, *The Gender of Money: Byzantine Empresses on Coins (324–802)*, "Gender & History" 12.3, 2000, p. 575–578; L. James, *Empresses...*, p. 101–106; K. Kotsis, *Defining Female Authority in Eighth-Century Byzantium: the Numismatic Images of the Empress Irene (797–802)*, "Journal of Late Antiquity" 5.1, 2012, p. 190; Z.A. Brzozowska, *Cesarzowa Bułgarów...*, p. 11–12.

[116] S. Maslev, *Die staatsrechtliche Stellung...*, p. 317; K.G. Holum, *Theodosian Empresses...*, p. 32–33, 65–66, 109–110, 123, 129–130; L. Brubaker, *Memories of Helena...*, p. 60; L. Garland, *Byzantine Empresses...*, p. 51; L. Brubaker, H. Tobler, *The Gender of Money...*, p. 578–580; А. Грабар, *Император в византийском искусстве*, Москва 2000, p. 44, 205; J. Herrin, *The Imperial Feminine...*, p. 15; L. James, *Empresses...*, p. 101–109; A. McClanan, *Representations of Early Byzantine Empresses*.

of the objects under discussion – aside from Verina's coins – include the male ruler. A representation of the imperial couple, on the reverse, is in turn characteristic of commemorative issues, celebrating rulers' weddings (e.g. of Licinia Eudoxia and Valentinian III in 437, of Pulcheria and Marcian in 450, or of Ariadne and Anastasios I in 491[117]). The oldest *sigilla* depicting the emperor and the empress also come from the 5th century; the images show e.g. Constantius III and Galla Placidia (from 421) or Theodosios II and Pulcheria (or Athenais-Eudokia), from the period 408–450[118].

With Ariadne's departure from the empire's political scene, the practice of depicting women on coins is abandoned for several decades. No coins or seals with the image of Euphemia, wife of Justin I, survive. Empress Theodora, the famous wife of Justinian I the Great, was most likely not depicted on coinage either; whether she used her own *sigillum* is likewise highly debatable[119].

The empress is once again included in the system of the official self-presentation of the Byzantine court in 565, most likely on the initiative of empress Sophia, the influential spouse of Justin II. Until 629, nearly all of her successors on the throne in Constantinople (Ino-Anastasia,

Image and Empire, New York 2002, p. 26–27, 40–41, 90–91; K. K o t s i s, *Defining Female Authority...*, p. 189–191; J. H e r r i n, *Late Antique Origins of the 'Imperial Feminine': Western and Eastern Empresses Compared*, "Byzantinoslavica" 74.1/2, 2016, p. 5–25; Z.A. B r z o z o w s k a, *Cesarzowa Bułgarów...*, p. 12.

[117] W. H a h n, *Moneta Imperii Byzantini: Rekonstruktion des Prägeaufbaues auf Synoptisch-Tabellarischer Grundlage*, vol. I, *Von Anastasius I. bis Justinianus I (491–565)*, Vienna 1973, p. 31; A.R. B e l l i n g e r, Ph. G r i e r s o n, *Catalogue of the Byzantine Coins in the Dumbarton Oaks Collection and in the Whittemore Collection*, vol. I, *Anastasius I to Maurice. 491–602*, Washington 1992, p. 4–5; L. B r u b a k e r, H. To b l e r, *The Gender of Money...*, p. 580–582; L. J a m e s, *Empresses...*, p. 105, 108–109; A. M c C l a n a n, *Representations...*, p. 27, 69, 90; A. Wa l k e r, *Numismatic and Metrological Parallels for the Iconography of Early Byzantine Marriage Jewelry. The Question of the Crowned Bride*, "Travaux et Mémoires" 16, 2010, p. 851–853, 861; Z.A. B r z o z o w s k a, *Cesarzowa Bułgarów...*, p. 12.

[118] W. S e i b t, M.L. Z a r n i t z, *Das Byzantinische Bleisiegel als Kunstwerk. Katalog zur Ausstellung*, Wien 1997, p. 29–31; Z.A. B r z o z o w s k a, *Cesarzowa Bułgarów...*, p. 12.

[119] A. M c C l a n a n, *Representations...*, p. 144; Z.A. B r z o z o w s k a, *Cesarzowa Bułgarów...*, p. 12–13.

Constantina, Leontia and Martina) were depicted on silver and bronze coins struck on their husbands' orders. However, a fundamental change occurred in the canon of coin imagery: contrary to the earlier tradition, the obverse now commonly includes a depiction of the imperial couple, full-length, *en face*, either in standing position or enthroned. The emperor is located on the left side of the composition, his spouse – on the right[120]. They are sometimes also accompanied by a portrayal of the imperial son (Maurice, for instance, was shown with Constantina and Theodosios, and Herakleios – with Martina and Herakleios-Constantine). Nonetheless, the *augusta*'s name – with the exception of some of the issues from the reign of Justin II and Sophia – never appears in the inscription[121]. Interestingly, several seals of imperial officials from the period 565–629 have survived; these include images of the imperial couple (Justin II and Sophia), or of the reigning emperor, his eldest son, and the empress (Maurice, Constantina and Theodosios, or Herakleios, Martina and Herakleios-Constantine)[122].

---

[120] When analyzing depictions on coinage and *sigilla*, we describe them from the viewer's perspective, following the system commonly employed in English-language publications. From the point of view of those depicted on a seal or coin, the directions would be reversed.

[121] W. H a h n, *Moneta Imperii Byzantini: Rekonstruktion des Prägeaufbaues auf Synoptisch-Tabellarischer Grundlage*, vol. II, *Von Justinus II. bis Phocas (565–610)*, Vienna 1975, p. 43–51, 57, 67, 71, 80–82; Ph. G r i e r s o n, *Byzantine Coins*, London – Berkeley – Los Angeles 1982, p. 44–48, 63–68, 86–88, 106–109, 120–126; A.R. B e l l i n g e r, Ph. G r i e r s o n, *Catalogue of the Byzantine Coins*, vol. I, p. 204–207, 220–239, 243–258, 320, 373–375; L. G a r l a n d, *Byzantine Empresses...*, p. 50–51, 55, 62; L. B r u b a k e r, H. T o b l e r, *The Gender of Money...*, p. 583–587; A. Г р а б а р, *Император...*, p. 34, 38, 44–47; L. J a m e s, *Empresses...*, p. 109–112; A. M c C l a n a n, *Representations...*, p. 144–146, 158–162; K. K o t s i s, *Defining Female Authority...*, p. 190–192; P. G k a n t z i o s D r á p e l o v á, *Byzantine Empresses on Coins in the Early Byzantine Period (565–610): a Survey of the Problems of Interpretation and Identification*, "Byzantinoslavica" 74.1–2, 2016, p. 75–91; Z.A. B r z o z o w s k a, *Cesarzowa Bułgarów...*, p. 13.

[122] N. O i k o n o m i d e s, *A Collection of Dated Byzantine Lead Seals*, Washington 1986, p. 22–25; L. J a m e s, *Empresses...*, p. 155; A. M c C l a n a n, *Representations...*, p. 161; *Catalogue of Byzantine Seals at Dumbarton Oaks and in the Fogg Museum of Art*, eds. E. M c G e e r, J. N e s b i t t, N. O i k o n o m i d e s, vol. V, *The East (continued)*, Washington 2005, p. 79; Z.A. B r z o z o w s k a, *Cesarzowa Bułgarów...*, p. 13.

During the years 629–780, Byzantine empresses were not depicted on coinage. There is but one extant seal from this period bearing an empress's name: it is the *sigillum* of Constantine IV and his wife Anastasia, dated to 679/680[123].

A breakthrough came with the reign of the empress Irene, who held regency for her son Constantine VI during the period 780–797 and subsequently reigned as the sole ruler of the empire (797–802). The empress had her image, title and name included on both (gold, silver and bronze) coins and on seals. During the initial period (780–792), she is depicted on the coins' obverse together with her son: they are shown *en face*, half-length. The figure of Constantine VI is located on the left side of the composition, and that of Irene – on the right. The empress's head is adorned by a diadem. In her left hand, she is holding a scepter topped with a cross, and in the right (780–790) – an orb. The iconographic model changes during the period 792–797: the obverse now shows an image of the *basilissa* alone, holding a scepter and an orb, while her son's portrayal is moved to the reverse. Having removed Constantine VI from power, Irene made one further modification, ordering her bust to be depicted on both sides of the coin[124]. Several seals of the empress from the period 797–802 survive as well; the images adorning them conform to the iconographic program of the coinage from the time of Irene's autocratic reign. The empress's likeness can also be found on the seals of imperial dignitaries. On artifacts from the years 780–797, she is depicted with her son; on later ones (801–802) – alone[125].

---

[123] L. J a m e s, *Empresses...*, p. 155; I. J o r d a n o v, *Corpus of Byzantine Seals from Bulgaria*, vol. III/1, Sofia 2009, p. 82–83; Z.A. B r z o z o w s k a, *Cesarzowa Bułgarów...*, p. 13–14.

[124] S. M a s l e v, *Die staatsrechtliche Stellung...*, p. 322–323; Ph. G r i e r s o n, *Byzantine Coins...*, p. 152–166; A.R. B e l l i n g e r, Ph. G r i e r s o n, *Catalogue of the Byzantine Coins*, vol. III, p. 337–351; L. G a r l a n d, *Byzantine Empresses...*, p. 87–88; L. B r u b a k e r, H. To b l e r, *The Gender of Money...*, p. 587–590; L. J a m e s, *Empresses...*, p. 112–114; J. H e r r i n, *Women in Purple...*, p. 76, 100; K. K o t s i s, *Defining Female Authority...*, p. 185–215; Z.A. B r z o z o w s k a, *Cesarzowa Bułgarów...*, p. 14.

[125] N. O i k o n o m i d e s, *A Collection...*, p. 52; *Catalogue of Byzantine Seals at Dumbarton Oaks and in the Fogg Museum of Art*, eds. J. N e s b i t t, N. O i k o n o m i d e s, vol. I, *Italy, North of the Balkans, North of the Black Sea*, Washington 1991, p. 162;

Fig. 7. Solidus with an image of empress Irene, Constantinople, 797–802.
Drawing (reconstruction): E. Myślińska-Brzozowska

Subsequent Byzantine empresses had at their disposal the models developed during Irene's reign. The next monarch whose name and image we
find on coins and seals is Theodora of Paphlagonia, wife of Theophilos
and regent from 842 until 856. During her husband's life, she appeared
on a gold coin only once – on a commemorative issue from the late 830s.
These coins are notable for their original iconography: the obverse shows
Theophilos accompanied by his spouse (on the right) and their eldest

L. J a m e s, *Empresses...*, p. 115; I. J o r d a n o v, *Corpus of Byzantine Seals...*, p. 428;
Z.A. B r z o z o w s k a, *Cesarzowa Bułgarów...*, p. 14.

daughter Thecla (on the left), while on the reverse there are the likeness-
es of two of his progeny – Anna and Anastasia. Having taken the reins
of power in 842, Theodora at first made use of the iconographic model
of the issues from the years 792–797. On the obverse of the coins struck
on her orders, we see the depiction of the *basilissa* holding a scepter and
an orb, and on the reverse – the image of her two children, Michael III
and Thecla (holding in her right hand the patriarchal cross). Having
restored the worship of icons in 843, Theodora made a further alteration:
she had Christ depicted on the obverse side of her coins, while the reverse
shows her together with her son. Relatively abundant sphragistic material
from the period 842–856 has also survived. On *sigilla* made after 842 we
find no figure imagery; instead, they only feature a legend mentioning
Michael, Theodora and Thecla, βασιλεῖς Ῥωμαίων. Artifacts created after
843 present Michael III on the obverse and his mother on the reverse.
Remarkably, the personal seal of empress Theodora, dated to 830–842,
also survived to our times – it does not show the *basilissa*, however, but
her husband[126].

One might get the impression that coins and seals from the 8th and
9th centuries only depicted empress mothers serving as regents during
their sons' minority, but never the wives of reigning emperors. However,
as can be seen from the above issue from the 930s, as well as from the
case of Eudokia Ingerina (wife of Basil I), such an impression would
be incorrect. The gold coins issued by Basil I ca. 882 show the images
of three royals: on the obverse, the bust of the emperor, and on the reverse
– Eudokia Ingerina and her stepson, Constantine[127].

---

[126] S. M a s l e v, *Die staatsrechtliche Stellung...*, p. 324; Ph. G r i e r s o n, *Byzantine
Coins...*, p. 175, 178; N. O i k o n o m i d e s, *A Collection...*, p. 57; A.R. B e l l i n g e r,
Ph. G r i e r s o n, *Catalogue of the Byzantine Coins*, vol. III, p. 12, 428, 457–465;
L. G a r l a n d, *Byzantine Empresses...*, p. 102–103; L. B r u b a k e r, H. T o b l e r, *The
Gender of Money...*, p. 594; J. H e r r i n, *Women in Purple...*, p. 191; K. K o t s i s, *Empress
Theodora: A Holy Mother*, [in:] *Virtuous or Villainess: The Image of the Royal Mother
form the Early Medieval to the Early Modern Era*, eds. C. F l e i n e r, E. W o o d a c r e,
Basingstoke 2016, p. 11–36; Z.A. B r z o z o w s k a, *Cesarzowa Bułgarów...*, p. 14–15.
[127] S. M a s l e v, *Die staatsrechtliche Stellung...*, p. 317–318; Ph. G r i e r s o n, *Byz-
antine Coins...*, p. 179, 185; A.R. B e l l i n g e r, Ph. G r i e r s o n, *Catalogue of the Byzantine
Coins*, vol. III, p. 489–490; Z.A. B r z o z o w s k a, *Cesarzowa Bułgarów...*, p. 15–16.

Fig. 8. Solidus with an image of empress Theodora of Paphlagonia, Constantinople, 842–843. Drawing (reconstruction): E. Myślińska-Brzozowska

The most valuable comparative material for the study of Bulgarian sigillography from the reign of Peter and Maria Lekapene comes from the coins and seals produced in Byzantium during 914–919, i.e. in the period of the regency of Zoe Karbonopsina, mother of Constantine VII Porphyrogennetos. Nearly all of the gold coins and lead *sigilla* produced on her orders were made according to one and the same design, with the obverse portraying Christ or the Mother of God, and the reverse – a likeness of the rulers. The busts of the emperor and the empress are depicted in an almost identical fashion as in Peter and Maria's seals. Constantine is on the left side of the composition, with Zoe to the right; they are holding the patriarchal cross between them, and on some of the artifacts, the mother's hand is above that of her son. The images are accompanied by an inscription identifying them as βασιλεῖς Ῥωμαίων. This same depiction of Zoe and Constantine can also be found on the obverse of the bronze coins from 914–919. Much rarer, on the other hand, are artifacts on which the bust of the young emperor is found on the obverse, while that of his mother – on the reverse (e.g. the *sigillum* from 918/919 or the bronze coins from Cherson)[128].

Consequently, in the light of the above analysis, one may state that the inclusion of Maria's image on the seals from 927–945 was a result of cultural transfer from Byzantium to Bulgaria. It is worth noting that the depiction of the empress had only disappeared from the coins and sigillographic material created within the empire a few years before the signing of the 927 peace treaty, due to the 919 deposition (termination of regency) of Zoe Karbonopsina, mother of Constantine VII[129]. Still, the practice was not discontinued in the later period: towards the end of his life, Peter could see Byzantine coins and seals with the image of empress Theophano, as regent for her minor sons[130].

The similarity between the seal images of the Bulgarian royal couple and the analogous depictions of Zoe and Constantine VII Porphyrogennetos from 914–919 is striking. One is, therefore, led to conclude that the creators of the Bulgarian *sigillum* modeled it on the Byzantine artifacts from 914–919[131].

Curiously, a dig in Preslav uncovered a lead *sigillum* from the 10th–11th century layer, almost entirely devoid of figural elements, belonging – according to the inscription – to *basilissa* Maria (Μαρήα βασήλησα).

---

[128] S. M a s l e v, *Die staatsrechtliche Stellung...*, p. 325; Ph. G r i e r s o n, *Byzantine Coins...*, p. 179–184; A.R. B e l l i n g e r, Ph. G r i e r s o n, *Catalogue of the Byzantine Coins*, vol. III, p. 530–569; L. G a r l a n d, *Byzantine Empresses...*, p. 120–121; Z.A. B r z o z o w s k a, *Cesarzowa Bułgarów...*, p. 16.

[129] S. M a s l e v, *Die staatsrechtliche Stellung...*, p. 325; Ph. G r i e r s o n, *Byzantine Coins...*, p. 179–184; A.R. B e l l i n g e r, Ph. G r i e r s o n, *Catalogue of the Byzantine Coins*, vol. III, p. 12, 530–569; L. G a r l a n d, *Byzantine Empresses...*, p. 120–121; Z.A. B r z o z o w s k a, *Cesarzowa Bułgarów...*, p. 16.

[130] S. M a s l e v, *Die staatsrechtliche Stellung...*, p. 326; Ph. G r i e r s o n, *Byzantine Coins...*, p. 184; A.R. B e l l i n g e r, Ph. G r i e r s o n, *Catalogue of the Byzantine Coins*, vol. III, p. 12; L. G a r l a n d, *Byzantine Empresses...*, p. 271; Z.A. B r z o z o w s k a, *Cesarzowa Bułgarów...*, p. 16.

[131] J. S h e p a r d, *A marriage...*, p. 143–144; Z.A. B r z o z o w s k a, *Cesarzowa Bułgarów...*, p. 16–17.

Some scholars are of the opinion that the artifact could be Maria's personal seal, manufactured after 945[132]. The use of a dedicated *sigillum privatum* by the Bulgarian tsaritsa would provide another piece of evidence suggesting that Byzantine ideas concerning the role of the imperial spouse became widespread in 10th-century Preslav. Suffice it to say that there are extant 10th–11th century seals of Byzantine empresses (e.g. Theodora), of eminent Constantinople ladies (usually titled *zoste patrikia*)[133], and of Rus' princesses (e.g. of Maria, daughter of Constantine IX Monomachos), the latter far from ignorant of the status of women at the palace in Constantinople[134].

Seal depictions are also the sole type of sources based on which one might attempt to reconstruct the official court dress of the Bulgarian tsaritsa in the 10th century, along with her insignia. No such data is available from archaeological digs, even from the aforementioned 'Preslav treasure.' As Georgi Atanasov's research shows, the diadem found in the collection could not have belonged to Maria, as it was intended for a very young woman – one of the daughters or granddaughters of the tsaritsa[135].

Since Maria and Peter were depicted on all of the *sigilla* holding the patriarchal cross, we are unable to conclude whether the Bulgarian

[132] Т. М и х а й л о в а, *Печат на "Мария Василиса" от Преслав*, "Нумизматика, сфрагистика и епиграфика" 3.2, 2007, p. 39–41; Т. Т о д о р о в, *Владетелският статут...*, p. 101–102; И. Й о р д а н о в, *Корпус на средновековните български печати...*, p. 119–121.

[133] S. M a s l e v, *Die staatsrechtliche Stellung...*, p. 324; Ph. G r i e r s o n, *Byzantine Coins...*, p. 175, 178; N. O i k o n o m i d e s, *A Collection...*, p. 56–57; A.R. B e l l i n g e r, Ph. G r i e r s o n, *Catalogue of the Byzantine Coins*, vol. III, p. 12, 428, 457–465; L. G a r l a n d, *Byzantine Empresses...*, p. 102–103; В.С. Ш а н д р о в с к а я, *Печати титулованных женщин Византии*, "Античная древность и средние века" 33, 2002, p. 89–101; J. H e r r i n, *Women in Purple...*, p. 191; Н. К ъ н е в, *Византийската титла...*, p. 191–198.

[134] В.Л. Я н и н, *Актовые печати Древней Руси X–XV вв.*, vol. I, *Печати X – начала XIII в.*, Москва 1970, p. 17–19, 33, 130, 173, 183–184, 210–211; A.V. M a i o r o v, *Eufrozyna Halicka. Córka imperatora bizantyńskiego na Rusi Halicko-Wołyńskiej (ok. 1176/1180 – po 1253)*, ed. D. D ą b r o w s k i, transl. R. S z p a k, Kraków 2016, p. 79.

[135] G. A t a n a s o v, *On the Origin, Function and the Owner of the Adornments of the Preslav Treasure from the 10th century*, "Archaeologia Bulgarica" 3.3, 1999, p. 81–94; i d e m, *Инсигниите...*, p. 224–243.

tsaritsa used a scepter and a sphere, i.e. the insignia we find in depictions of Byzantine empresses of the 8th–9th centuries. The diadem and robes worn by Maria as portrayed on the artifact under examination do bear a marked resemblance to the elements of clothing depicted on seals and coins of Zoe Karbonopsina (914–919), as well as on a mid-10th century ivory tablet showing a full-figure Byzantine imperial couple: Romanos II and Bertha-Eudokia[136].

The diadem on Maria's head is a middle Byzantine *stemma* of the female type. On many of the seals of Maria and Peter from 927–945, we see long, shoulder-length *prependoulia* (triple pearl pendants), as well as a richly decorated headband with a cross on top and two conical pinnacles on each side[137]. Due to the poor state of preservation of the seals' outer parts, it is significantly more challenging for scholars to ascertain what type of robe the tsaritsa is wearing: a *loros* or a chlamys[138].

---

[136] Г. А т а н а с о в, *Инсигниите...*, p. 99, 186, 256; M.G. P a r a n i, *The Romanos Ivory and the New Tokali Kilise: Imperial Costume as a Tool for Dating Byzantine Art*, "Cahiers archéologiques. Fin de l'antiquité et moyen-âge" 49, 2001, p. 15–28; Т. Т о д о р о в, *България...*, p. 163; i d e m, *Владетелският статут...*, p. 104; Z.A. B r z o z o w s k a, *Cesarzowa Bułgarów...*, p. 17.

[137] J. S h e p a r d, *A marriage...*, p. 144; Г. А т а н а с о в, *Инсигниите...*, p. 185–186; И. Й о р д а н о в, *Корпус на печатите...*, p. 58–59; M.G. P a r a n i, *Reconstructing the Reality of Image. Byzantine Material Culture and Religious Iconography (11th–15th Centuries)*, Leiden – Boston 2003, p. 28–30; Т. Т о д о р о в, *България...*, p. 162, 255–256; i d e m, *Владетелският статут...*, p. 103; Г. А т а н а с о в, *Печатите на българските владетели от IX–X в. в Дръстър (Силистра)*, [in:] *От тука започва България. Материали от втората национална конференция по история, археология и културен туризъм "Пътуване към България", Шумен 14–16.05. 2010 година*, ed. И. Й о р д а н о в, Шумен 2011, p. 287; K. K o t s i s, *Defining Female Authority...*, p. 205; Н. К ъ н е в, *Четири непубликувани оловни печата от района на Шумен*, "Историкии" 5, 2012, p. 63; Z.A. B r z o z o w s k a, *Cesarzowa Bułgarów...*, p. 17.

[138] J. S h e p a r d, *A marriage...*, p. 144; Г. А т а н а с о в, *Инсигниите...*, p. 186; И. Й о р д а н о в, *Корпус на печатите...*, p. 58–59; Т. Т о д о р о в, *България...*, p. 162, 255–256; i d e m, *Владетелският статут...*, p. 103; Г. А т а н а с о в, *Печатите...*, p. 287; Н. К ъ н е в, *Четири непубликувани оловни печата...*, p. 63; П. П а в л о в, *Години на мир и "ратни беди" (927–1018)*, [in:] Г. А т а н а с о в, В. В а ч к о в а, П. П а в л о в, *Българска национална история*, vol. III, *Първо българско царство (680–1018)*, Велико Търново 2015, p. 432; Z.A. B r z o z o w s k a, *Cesarzowa Bułgarów...*, p. 17–18.

Both of these, we may note, were a part of the official court attire of Byzantine empresses[139].

[139] A.R. B e l l i n g e r, Ph. G r i e r s o n, *Catalogue of the Byzantine Coins*, vol. III, p. 122–123; J. H e r r i n, *The Imperial Feminine...*, p. 16; M.G. P a r a n i, *The Romanos Ivory...*, p. 18; e a d e m, *Reconstructing...*, p. 12–27, 38–39; M. S m o r ą g-R ó ż y c k a, *Bizantyńsko-ruskie miniatury Kodeksu Gertrudy. O kontekstach ideowych i artystycznych sztuki Rusi Kijowskiej XI w.*, Kraków 2003, p. 98-99; K. K o t s i s, *Defining Female Authority...*, p. 205–208, 213; Z.A. B r z o z o w s k a, *Cesarzowa Bułgarów...*, p. 18.

VIII

Zofia A. Brzozowska
Mirosław J. Leszka

Towards Eternity

Two Byzantine authors mention Maria's death in their chronicles: John Skylitzes and John Zonaras (relying on the former). The account of interest to us is located in the part of the narrative devoted to the final stage of emperor Romanos II's life[1]. Thus, several scholars are inclined to assume that Peter's wife died at the same time as Constantine VII Porphyrogennetos's son, i.e. in 963[2].

Nonetheless, the particulars of the two chroniclers' narrative need to be taken into account. They mention Maria's demise in a somewhat incidental manner, focusing their attention on something rather different: Peter's efforts to renew the peace treaty of 927. The necessity to reconfirm the provisions of the treaty – by then decades old – was the result of the

---

[1] John Skylitzes, p. 255; John Zonaras, XVI, 23, p. 495; John Zonaras (Slavic), p. 146.

[2] S. Georgieva, *The Byzantine Princesses in Bulgaria*, "Byzantinobulgarica" 9, 1995, p. 169–170; T. Тодоров, *България през втората и третата четвърт на X век: политическа история*, София 2006 [unpublished PhD thesis], p. 160; idem, *Владетелският статут и титла на цар Петър I след октомври 927 г.: писмени сведения и сфрагистични данни (сравнителен анализ)*, [in:] *Юбилеен сборник. Сто години от рождението на д-р Васил Хараланов (1907–2007)*, Шумен 2008, p. 102; С. Звездов, *Българо-византийските отношения при цар Петър*, "Минало" 2016, 3, p. 15.

accession of a new emperor in Constantinople, not of the Bulgarian tsarit-sa's death[3]. Hence, the year 963 should be considered a *terminus ante quem* of Maria's death, rather than its specific date. Perhaps, then, those scholars who argue that Maria departed this life in the early 960s are correct[4].

Attempts have been made to link the deterioration of Bulgarian-Byzantine relations with Maria Lekapene's death. There can be no doubt that Peter's foreign policy, aimed at preserving the country's possessions without engaging in armed conflicts, was successful through the mid-960s – that is, throughout Maria's stay in the court in Preslav. After decades of wars waged by Symeon, the Bulgarian empire enjoyed a long period of peace[5]. Only after Maria's death did the relations between the two countries change, progressing from increased intensity to marked dete-rioration. It may have been in 963, during Theophano's regency, that the 927 peace was renewed[6]. Some scholars have argued that Peter and Maria's sons were sent to Constantinople as hostages at that point[7]. However,

---

[3] M.J. L e s z k a, K. M a r i n o w, *Carstwo bułgarskie. Polityka – społeczeństwo – gospo-darka – kultura. 866–971*, Warszawa 2015, p. 174.

[4] J. S h e p a r d, *A marriage too far? Maria Lekapena and Peter of Bulgaria*, [in:] *The Empress Theophano. Byzantium and the West at the turn of the first millennium*, ed. A. D a v i d s, Cambridge 1995, p. 147; С. З в е з д о в, *Българо-византийските отно-шения при цар Петър…*, p. 15; i d e m, *Българо-византийските отношения при цар Петър I*, София 2016, p. 44–45.

[5] For more on the issue of Peter's foreign policy (mainly with regard to the period after Maria's death, however) see: M.J. L e s z k a, K. M a r i n o w, *Carstwo bułgarskie…*, p. 167–186.

[6] This can be inferred from John Skylitzes's relation (p. 255). However, it must be noted that the Byzantine historian's account is far from precise, recounting events that took place over the period of six years in a single sentence. Doubts can also be raised as to the reasons for renewing the treaty. It seems that this fact should be linked with Romanos II's death, rather than Maria's. As for the reliability of Skylitzes's account, or the lack thereof, see: И. Б о ж и л о в, В. Г ю з е л е в, *История на средновековна България. VII–XIV в.*, София 2006, p. 305, fn. 25; p. 307, fn. 51. The fragment in question is likely to be an interpolation.

[7] В.И. З л а т а р с к и, *История на българската държава през средните векове*, vol. 1/2, *Първо българско Царство. От славянизацията на държавата до падането на Първото царство (852–1018)*, София 1927, p. 569, 592; Blagoev (Н.П. Б л а г о е в, *Българският цар Роман*, "Македонски преглед" 6.3, 1930, p. 19–22), believed that Peter's sons did not stay in Constantinople in 963 as hostages: rather, they went to the city in connection with Romanos II's death. Pavlov (П. П а в л о в, *Векът на цар*

it must be noted that this view, which is based on John Skylitzes's account, should be treated with great caution: Maria and Peter's sons may have only appeared in the Byzantine capital later, if at all[8].

The Byzantine-Bulgarian peace, signed in 927 and sealed by the marriage of Maria and Peter, was broken in the winter of 965/966 or 966/967[9].

Самуил, София 2014, p. 27–28), in turn, argues that Peter's sons arrived in the Byzantine capital for educational purposes, just like their grandfather one hundred years earlier. John Skylitzes (p. 328) provides us with the intriguing information according to which Romanos was castrated on orders from *parakoimomenos* Joseph. The latter is identified as Joseph Bringas, a cornerstone of Theophano's regency, which implies that the event in question took place in 963. This information is also doubtful, however. It appears in the context of the account of Romanos's escape from Byzantium in the 970s and the 980s. For this reason, some of the scholars who take John's account at face value date this event to 971, connecting it with the concerns about the use of Romanos's children in the struggle for the imperial throne (let us recall Romanos Lekapenos's grandson!). An Armenian author called A s o c h i k (p. 185–186) also writes that Romanos was a eunuch, but he does not mention his name directly.

[8] J o h n   S k y l i t z e s, p. 255. Treating the fragment literally, one is led to believe that Peter and Maria's sons arrived in Constantinople shortly before their father's death. If this was the case, the event should be dated to 968 rather than 963, as Peter is known to have died on January 30th, 969.

[9] The dating of the event is in dispute; some scholars opt for 965/966, while others contend that it should be dated to 966/967. It seems that the latter date is more plausible. Arguments in favor of both options can be found in the following works: В.И. З л а т а р с к и, *История...*, p. 570, 572, 577–578, fn. 4; Н.П. Б л а г о е в, *Критичен поглед върху известията на Лъв Дякон за българите*, "Македонски преглед" 6.1, 1930, p. 27–31; S. R u n c i m a n, *The History of the First Bulgarian Empire*, London 1930, p. 198–201; Р.О. К а р ы ш к о в с к и й, *О хронологии русско-византийской войны при Святославе*, "Византийский Временник" 5, 1952, p. 138; B. S t o k e s, *The Background and Chronology of the Balkan Campaigns of Svyatoslav Igorevich*, "The Slavonic and East European Review" 40/94, 1961, p. 44–57; R. B r o w n i n g, *Byzantium and Bulgaria. A comparative studies across the Early Medieval Frontier*, London 1975, p. 70–71; А.Н. С а х а р о в, *Дипломатия Святослава*, Москва 1982, p. 102, 108; J.V.A. F i n e, *The Early Medieval Balkans: a Critical Survey from the Sixth to the Late Twelfth Century*, Ann Arbor 1983, p. 163, 181–182; С.А. И в а н о в, *Византийско-болгарские отношения в 966–969 гг.*, "Византийский Временник" 42, 1981, p. 90; В. Т ъ п к о в а - З а и м о в а, *Падане на Североизточна България под византийска власт*, [in:] *История на България в четиринадесет тома*, vol. II, *Първа българска държава*, София 1981, p. 389; И. Б о ж и л о в, В. Г ю з е л е в, *История...*, p. 295, 306, fn. 36; J. B o n a r e k, *Przyczyny i cele bułgarskich wypraw Światosława a polityka Bizancjum w latach sześćdziesiątych X w.*, "Studia Historyczne" 39, 1996, p. 77, fn. 183;

Peter sent his envoys to Constantinople to demand from the Byzantines
the payment of the annual tribute, which they were required to pay under
the terms of the 927 peace treaty. It is believed that, in response, the emperor
called the Bulgarians a dirty, wicked and base Scythian tribe, and dubbed
Peter, to whom he referred three times as a slave, an archont wearing and
chewing skins. This must have been a huge insult[10]. Thus, Nikephoros II
Phokas rejected the Bulgarian demands and instigated Kievan prince
Svyatoslav to invade the Bulgarian lands. By provoking this invasion,
the emperor attempted to neutralize Bulgaria in view of Byzantium's
conflicts with Otto I and the Arabs. He was concerned about Peter's
policy, which, geared towards achieving a rapprochement with Otto I and
establishing peaceful relations with Hungary, disregarded the interests
of Byzantium[11].

Under such circumstances, the so-called deep peace, indelibly linked
with Maria, faded into nothingness.

An interesting aspect of the issue of dating Maria's death has been
illuminated by Todor Todorov. The scholar draws attention to the following fact: Liudprand of Cremona, who mentioned Symeon I the Great,
Romanos I Lekapenos, Christopher, Maria and Peter in his *Antapodosis*
(written in the years 958–962), pointed out that the Bulgarian tsar was
the only one still among the living. Perhaps, then, the tsaritsa – like her
father-in-law, grandfather and father – died somewhat earlier than is
commonly assumed, i.e. sometime before the bishop of Cremona started
writing his account[12].

K. M a r i n o w, *Hémos comme barrière militaire. L'analyse des écrits historiques de Léon
le Diacre et de Jean Skylitzès au sujet de la campagne de guerre des empereurs byzantins
Nicéphore II Phocas en 967 et de Jean I Tzymiscès en 971*, "Bulgaria Mediaevalis" 2, 2011,
p. 444–445, fn. 5.

[10] L e o   t h e   D e a c o n, IV, 5. This conclusion is confirmed by the account
of T h e o p h y l a k t o s   o f   O h r i d (*Letters*, 4–5), writing with disgust about the
Bulgarians. According to the bishop, they stank of goatskin. See also: J. S h e p a r d,
A marriage..., p. 138.

[11] П. П а в л о в, *Векът...*, p. 31. On Svyatoslav's actions against Bulgaria cf.:
M.J. L e s z k a, K. M a r i n o w, *Carstwo bułgarskie...*, p. 176–186 (the work contains
a wider bibliography).

[12] Т. Т о д о р о в, *България...*, p. 161; i d e m, *Владетелският статут...*, p. 103.

At this point, it is also worth noting that the literature on the subject features occasional attempts to link Maria's death with the removal of her name and images from the official seals of the Bulgarian monarch. If one were to accept this assumption, one would have to date Maria's demise significantly earlier, around 945[13]. However, it would be rather difficult to reconcile such dating with John Skylitzes' account.

We do not know anything about the circumstances of Maria's death. We can only guess that she ended her life as a lay person, without donning monastic robes in her later years. It seems that if the tsaritsa had decided to undertake such transition, it would have been noted by Bulgarian writers, who devoted their attention primarily to those female royals who ended their earthly existence in a monastery[14].

The fact that Maria showed no interest in living in a monastic community may have been one of the reasons why she was almost entirely absent from the historical memory of medieval Bulgarians. It is worth asking what other factors determined why Maria, a woman who hailed from an imperial family and whose marriage to Peter was a point of pride for him and his subjects, was forgotten during subsequent centuries.

Among the causes of this phenomenon one should indicate primarily the lack of a native, Old Bulgarian historiographical tradition. After all, there is not a single extant chronicle from tsar Peter's times that would include a description and evaluation of his rule. It should be pointed out that the memory of the role of princess Anna Porphyrogennete, wife of Vladimir I, in the process of Christianization of East Slavs survived in medieval Rus' writings mainly owing to the account in the *Russian Primary Chronicle* (the work that inspired the creators of the subsequent

---

[13] J. S h e p a r d, *A marriage...*, p. 147; В. Г ю з е л е в, *Значението на брака на цар Петър (927–969) с ромейката Мария-Ирина Лакапина (911–962)*, [in:] *Културните текстове на миналото – носители, символи, идеи*, vol. I, *Текстовете на историята, история на текстовете. Материали от Юбилейната международна конференция в чест на 60-годишнината на проф. д.и.н. Казимир Попконстантинов, Велико Търново, 29–31 октомври 2003 г.*, София 2005, p. 27; Т. Т о д о р о в, *България...*, p. 160–161; i d e m, *Владетелският статут...*, p. 102–103.

[14] Г. Н и к о л о в, *Български царици от Средновековието в "ангелски образ"*, "Годишник на Софийския университет Св. Климент Охридски" 93 (12), 2003, p. 299–303.

annals). The Old Bulgarian authors, on the other hand, did not create their own vision of Peter and Maria's reign, one that would have been independent of Byzantine chronicles translated into Slavic.

The fact that the sources dedicated to tsar Peter as a saint of the Bulgarian Church are silent on the subject of Maria may be explained by the specific character of this ruler's cult. It has been noted repeatedly in the literature on the subject that, contrary to many other monarchs from the sphere of *Slavia Orthodoxa*, he was worshipped not as the one responsible for Christianizing his country, but as the saint who deepened the Christian piety of Bulgarians. For this reason, works devoted to Peter focus on monastic themes in particular. They highlight the spiritual connection between the ruler and St. John of Rila, as well as his personal predilection for monastic life and the fact that he accepted the Little Schema near the end of his life[15]. There were even frequent efforts, for example in the *Tale of the Prophet Isaiah* or in the 13th-century *Officium*, to paint the picture of Symeon's son as a man who lived a semi-ascetic life and remained unmarried[16]. In this model, there was simply no room for a woman or wife, even one of such high birth as Peter's Byzantine consort – daughter and granddaughter of Constantinopolitan emperors.

[15] I. B i l i a r s k y, *Saint Jean de Rila et saint tsar Pierre. Les destins des deux cultes du Xᵉ siecle*, [in:] *Byzantium and the Bulgarians (1018–1185)*, eds. K. N i k o l a o u, K. T s i k n a k i s, Athens 2008, p. 172–174; i d e m, *St. Peter (927–969), Tsar of the Bulgarians*, [in:] *State and Church. Studies in Medieval Bulgaria and Byzantium*, eds. V. G j u z e l e v, K. P e t k o v, Sofia 2011, p. 187–186; M.J. L e s z k a, *Rola cara Piotra (927–969) w życiu bułgarskiego Kościoła. Kilka uwag*, "Vox Patrum" 66, 2016, p. 435–437.
[16] *Tale of the Prophet Isaiah*, p. 17; *Liturgical text dedicated to St. Peter*, p. 392. Cf. Д.И. П о л ы в я н н ы й, *Царь Петр в исторической памяти болгарского средневековья*, [in:] *Средновековният българин и "другите". Сборник в чест на 60-годишнината на проф. дин Петър Ангелов*, eds. А. Н и к о л о в, Г.Н. Н и к о л о в, София 2013, p. 143–145.

Final Remarks

The views of those historians who see in Maria Lekapene an agent of Constantinople at the Preslav court, as well as an ardent propagator of Byzantine culture on Bulgarian soil, are clearly exaggerated; they find no confirmation in the available source material. Firstly, one needs to remember that Maria was a ruler of a people whose political and intellectual elites were already quite familiar with the cultural achievements of the Byzantine Empire. Secondly, it would be problematic to consider her as a person exerting a dominant influence on either the foreign or the domestic policy of Peter. None of the medieval Bulgarian texts that have survived to our time include even the slightest mention of the tsaritsa's public activities. The message of the Byzantine sources is also enigmatic, only informing us about the fact that on several occasions, Maria visited Constantinople with her children to see her relatives.

We are unlikely to ever learn what caliber of person Maria was, how strong her character was, or what her personal goals and ambitions were. Apparently, the Byzantine chroniclers only displayed interest in her feelings on one occasion. Near the end of the narrative about the events of 927, they mention the ambivalent emotions that accompanied young Maria during the journey to her new homeland: Maria was sad to have to part with her parents, relatives and the palace in Constantinople, but at the same time she was full of joy at the thought that she had not only married a man of imperial status, but had also been proclaimed a ruler of the Bulgarians herself. With a considerable dose of good will, one might interpret the passage as implying that Maria associated her marriage to Peter not only with hope of life stability, but also with an opportunity to realize her own political aspirations. In most likelihood, however, the Byzantine historians attributing these thoughts to her merely wanted to reassure their readers that no harm was done: while the Byzantine imperial princess did marry a foreigner, which had not happened in the past, he was the ruler of a powerful Christian state, so that being his spouse and a co-ruler of his people was no disgrace for her.

One thing is completely clear: during Maria Lekapene's reign, the key elements of the idea of the *imperial feminine* were assimilated in Bulgaria. In their descriptions of Peter's spouse, Greek authors employ all three titles that were used to denote Byzantine empresses: *augusta*, *basilissa* and *despoina*. Unfortunately, we are not able to ascertain how Maria's own 10th-century Slavic subjects addressed her; in all probability, the term *cěsarica* was used at that time. The inclusion of Maria's image on the seals made on her husband's orders in the years 927–945 was a result of the reception of Byzantine models as well. Likewise, the diadem and the official court attire of the Preslav tsaritsa were faithful copies of the *stemma* and dress of Constantinopolitan empresses. Sadly, however, the lack of sources other than the aforementioned sphragistic material does not allow us to confirm beyond doubt whether Maria indeed wore such clothes.

Another fact is noteworthy. Maria sat on the throne in Preslav for a grand total of 36 years, during which entire time Bulgaria enjoyed peaceful relations with the Byzantine empire. Therefore, it would appear that even if the granddaughter of Romanos I Lekapenos was not a sufficiently colorful and strong personality to enter the collective memory of her Slavic subjects, her lifelong mission – ensuring the stability of the peace concluded in 927 – was certainly fulfilled!

In fact, it is difficult to establish who Maria really was. Remarks about her in the sources are exceedingly sparse, and many of those that do exist are rather conventional in nature. One may get the impression that she represented the type of female royal – or even more broadly, woman – who usually escapes the attention of chroniclers. She probably did not display exceptional intellectual qualities or political abilities, nor was she notable for her piety or moral virtues to a degree that would have elevated her into the ranks of the saints of the Bulgarian Church – in the way her husband was. On the other hand, she did not commit any deeds that would have gained her infamy (which would have likely attracted the attention of the relevant authors). One may suppose that Maria went through her life quietly and without seeking fame: for more than three decades, she was a faithful wife and mother, raising heirs to the Bulgarian throne. She did what was expected of her, both in private life and in the public sphere. Her actions, therefore, drew the interest of neither the medieval Bulgarian historiographers nor the Byzantine chroniclers. Her case makes one muse on the historic role of an individual who remained in the shadows (out of their own volition or for independent reasons), unnoticed and unappreciated by those surrounding her – a 'supporting actress' who, ultimately, may have turned out to be irreplaceable.

Appendix

Zofia A. Brzozowska

Maria Lekapene and Peter in Medieval Rus' Historiography – fragments of the *Hellenic and Roman Chronicle* of the second redaction

The *Hellenic and Roman Chronicle* is a unique piece of medieval Rus' historiography. Its anonymous authors embarked upon the remarkable task of presenting the beginnings of the state of the Rurik dynasty against the background of universal history. In accordance with the tradition of Byzantine literature, their account begins with the creation of the world. This preliminary motive is followed by a detailed summary of Old Testament events as well as an account of the conquests of Alexander the Great. Subsequently, much space is devoted to the history of Rome. The authors outline the circumstances of the rise of the city on the Tiber and trace its further history, covering all the eras into which it is divided: the Roman kings, the Republic, the Principate and the Dominate. They also relate the history of the Christian empire with Constantinople as its capital. Its beginnings are linked with the reign of Constantine I the Great, the founder of the city on the Bosporos and the first Roman emperor who turned toward the new religion. Interestingly, the systematic account of the history of Byzantium, extending into the reign of Romanos I Lekapenos (which paralleled that of Igor, prince of Kievan Rus'), contains numerous references to the Bulgarian state and those who ruled it. Of particular note among the latter are Symeon I the Great and his son Peter, married to Maria Lekapene[1].

The authors drew on both older Rus' historiography and on Byzantine sources, especially the *Chronicle of John Malalas* and the *Chronicle of George the Monk*, including the latter's anonymous continuation[2]. The Rus' authors probably had no access to the Greek originals, but relied on their Slavic translations completed in Bulgaria in the late 10th or early 11th century[3]. Certain sections of the source under discussion contain obvious borrowings and *verbatim* excerpts from the Slavic translations of both chronicles.

The *Hellenic and Roman Chronicle* survives in two variants. The first redaction spans four copies: ГИМ, Синод. собр., № 280 (16th cent.); ГИМ, собр. Уварова, № 10/1334 (16th cent.); РНБ, собр. Погодина, № 1437 (16th cent., only containing half of the original text) and БАН, 45.10.6 (15th cent., fragmentary)[4].

---

[1] О.В. Т в о р о г о в, *Летописец Еллинский и Римский*, [in:] *Словарь книжников и книжности Древней Руси (вторая половина XIV–XVI в.)*, ed. Д.С. Л и х а ч е в, vol. II, Ленинград 1989, p. 18.

[2] Д.С. Л и х а ч е в, *Еллинский летописец второго вида и правительственные круги Москвы конца XV в.*, "Труды Отдела древнерусской литературы" 6, 1948, p. 104; Б.М. К л о с с, *К вопросу о происхождении Еллинского летописца второго вида*, "Труды Отдела древнерусской литературы" 27, 1972, p. 371–375; О.В. Т в о р о г о в, *Древнерусские хронографы*, Ленинград 1975, p. 141–143; i d e m, *Летописец Еллинский и Римский...*, p. 18–19; i d e m, *Летописец Еллинский и Римский: текстологические проблемы*, "Труды Отдела древнерусской литературы" 52, 2001, p. 64; А.Г. Б о б р о в, *К вопросу о времени и месте создания Летописца Еллинского и Римского второй редакции*, "Труды Отдела древнерусской литературы" 55, 2004, p. 86–87; В.В. К о л е с о в, *Заметки о языке Летописца Еллинского и Римского второй редакции (К вопросу о месте и времени составления)*, "Труды Отдела древнерусской литературы" 55, 2004, p. 91; Т. В и л к у л, *Літопис і хронограф. Студії з домонгольського київського літописання*, Київ 2015, p. 372.

[3] Н.А. М е щ е р с к и й, *Источники и состав древней славяно-русской переводной письменности IX–XV вв.*, Ленинград 1978, p. 88–89; О.В. Т в о р о г о в, *Летописец Еллинский и Римский...*, p. 18–19; i d e m, *Летописец Еллинский и Римский: текстологические...*, p. 64–72.

[4] Б.М. К л о с с, *К вопросу...*, p. 379; О.В. Т в о р о г о в, *Летописец Еллинский и Римский...*, p. 18.

The second redaction of the *Hellenic and Roman Chronicle* must have arisen in the first half of the 15[5] century. The account of universal history, which the original version of the source takes to the year 948, was enhanced with a list of Byzantine emperors and the years of their reign, beginning with Nikephoros II Phokas (963–969) and ending with Manuel II Palaiologos (1391–1425). This version also contains an account of the capture of Constantinople by the Crusaders in 1204 (taken most probably from the *Novgorod First Chronicle*) as well as two brief narratives regarding places of worship to be found in the Byzantine capital: the icon of the Virgin Hodegetria and the robe of the Theotokos kept in the church in Blachernai[6]. Since the authors fail to mention the fall of Constantinople to the Turks in 1453, it can be assumed that the second redaction of the chronicle was completed before that event[7].

The later 15th century also yielded a number of copies representing the second redaction of the text: БАН, 33.8.13 (last third of 15th cent., incomplete – missing initial part); РГБ, собр. Пискарева, № 162 (1485, presently divided into two parts – 1. РНБ, Кир.-Белоз. собр., № 1/6 and 2. ГИМ, Синод. собр., № 86); ГИМ, Чуд. собр., № 51/353 (late 15th cent.); РНБ, F.IV.91 (late 15th cent.). Other copies arose even later: БАН, Арханг. собр., С 18 (turn of 15th/16th cent.); РНБ, Соф. собр., № 1520 (16th cent., fragmentary); РНБ, собр. ОЛДП, F.33 (16th cent.); РГБ, собр. Егорова, № 867 (mid-16th cent.); СПб. ГУ, НБ, № 108 (early 17th cent.); РГБ, Калуж. собр. (Ф. 738), № 104 (second quarter of 17th cent., fragmentary) and РГБ, собр. Ундольского, № 720 (16th cent., heavily distorted text)[8].

---

[5] А.Г. Б о б р о в, *К вопросу...*, p. 89; В.В. К о л е с о в, *Заметки...*, p. 91–92; Т.В. А н и с и м о в а, *Хроника Георгия Амартола в древнерусских списках XIV– XVII вв.*, Москва 2009, p. 31.

[6] Д.С. Л и х а ч е в, *Еллинский летописец...*, p. 104; Б.М. К л о с с, *К вопросу...*, p. 375; О.В. Т в о р о г о в, *Древнерусские хронографы...*, p. 147; i d e m, *Летописец Еллинский и Римский...*, p. 18–19; А.Г. Б о б р о в, *К вопросу...*, p. 87.

[7] Б.М. К л о с с, *К вопросу...*, p. 375–376; О.В. Т в о р о г о в, *Древнерусские хронографы...*, p. 159; i d e m, *Летописец Еллинский и Римский...*, p. 18; Т.В. А н и с и м о в а, *Хроника Георгия Амартола...*, p. 31.

[8] Д.С. Л и х а ч е в, *Еллинский летописец...*, p. 102–103; Б.М. К л о с с, *К вопросу...*, p. 370; О.В. Т в о р о г о в, *Летописец Еллинский и Римский...*, p. 19; i d e m, *Летописец*

* * *

The parts of the second redaction of the *Hellenic and Roman Chronicle* devoted to Peter and Maria Lekapene are quite extensive. In the most representative copy of the source, БАН, 33.8.13 (dated to the last third of the 15th century), they take six columns of semi-uncial (*poluustav*) text – fol. 287d–288d, 290a–290b, 290d. However, an analysis of the fragment permits us to claim that it constitutes nothing other than a revised version of the Slavic translation of the relevant passages from the *Continuation of George the Monk*, specifically its so-called redaction B.

It would take us too far afield of the main topic to discuss the circumstances of how the translation of the *Chronicle of George the Monk* (as well as its continuation) was incorporated into Slavic literature. There is a huge body of scholarly literature dealing with this issue[9]. Most scholars, to summarize the long debate, are of the opinion that the translation came into being in Bulgaria in the late 10th or early 11th century and was quickly transferred to Rus', where it was further edited[10]. Some, e.g. Ludmila Gorina, maintain that the *Chronicle of George the Monk* (including its continuation containing the account of the 10th-century events) found its way into Old Rus' writings through some Bulgarian historiographical text that reached Rus' after 1018[11]. Others, however, argue for the Rus' origin of the oldest Slavic translation of the *Chronicle of George the Monk*[12].

Еллинский и Римский: текстологические..., p. 57–64; Ю.Д. Р ы к о в, *Новонайденный фрагмент Летописца Еллинского и Римского второй редакции*, "Труды Отдела древнерусской литературы" 55, 2004, p. 72.

[9] See: О.В. Т в о р о г о в, *Хроника Георгия Амартола*, [in:] *Словарь книжников и книжности Древней Руси (XI – первая половина XIV в.)*, ed. Д.С. Л и х а ч е в, Ленинград 1987, p. 469–470; В. М а т в е е н к о, Л. Щ е г о л е в а, *Временник Георгия Монаха (Хроника Георгия Амартола). Русский текст, комментарий, указатели*, Москва 2000, p. 532–543.

[10] Н.А. М е щ е р с к и й, *Источники...*, p. 78–79; О.В. Т в о р о г о в, *Хроника Георгия Амартола...*, p. 468–469.

[11] Л.В. Г о р и н а, *Болгарский хронограф и его судьба на Руси*, София 2005, p. 80–85.

[12] В. М а т в е е н к о, Л. Щ е г о л е в а, *Временник Георгия Монаха...*, p. 6; Т.В. А н и с и м о в а, *Хроника Георгия Амартола...*, p. 28.

The translation survives in a dozen or so copies, representing two variants of the text. Thus, there are four manuscripts containing the earlier redaction of the Slavic translation of the chronicle: the oldest of them is dated to the beginning of the 14th century (РГБ, Троицкое собр. Ф. 173/I [МДА], № 100), while the remaining ones originated in the 14th–16th centuries. However, copies representing the older redaction of the translation are of no use for our research, as this variant of the *Chronicle of George the Monk* only reaches the year 553[13]. The later redaction of the text, textologically dependent on the original one, is likewise known from roughly a dozen copies (some complete and some fragmentary), dating from the 15th–17th centuries. The manuscript РГБ, собр. Ундольского (Ф. 310), № 1289, from the turn of the 15th and 16th centuries, is considered the most representative of them all[14].

* * *

In the relevant fragments of the *Hellenic and Roman Chronicle* of the second redaction, the content of the Byzantine source was reproduced in an unabridged form and without any secondary additions. The differences between the text of БАН, 33.8.13 (fol. 287d–288d, 290a–290b, 290d) and that of its copy РГБ, собр. Ундольского (Ф. 310), № 1289 (fol. 396-397', 399-399', 400) – on which the Slavic translation of the *Continuation of George the Monk* (redaction B) is based – are limited to the stylistic and redactional levels, disregarding changes apparently caused by the copyist's misunderstanding of the original:

---

[13] О.В. Т в о р о г о в, *Древнерусские хронографы...*, p. 12; i d e m, *Хроника Георгия Амартола...*, p. 469; В. М а т в е е н к о, Л. Щ е г о л е в а, *Временник Георгия Монаха...*, p. 8–9; Т.В. А н и с и м о в а, *Хроника Георгия Амартола...*, p. 41–70, 83–88, 124–131, 211–222.

[14] О.В. Т в о р о г о в, *Древнерусские хронографы...*, p. 12; i d e m, *Хроника Георгия Амартола...*, p. 469; Т.В. А н и с и м о в а, *Хроника Георгия Амартола...*, p. 89–123, 131–171, 187–196, 223–257.

Hellenic and Roman Chronicle of the second redaction (БАН, 33.8.13)	Slavic translation of the *Continuation of George the Monk* (РГБ, собр. Ундольского [Ф. 310], № 1289)	Greek text
воиною на гръкы пре-шедша, страх нъккыи гръком творяще (fol. 288a)	на грекы изидоша вои-ною и в Македонию преидоша, страх нъкко-торыи греком творяще (fol. 396')	βουλὴν οὖν ποιησάμενοι κατὰ ʽΡωμαίων ἐκστρα-τεύουσιν καὶ ἐν Μακεδονίᾳ καταλαμβάνουσιν, φόβον, ὡς εἰκός, τοῖς ʽΡωμαίοις ἐμποιήσοντες
съ всъм болгарьскым чиномь (fol. 288c)	съ всъм воларском чиномъ (fol. 397)	πάσῃ τῇ συγκλήτῳ
жену от своего отечь-ствиа от Арменна сущии странъ (fol. 290a)	женоу ѿ своего ѿьствиа ѿ Арменнак соущии странъ (fol. 399)	καὶ γυναῖκα ἐκ τῆς αὐτοῦ πατρίδος τῆς τῶν ʼΑρμενιάκων

The parts of the second redaction of the *Hellenic and Roman Chronicle* devoted to Peter and Maria Lekapene can be considered a variant of the relevant fragments from the *Continuation of George the Monk*, redaction B. Apart from the aforementioned passages with regard to which the *Hellenic and Roman Chronicle* diverges from the Slavic translation of redaction B of the *Continuation of George the Monk*, the comparison between the source in question and the Greek text of the Byzantine chronicle merely enables us to indicate a few divergences (or terminological peculiarities) that the authors of the *Hellenic and Roman Chronicle* took directly from the Slavic translation of the source. The most important of these divergences are as follows:

- Bulgarian rulers' titles: in the account of the events taking place before the signing of the peace treaty in 927, under which the Byzantines recognized Peter's right to use his imperial title,

Bulgarian rulers are referred to as кнѧзь (which corresponds to Greek ἄρχων); in the account of the events that followed the treaty in question, the son of Symeon is referred to using the appellative цѣрь (Greek βασιλεύς).

- The source is, as was the case with all Old Rus' texts, consistent in referring to the Byzantines as Greeks (грѣккы) and not Romans (Ῥωμαῖοι).

- Bulgaria's neighbors – the author of the Slavic translation of the *Continuation of George the Monk* and later the authors of the *Hellenic and Roman Chronicle* mention that in 927, Peter's state was in danger of being invaded by the Hungarians (угры), while Byzantine historiographers mention the Turks (Τοῦρκοι) in this context.

Text of the source in the Old Russian original

Text according to the copy БАН, 33.8.13, dated to the last third of the 15ᵗʰ century. Reprinted from: *Летописец Еллинский и Римский*, vol. I, *Текст*, ed. О.В. Т в о р о г о в, Санкт-Петербург 1999, p. 497–498, 500, 501.

(fol. 287d) Мѣсяца мая 27 день и индикта 15 Cумеонъ, князь болгарьскыи, на ховраты подвиже воину. Съступу бывшу, и побѣжденъ бысть и, сущии под нимь вошью, зѣло исъсѣче. Тѣм неисцѣлною волѣзнию по срѣдцу ятъ, погыбе безаконновавъ всуе. Петра, сына своего, постави княземь, егоже имѣаше от другыя ему суща жены, сестры Георгиа, ‖(fol. 288a) иже и Съсубыла, поручника того чядомъ своим остави. Михаила же, сущаго от прьвыя жены своея, постриже минихом. Иоан же и Бѣньяминь, Петрова брата, одеждею болгарьскою украшена вяста. Сущии округъ языци, увѣдавше Cумеоново умерътвие, – ховратѣ и угры и прочии, воевати начаша на болгары и прочии съвѣт творяху. Гладу же велию с пругы болгарьскому языку крѣпко одержиму, бояху бо ся инѣх языкъ пришествиа, бояху бо ся паче

и грѣчькаго наитья, съвѣт убо створше, воиною на грѣкы прешедша,
страх нѣкыи грѣком творяще.

По сих же пакы увѣдавше, яко хощет на ня царь воиною изити
Романъ, посласта Петръ и Георгии отаи нѣкоего мниха, Калокуръ
именуема именем, арменьянинъ, златом запечатану грамоту нося.
Исповѣдаше же сущее въ грамотѣ, яко съ грѣкы миръ люба имѣти
и любими суть миръ сложити, о брачную створити куплю. Такого убо
мниха царь с любовию ǀ(fol. 288b) приатъ, абие посла в лодьи глаго-
лемѣи дромонъ, мниха Феодосья, глаголема Явукиа, и Василья кли-
рика родьянина, да о мирѣ глаголати с болгары и в Несембрьистѣмь
градѣ. Прѣжде бо Небриа наричаемь от Фрака, бо вселивше его,
и Врию, нѣкыих фракишан градѣм глаголемѣмь, лучее же Несембриа
именуемо. Се же пришедше, и ключимая сии глаголааше, изидоша
купно съ Стефаном болгарином берегом, позаду же ею приде Георгии
Соруcбыля и Сумеон Клутороканъ и Усапсъ и Сумеонъ, старѣишинъ
Болгарьстѣи земли, тъ обрѣт на женитву. К симже възвлюбленикъ
его Стефанъ, и Минъ и Клаготинъ. Крон же Миникъ, утвердишася
къ цареви Роману.

Видѣвши же дщерь Христофора царя, именем Марью, и повелику
люба имъ бяше. Написаша к Петрови въскорѣ да приидет, съгласную
грамоту створше о устроении мира. Посланъ же Никита магистръ,
сват Роману царю, срѣсти, привести Петра даже и до Костянтина-
града. Болгарину убо Петрови пришедшю, въ трииру, глаголемыи
олядь, царь Романъ вшед, Влахерну прииде, и Петра к нему идуща
видѣ, и цѣлова и. Егда же межи собою ключимая бесѣдоваста,
и написаста ǁ(fol. 288c) съгласная о мирѣ и брачную куплю промежи
сих приимающу и разумну правляющу промежи грѣкы и болгары
протовестиарьемь Феофаномъ. Въ 8 день мѣсяца октяб(ря) изиде
патриархъ Стефанъ купно с Феофаном протовестиарьем, съ Марьею,
Христофоровою дщерью, и съ всѣм болгарьскым чиномь въ церковь
Прѣсвятыя Богородица въ Пигии, да благословить Петра и Марью,
брачныя вѣнца на главѣ ею положит, дружащу же Феофану прото-
вестиарью и Георгию Соруcбыли.

Свѣтлѣи же и многоразличнѣи трапезѣ бывши, и всѣм ядущим
браку свѣтлу устроену, и вниде протовестиарии купно съ Марьею,

Христофора царя дъщерью, въ град, в 3 день бракъ створи Романъ
и пиръ свѣтелъ ў примоста ў Пигиинаго, украсивъ запоны шелковы-
ми. Ў того примоста царева лодья, рекомаа дромонъ, стоящу, идеже
обѣда царъ Романъ с Петромъ болгариномъ, купно с Костянтином
зятем, и съ Христофором, сыномъ своим. Болгаром же прю немалу
створшим, прежде славят Христофора, потом же Костя(fol. 288d)
нтина, послуша прекословиа их Романъ царь бысть же егоже про-
сиша. И вся еже о брацѣ свершишяся, хотящи же Марьи в Болгары
шествовати с мужемъ своим с Петромъ, родителя ея изидоста до
Евдома купно с Феофаном протовестиариемъ, обѣдавше ту с Петром.
Хотящим же им ити прочь, объемшим дщерь и многы слезы про-
льявшим, яко лишающимся срѣдца своего възлюбленаго, и своего
зятя цѣловавша. И сию в руцѣ предавша, въ царствие обратившеся.
Марьи же к болгарьскым рукамъ преданѣ, в болгары шествующе,
радующися купно и печялующися, зане родитель възлюбленых лиша-
ющися и царьскых домовъ и обычаи в родѣ еи сущих; радующися,
яко причтася мужю цаю и владычиця болгаром наречена. Идущи убо
и богатство носящи всякое и пристрои безъ числа.

[...]

(fol. 290a) Петра же болгарина сложися убити его брат его Иоан съ
иными велможами Сумеонѣми. Ятом бывшим имъ, ибо Иоаннъ бьем
и затворенъ бысть в темници, прочии же въ мукы многы впадоша.
Сих бо вѣсти посла Петръ к Роману царю. Посла царь миниха Иоана,
иже бѣ прежде ректоръ, и вину творя, яко измѣну створити ему
держимых плѣнникь, поистинѣ же Иоанна яти и в Костянтинъ-
град вести, якоже бысть. Въшед бо купно съ Иоаномъ в лодьи,
от Месимбриа прииде в Костянтинъ-град. И не по мнозѣ мнишь-
скую скыму отвергъ и жену просивъ, и се абие дасть ему царь
дом, и села, и стяжаниа многа и жену от своего отечьствиа от
Ярмениа сущии странѣ, бракъ же свѣтелъ в кесаревѣ дому створи,
Христофору же царю Иоану миниху, бывшему ректору, дружившю. Нь
и Михаилъ мних и тъ брат Петровъ, съ тщаниемъ хотя болгарь-
скую власть приати, въступи самъ в болгарьскыи град, и к сему

|(fol. 290b) прибѣгоша, от Петровы власти отступиша, скуфянѣ, егоже по житенскаго испроверженна наидоша сии въ Грѣчьскую страну, яко ключитися симъ от Македити сквозѣ Стримона на Еладу и на Никополии внити, ту сущая вся плѣнити. Никополии же рекомыи побѣдныи град, наречень бысть по имени его Августа, побѣди же его честныи, на Антониа и Клеопатру побѣду створи, Егупетскую власть под римляны подклони.

[...]

(fol. 290d) И преждереченнаго царя Романа внука, жена же Петра болгарина, многажды в Костянтинъ-град прииде, своего отца и дѣда присѣтить. Прочее же с троим дѣтеи прииде, уже Христофору, отцу еи, умершю. И много богатство у дѣда своего вземши, съ честью многою възвратися.

Translation

On May 27th, the fifteenth indiction [927], Symeon, prince of Bulgaria, set out on an armed expedition against the Croats. The battle that broke out ended in his defeat and those who served under him were killed. As a result, his heart was struck with an incurable disease; he died, having committed a crime in vain[15]. He designated his son Peter (whom he had by his second wife, George Sursuvul's sister) as prince. George became the guardian of his children. Michael,

---

[15] The information that Symeon I the Great died because of a heart attack caused by a traumatic experience (the defeat that the Bulgarian troops suffered at the hands of the Croats) appears in redaction B of the *Continuation of George the Monk*, the *Chronicle of Symeon Logothete* and the *Continuation of Theophanes*. The latter is based on the first two, although it enriches the account by mentioning Symeon's loss of mental capacities: *[Symeon], overcome by dementia [...] lost his mind* (Continuator of Theophanes, p. 412).

whom he had by his first wife, was tonsured a monk. John and Benjamin, Peter's brothers, were adorned with Bulgarian robes. The surrounding nations (Croats, Hungarians and others)[16], having learned about Symeon's death, established an alliance and started a war against the Bulgarians. Overwhelmed with great hunger due to the locust, the Bulgarian nation was afraid of being invaded by other peoples, especially by the Greeks. Having reached a decision, the Bulgarians set out to attack the Greeks, for whom they posed a certain threat[17].

Subsequently, having learned that emperor Romanos [I Lekapenos] was planning to attack them, Peter and George secretly dispatched an Armenian monk by the name of Kalokir[18]. The monk carried a document protected with a golden seal in which they declared that they sought peace with the Greeks and were ready to conclude a peace treaty and a marriage agreement. Having received the monk with love, the emperor immediately sent a monk named Theodosios, known as Abukes[19], and clergyman Basil of Rhodes[20] in a boat called a *dromon* to negotiate peace with the Bulgarians in the city of Mesembria. The city had earlier been called Nebria or Bria, after the name of a Thracian who had settled there; it had been referred to as 'the city of certain Thracians.' Thus, it

---

[16] The Byzantine authors mention the Turks (Τοῦρκοι) here. In reality, Bulgaria faced a threat from the Hungarians.

[17] Here, the authors of the second redaction of the *Hellenic and Roman Chronicle* neglected to mention a significant detail that is recorded in the Byzantine sources as well as in the Slavic translation of the *Continuation of George the Monk*, namely the capture of the theme of Macedonia by the Bulgarian army.

[18] Kalokir – a monk from Armenia. In 927, he was sent as an envoy to Constantinople. We have no knowledge of what happened to him later.

[19] Theodosios Abukes – a monk. In 927, he was sent by Romanos I Lekapenos as an envoy to Peter. This is the only episode from his life that is mentioned in primary sources.

[20] Actually, Constantine of Rhodes (about 870/880–after 931) – son of John and Eudokia, who settled in Lindos on the island of Rhodes. In 908 he found his way to the court of emperor Leo VI the Wise. After the latter's death, he remained in the circle of Constantine VII Porphyrogennetos. In 927, along with Theodosios Abukes, he was sent by Romanos I Lekapenos as an envoy to Bulgaria's ruler. The anonymous author of the *Continuation of George the Monk*, and later the authors of the second redaction of the *Hellenic and Roman Chronicle*, presumably call him Basil because of the name's phonetic similarity to the title which Constantine wore at the time: βασιλικὸς κληρικός (imperial clergyman).

is better to call it Mesembria[21]. Upon their arrival, the envoys discussed the relevant issues and set out with Stephen the Bulgarian[22] along the shore. They were followed by George Sursuvul, *kalutarkan* and *sampsis* Symeon, and Symeon who became a dignitary in the Bulgarian lands by marriage, and his beloved Stephen, *menikos*, *magotinos*, *kronos* and *menikos*. They all appeared before emperor Romanos[23].

When they saw emperor Christopher's daughter Maria, they found her very attractive and, having first prepared the peace agreement, wrote to Peter to come as fast as he could. Niketas Magistros, a relative of emperor Romanos[24], was sent out to meet Peter on the way and bring him to Constantinople. When the Bulgarian arrived, emperor Romanos, having boarded a trireme, i.e. a ship, sailed to Blachernai[25], saw Peter coming

---

[21] Mesembria – today's Nesebar. A harbor city on the western coast of the Black Sea, it was indeed founded by the Thracians, and it was known by the name of *Menebria* in the earliest period of its existence. In the 6th century BC, it was transformed into a Greek colony inhabited by settlers from Megara. In the 9th–10th centuries, the Byzantines lost Mesembria to the Bulgarians a number of times, and vice versa. In 927, it remained under Bulgarian rule.

[22] Stephen the Bulgarian, *kauchan* (?), was Peter's close relative. Some scholars believe that he was his cousin, the son of Symeon I the Great' brother (П. П а в л о в, *Стефан*, [in:] i d e m, И. Л а з а р о в, П. П а в л о в, *Кой кой е в средновековна България*, София 2012, p. 625), or nephew. He was one of the most influential people in Bulgaria at the time.

[23] On the composition of the Bulgarian legation see: chapter III. The person referred to as *his beloved Stephen* (**възлюбленикъ его Стефанъ**) is probably Stephen the Bulgarian (В.И. З л а т а р с к и, *История на българската държава през средните векове*, vol. 1/2, *Първо българско Царство. От славянизацията на държавата до падането на Първото царство (852–1018)*, София 1927, p. 523, fn. 4). The names of the posts mentioned here (*kalutarkan*, κουλου τερκανὸς, καλου τερκάνος, **къλу/кλу торока-нъ**; *sampsis*, σαμψής, **саmъчи**; *magotinos*, μαγοτῖνος, **клогатинъ**; *kronos*, κρόνος, **кронъ**; *menikos*, μηνικός, **минникъ**) are of Proto-Bulgar origin. Cf.: Т. С л а в о в а, *Владетел и администрация в ранносредновековна Бълагария. Филологически аспекти*, София 2010, p. 81–83, 105–129.

[24] Niketas (about 870–after 946) – *magistros*, descended from a Slavic family from the Peloponnesos. He was the father of Sophia, Maria Lekapene's mother. In 928, for his involvement in the plot against emperor Romanos I (he was believed to have encouraged his son-in-law to seize power), he was expelled from Constantinople and forced to become a monk.

[25] Blachernai – an area of Constantinople situated in the northwestern part of the city, on the southern bank of the Golden Horn inlet. Outside of the Theodosian walls,

his way and kissed him. After discussing the relevant issues, they composed the peace and marriage arrangement to be signed by both parties. *Protovestiarios* Theophanes[26] skillfully mediated between the Greeks and the Bulgarians. On October 8th, patriarch Stephen[27], accompanied by *protovestiarios* Theophanes, Christopher's daughter Maria, and all Bulgarian dignitaries[28] set out for the Church of the Virgin Mary in Pege[29] to bless Peter and Maria and to put wedding wreaths on their heads in the presence of *protovestiarios* Theophanes and George Sursuvul.

Once the brilliant, multi-course feast appropriate for an extraordinary wedding was over, the *protovestiarios* and Maria, Christopher's daughter, returned to the city. On the third day, Romanos organized a wedding

---

the area became included in the fortification line during the reign of Herakleios. The church, which appears in a number of sources, was in fact a complex of three buildings (the Great Church, the Holy Reliquary Chapel and the Holy Bathhouse), founded by empress Pulcheria. The most precious relic kept in the chapel was the robe of the Theotokos, brought to Constantinople from the Holy Land in the second half of the 5th century. An icon of the Virgin Mary was also kept there. It was believed that the Blachernai relics and Mary's image saved the Byzantine capital from foreign invasions many a time (for instance, in 626 against the Persians and the Avars and in 860 against the Rus').

[26] Theophanes – *protovestiarios*. After 925, he is also referred to in the sources as ὁ πατρίκιος Θεοφάνης ὁ παραδυναστεύων. In the years 941–946, he held the office of *parakoimomenos*. He enjoyed the trust of Romanos I Lekapenos as his adviser and had a great impact on the course of the peace negotiations in 927.

[27] Stephen II of Amaseia (died in 928) – patriarch of Constantinople in the years 925–928.

[28] The account of the second redaction of the *Hellenic and Roman Chronicle* is corrupt here, probably because of an error committed by a copyist. In the Slavic translation of the *Continuation of George the Monk*, this part of the text contains the phrase съ всѣм болярьскомъ чиномъ (РГБ, собр. Ундольского [Ф. 310], № 1289, fol. 397), which approximates the Greek πάσῃ τῇ συγκλήτῳ (*with the whole Senate*) much more closely.

[29] The church in the Monastery of the Holy Mother of the Life-Giving Spring (Μονὴ τῆς Θεοτόκου τῆς Πηγῆς) – situated in the suburbs of Constantinople, outside the wall of Theodosios II, south-west of the city. It owes its name to the nearby spring, giving rise to water with healing powers. The oldest church was erected here in the 6th century, in the last years of the reign of Justinian I the Great. The church was renovated and rebuilt a number of times, e.g. by empress Irene (after the 790 earthquake) and Basil I (after another cataclysm in 869). In September 923, the church was destroyed by the Bulgarian troops; Romanos I Lekapenos took on the task of rebuilding it.

ceremony and a lavish feast at the waterside in Pege, which was embellished with silk curtains. An imperial boat called a *dromon* was moored at the quay; emperor Romanos, Peter the Bulgarian, [Romanos's] son-in-law Constantine[30] and [Romanos's] son Christopher enjoyed their meal on it. The Bulgarians raised a major objection, calling for Christopher to be praised first and Constantine second. Emperor Romanos heeded their protests and they obtained what they requested. When all the matters regarding the wedding were completed, and Maria was to set out with her husband Peter for Bulgaria, her parents, accompanied by *protovestiarios* Theophanes, went to the Hebdomon[31], where they had dinner with her and Peter. As the newly married couple were to leave, the parents embraced their daughter, shedding torrents of tears as if they were losing their beloved heart, and kissed their son-in-law. Having entrusted her in his hands, they returned to the empire. Maria, remaining in the care of the Bulgarians, went to their country, happy and sad at the same time, for she had been deprived of her parents, the imperial chambers and the customs adhered to by her family. However, she rejoiced at having married a man who was an emperor and at having been titled ruler of the Bulgarians. Leaving, she carried all kinds of riches and innumerable objects with her.

[...]

Peter's brother John[32] and Symeon's other dignitaries conspired to kill Peter. When they were captured, John was flogged and imprisoned while the rest were subjected to severe torture. Peter informed emperor Roma-

---

[30] Constantine VII Porphyrogennetos – Byzantine emperor (913–959).

[31] The Hebdomon – a suburb of Constantinople, situated south-west of the city, on the northern coast of the Sea of Marmara. Military units were stationed and trained here. Besides, the Hebdomon was the site of ceremonies attended by the emperor; he would greet armies returning from military expeditions there, as well as review units and receive parades. He would be welcomed there himself by the patriarch, the senate and the people when returning from campaigns he commanded. The Hebdomon also witnessed imperial proclamations. Finally, in view of its picturesque location overlooking the Sea of Marmara, the area served as the emperor's summer residence.

[32] On the plot led by John see: chapter VI.

nos of what had happened. The emperor sent a monk named John[33], who had once been a *rhaiktor*, under the excuse of arranging the exchange of captives. In reality, he was to take John and bring him to Constantinople; and this is what happened. Having boarded a ship with John, he went from Mesembria to Constantinople. Before long, he renounced his monastic vows and asked for a wife. The emperor immediately gave him a house, villages, many riches and a wife coming from Armenia[34], [Romanos's] native country. He also organized a solemn wedding in his co-emperor's house (emperor Christopher and monk John, former *rhaiktor*, served as the groomsmen). Monk Michael[35], who was also Peter's brother, filled with desire to seize power in Bulgaria and took control of one of Bulgaria's strongholds. He was joined by Scythians[36] who had rebelled against Peter. When Michael died, his supporters found themselves in Greece, having managed to cross from Maketidos[37] through Strymon[38]

---

[33] John – a monk, former *rhaiktor*. The oldest source information about him comes from 921, at which time he was (along with Leo and Potos Argyros) in command of the imperial troops dispatched by Romanos I Lekapenos to fend off Symeon I the Great's army ravaging the vicinities of Constantinople. The clash with the Bulgarians ended in defeat and John fled the battlefield. In 929, he was one of the envoys sent to Preslav to exchange captives. The emissaries were entrusted with the task of bringing Peter's brother, John, to Constantinople.

[34] The Byzantine sources, the Slavic translation of the *Continuation of George the Monk* and even the copies of the second redaction of the *Hellenic and Roman Chronicle* refer to the Armeniac theme here.

[35] On the plot led by Michael see: chapter VI.

[36] This ethnonym probably refers to the Bulgarians.

[37] Maketidos – the term is unclear. It appears in redaction B of the *Continuation of George the Monk*, in the *Continuation of Theophanes* (ἀπὸ Μακέτιδος) as well as in the Slavic translation of the *Continuation of George the Monk* (ѿ Макетнда). A different variant is to be found in the oldest copies of the *Hellenic and Roman Chronicle*: ѡт Макединн. The publisher of the text of the second redaction of the *Hellenic and Roman Chronicle*, Oleg V. Tvorogov, considers it to be *a stronghold in Bulgaria*, thus drawing a distinction between Macedonia and the toponym under discussion. The same approach can be found in Vasily M. Istrin's edition of the Slavic translation of the *Continuation of George the Monk* and in Yakov N. Lyubarsky's translation of the *Continuation of Theophanes* into contemporary Russian. Cf.: chapter VI.

[38] Strymon – today's Strymonas/Struma, a river originating in the Vitosha mountain range near Sofia and discharging into the Thracian Sea.

to Hellas[39] and Nikopolis[40], taking possession of everything they encountered. Nikopolis, called the city of victory, received its name to commemorate the victory which honorable Augustus achieved over Antony and Cleopatra – he subjugated Egypt for the Romans[41].

[...]

Emperor Romanos's granddaughter, Peter the Bulgarian's wife, came to Constantinople on many occasions to visit her father and grandfather. For the last time, she arrived with three children already after her father Christopher's death. Having received many riches from her grandfather, she returned to Bulgaria with great honors.

[39] Hellas – by this term, the author probably means Epiros, where Michael's supporters settled after reaching Byzantine territory.

[40] Nikopolis – a city in Epiros situated on the Ambracian Gulf (Ionian Sea). Founded by Octavian Augustus after his victory over Mark Antony in 31 BC, in the 930s it remained under Byzantine rule. A theme of Nikopolis also existed, with Naupaktos as its capital.

[41] Here, the author of redaction B of the *Continuation of George the Monk*, and later the authors of the *Hellenic and Roman Chronicle*, refer to the events that took place in 31 BC, i.e. the Battle of Actium, in which Octavian Augustus's fleet overpowered the ships of Cleopatra VII (the last queen of Egypt) allied with Mark Antony. A year later, Egypt came under Roman rule.

Bibliography

Sources

Asochik

Der Stephanos von Taron armenische Geschichte, transl. H. G e l z e r, A. B u r c k h a r d t, Leipzig 1907.

Basilika

Basilicorum libri LX, vol. I–VIII, eds. J. S c h e l t e m a, D. H o l w e r d a, N. Va n D e r Wa l, Amsterdam 1953–1988.

Beneševič's Taktikon

N. O i k o n o m i d è s, *Les listes de préséance byzantines des IXe et Xe siècles*, Paris 1972, p. 237–253.

Constantine VII Porphyrogennetos, *The Book of Ceremonies*

Constantini Porphyrogeniti De caeremoniis aulae byzantinae, ed. I.I. R e i s k e, Bonnae 1829.

C o n s t a n t i n e   P o r p h y r o g e n n e t o s, *The Book of Ceremonies*, transl. A. M o f f a t, M. Ta l l, Leiden 2012.

Constantine VII Porphyrogennetos, *On the Governance of the Empire*

Constantine Porphyrogenitus, *De administrando imperio*, ed., transl. G. Moravcsik, Washington 1967.

Constantine VII Porphyrogennetos, *On the Themes*

Constantino Porfirogenito, *De thematibus*, ed. A. Pertusi, Citta del Vaticano 1952.

Continuator of George the Monk

Georgius Monachus, *Vitae imperatorum recentiorum*, ed. I. Bekker, Bonnae 1838, p. 761–924.

Continuator of George the Monk (Slavic)

В.М. Истрин, *Книгы временыя и образныя Георгия Мниха. Хроника Георгия Амартола в древнем славянорусском переводе. Текст, исследование и словарь*, vol. I, Петроград 1920.

Continuator of Theophanes

Theophanes Continuatus, eds. B.G. Niebuhr, I. Bekker, Bonnae 1838.
Theophanis Continuati. Libri I–IV, ed., transl. M. Featherstone, J. Signes Codoñer, Boston–Berlin 2015.

Cosmas the Priest

Ю.К. Бегунов, *Козма Пресвитер в славянских литературах*, София 1973, p. 297–392.
Kosma Prezbiter, *Mowa polemiczna przeciwko heretykom (fragmenty)*, eds. M. Skowronek, G. Minczew, [in:] *Średniowieczne herezje dualistyczne na Bałkanach. Źródła słowiańskie*, eds. G. Minczew, M. Skowronek, J.M. Wolski, Łódź 2015, p. 67–125.

Digest of Justinian

Institutiones, Digesta, eds. P. Krüger, T. Mommsen, Berlin 1928.
The Digest of Justinian, vol. I, transl. A. Watson, Philadelphia 1998.

Eusebios of Caesarea

Eusebius Caesariensis, *Vita Constantini*, ed. F. Winkelmann, Berlin–New York 2008.

Evagrios Scholastikos

The Ecclesiastical History of Evagrius with Scholia, eds. J. Bidez, L. Parmentier, London 1898.

The Ecclesiastical History of Evagrius Scholasticus, transl., introd. M. Whitby, Liverpool 2000.

George the Monk

Georgii monachi, dicti Hamartoli, Chronicon, ed. E. de Muralt, St. Petersburg 1859.

Hellenic and Roman Chronicle

Летописец Еллинский и Римский, ed. О.В. Творогов, vol. I, Санкт-Петербург 1999.

John Malalas

Ioannis Malalae Chronographia, ed. I. Thurn, Berolini–Novi Eboraci 2000.

John Skylitzes

Ioannis Scylitzae Synopsis historiarum, ed. I. Thurn, Berolini–Novi Eboraci 1973.

John Skylitzes, *A Synopsis of Byzantine History 811–1057*, transl. J. Wortley, Cambridge 2010.

John Zonaras

Ioannis Zonarae Epitomae historiarum, ed. Th. Büttner-Wobst, Bonnae 1897.

John Zonaras (Slavic)

В.И. Срезневский, *Симеона Метафраста и Логофета описание мира от бытия и летовниксобран от различных летописец. Славянский перевод Хроники Симеона Логофета с дополнениями*, Санкт-Петербург 1905, p. 144–186.

Leo the Deacon

Leonis Diaconi Caloensis Historiae, ed. C.B. Hase, Bonnae 1828.

History of Leo the Deacon. Byzantine Military Expansion in the Tenth Century, ed., transl. A-M. T a l b o t, D.F. S u l i v a n, with assistance G.T. D e n n i s, S. M c G r a t h, Washington 2006.

Leo Grammatikos

Leonis Grammatici Chronographia, ed. I. B e k k e r, Bonnae 1842.

Letter of the Patriarch Theophylact to Tsar Peter

Iv. D u j č e v, *L'epistola sui Bogomili del patriarcha Teofilatto*, [in:] i d e m, *Medioevo bizantinoslavo*, vol. I, Roma 1965, p. 283–315 (text on p. 311–315).

List of Bulgarian Archbishops

И. Б о ж и л о в, *Българската архиепископия XI–XII в. Списъкът на българските архиепископи*, София 2011, p. 93–131.

Liturgical text dedicated to St. Peter

Й. И в а н о в, *Български старини из Македония*, София 1970, p. 383–394.

Liudprand of Cremona, *Embassy*

L i u d p r a n d u s C r e m o n e n s i s, *Relatio de legatione constantinopolitana*, [in:] *Liudprandi Cremonensis Antapodosis, Historia Ottonis, Relatio de legatione constantinopolitana*, ed. P. C h i e s a, Turnholti 1998, p. 185–218.

The Embassy of Liudprand, [in] *The Complete Works of Liudprand of Cremona*, transl. P. S q u a t r i t i, Washington 2007, p. 238–284.

Liudprand of Cremona, *Retribution*

L i u d p r a n d u s C r e m o n e n s i s, *Antapodosis*, [in:] *Liudprandi Cremonensis Antapodosis, Historia Ottonis, Relatio de legatione constantinopolitana*, ed. P. C h i e s a, Turnholti 1998, p. 5–150.

L i u d p r a n d o f C r e m o n a, *Retribution*, [in] *The Complete Works of Liudprand of Cremona*, transl. P. S q u a t r i t i, Washington 2007, p. 41–202.

Maqqari

A l - M a q q a r i, *The History of the Mohammedan Dynasties in Spain*, transl. P. d e G a y a n g o s, London–New York 1964.

Nicholas Mystikos

Nicholas I Patriarch of Constantinople, *Letters*, ed., transl. R.J.H. Jenkins, L.G. Westerink, Washington 1973.

Nikon Chronicle

Летописный сборник, именуемый Патриаршею или Никоновскою летописью, Санкт-Петербург 1862 [=Полное Собрание Русских Летописей IX].

Novellae

Novellae, eds. R. Schöll, G. Kroll, Berlin 1928.

On Justiniana Prima's canonical position

Περὶ τῆς Πρώτης καὶ Δευτέρας Ἰουστινιανῆς ἐκ τῶν μετὰ τὸν κώδικα νεαρῶν τίτλος β´ δυάταξις γ´, [in:] G. Prinzing, *Entstehung und Rezeption der Justiniana Prima-Theorie im Mittelalter*, "Byzantinobulgarica" 5, 1978, p. 279, 37–42 (Scor. gr. X–II–10, fol. 377r.).

On the Treaty with the Bulgarians

I. Dujčev, *On the Treaty of 927 with the Bulgarians*, "Dumbarton Oaks Papers" 32, 1978, p. 254–288.

Prokopios, *On the Wars*

Procopius, *History of the Wars*, vol. I–V, transl. H.B. Dewing, London 1914–1928.

Prokopios, *Secret History*

Procopius, *The Anecdota or Secret History*, transl. H.B. Dewing, London 1935.

Pseudo-Symeon Magistros

Pseudo-Symeon (Symeon Magister), *Chronographia*, [in:] *Theophanes Continuatus*, eds. B.G. Niebuhr, I. Bekker, Bonnae 1838, p. 601–760.

Rūdhrāwarī

Continuation of the Experiences of the Nations by Abu Shuja' Rudhrawari, Vizier of Muqtadi and Hilal b. Muhassin, Vizier's secretary in Baghdad, transl. D.S. Margoliouth, [in:] *The Eclipse of the Abbasid Caliphate. Original Chronicles of the Fourth Islamic Century*, eds. H.F. A m e d r o z, D.S. M a r g o l i o u t h, vol. VI, London 1921.

Russian Chronograph

Русский хронограф. Хронограф редакции 1512 г., Санкт-Петербург 1911 [=Полное Собрание Русских Летописей, vol. XXII/1].

Russian Primary Chronicle

Лаврентьевская летопись, Ленинград, 1926–1928 [=Полное Собрание Русских Летописей, vol. I].

The Russian Primary Chronicle. Laurentian Text, transl. S.H. C r o s s, O.P. S h e r-b o w i t z-W e t z o r, Cambridge 1953.

Symeon Logothete

Symeonis Magistri et Logothetae Chronicon, ed. S. W a h l g r e n, Berolini–Novi Eboraci 2006.

Symeon Logothete (Slavic)

В.И. С р е з н е в с к и й, *Симеона Метафраста и Логофета описание мира от бытия и летовниксобран от различных летописец. Славянский перевод Хроники Симеона Логофета с дополнениями*, Санкт-Петербург 1905.

Synodikon of Tsar Boril

Борилов синодик. Издание и превод, eds. И. Б о ж и л о в, А. Т о т о м а н о в а, И. Б и л я р с к и, София 2010.

Tale of the Prophet Isaiah

I. B i l i a r s k y, *The Tale of the Prophet Isaiah. The Destiny and Meanings of an Apocryphal Text*, Leiden–Boston 2013, p. 13–27.

Theodore Anagnostes

T h e o d o r o s A n a g n o s t e s, *Kirchengeschichte*, ed. G. Ch. H a n s e n, Berlin 1995.

Theodore Daphnopates

Théodore Daphnopatès, *Corréspondance*, ed., transl. J. Darrouzès, L.G. Westerink, Paris 1978.

Theophanes

Theophanes, *Chronographia*, ed. C. de Boor, vol. I, Lipsiae 1883.

Theophylaktos of Ohrid

Theophylacte d'Achrida, *Lettres*, ed., transl. P. Gautier, Thessalonique 1986.

Theophylaktos Simokattes

Theophylacti Simocattae Historiae, ed. C. de Boor, Lipsiae 1887.

Yahyā of Antioch

Histoire de Yahya-ibn-Saʿïd d'Antioche, continuateur de Saʿïd-ibn-Bitriq, eds. I. Kratchkovsky, A. Vasiliev, vol. II, Paris 1932 [=*Patrologia Orientalis*, vol. XXIII/3]. ·

Modern Scholarship

A l e k s a n d r o v E., *The International Treaties of Medieval Bulgaria (Legal Aspects)*, "Bulgarian Historical Review" 17.4, 1989, p. 40–56.

A n g e l i d i Ch., *Pulcheria. La castità al potere (399–c. 455)*, Milano 1998.

A n g e l o v a S., P r i n z i n g G., *Das mutmassliche Grab des Patriarchen Damian: zu einem archäologischen Fund in Dristra/Silistria*, [in:] *Средновековна християн-ска Европа. Изток и запад. Ценности, традиции, общуване*, eds. В. Г ю з е л е в, А. М и л т е н о в а, София 2002, p. 726–730.

A r r i g n o n J.P., *Les relations internationales de la Russie Kiévienne au milieu du Xe siècle et le baptême de la princesse Olga*, [in:] *Actes des congrès de la Société des histo-riens médiévistes de l'enseignement supérieur public. 9e congrès*, Dijon 1978, p. 167–184.

A t a n a s o v G., *On the Origin, Function and the Owner of the Adornments of the Preslav Treasure from the 10th century*, "Archaeologia Bulgarica" 3.3, 1999, p. 81–94.

B a n a s z k i e w i c z J., *Jedność porządku przestrzennego, społecznego i tradycji początków ludu. (Uwagi o urządzeniu wspólnoty plemienno-państwowej u Słowian)*, "Przegląd Historyczny" 77, 1986, p. 445–466.

B e l l i n g e r A.R., G r i e r s o n Ph., *Catalogue of the Byzantine Coins in the Dumbarton Oaks Collection and in the Whittemore Collection*, vol. I, *Anastasius I to Maurice. 491–602*, Washington 1992.

B e l l i n g e r A.R., G r i e r s o n Ph., *Catalogue of the Byzantine Coins in the Dumbarton Oaks Collection and in the Whittemore Collection*, vol. III, *Leo III to Nicephorus III. 717–1081*. Washington 1993.

B e n s a m m a r E., *La titulature de l'impératrice et sa signification. Recherches sur les sources byzantines de la fin du VIIIe siècle à la fin du XIIe siècle*, "Byzantion" 46, 1976, p. 243–291.

B i l i a r s k y I., *Saint Jean de Rila et saint tsar Pierre. Les destins des deux cultes du Xe siecle*, [in:] *Byzantium and the Bulgarians (1018–1185)*, eds. K. N i k o l a o u, K. T s i k n a k i s, Athens 2008, p. 161–174.

B i l i a r s k y I., *St. Peter (927–969), Tsar of the Bulgarians*, [in:] *State and Church. Studies in Medieval Bulgaria and Byzantium*, eds. V. G j u z e l e v, K. P e t k o v, Sofia 2011, p. 173–188.

B o n a r e k J., *Przyczyny i cele bułgarskich wypraw Światosława a polityka Bizancjum w latach sześćdziesiątych X w.*, "Studia Historyczne" 39, 1996, p. 287–302.

B o r o ń P., *Kniaziowie, królowie, carowie... Tytuły i nazwy władców słowiańskich we wczesnym średniowieczu*, Katowice 2010.

B o ž i l o v I., *L'ideologie politique du tsar Syméon: pax Symeonica*, "Byzantinobulgarica" 8, 1986, p. 73–88.

B r a l e w s k i S., *Konstantynopolitańskie kościoły*, [in:] *Konstantynopol–Nowy Rzym. Miasto i ludzie w okresie wczesnobizantyńskim*, eds. M.J. L e s z k a, T. W o l i ń s k a, Warszawa 2011, p. 132–151.

B r o k a a r W.G., *Basil Lecapenus*, "Studia bizantina et neohellenica Neerlandica" 3, 1972, p. 199–234.

B r o w n i n g R., *Byzantium and Bulgaria. A comparative studies across the Early Medieval Frontier*, London 1975.

B r z o z o w s k a Z.A., *Car i caryca czy cesarz i cesarzowa Bułgarów? Tytulatura Piotra i Marii-Ireny Lekapeny w średniowiecznych tekstach słowiańskich (Jak powinniśmy nazywać władców bułgarskich z X stulecia)*, "Die Welt der Slaven" 62, 2017, p. 17–26.

B r z o z o w s k a Z.A., *Cesarzowa Bułgarów, Augusta i Bazylisa – Maria-Irena Lekapena i transfer bizantyńskiej idei kobiety-władczyni (imperial feminine) w średniowiecznej Bułgarii*, "Slavia Meridionalis" 17, 2017, p. 1–28.

B r z o z o w s k a Z.A., *Geneza tytułu "car" w świetle zabytków średniowiecznego piśmiennictwa słowiańskiego*, "Die Welt der Slaven" 46, 2012, p. 34–39.

B r z o z o w s k a Z.A., *The Image of Maria Lekapene, Peter and the Byzantine-Bulgarian Relations Between 927 and 969 in the Light of Old Russian Sources*, "Palaeobulgarica" 41.1, 2017, p. 40–55.

B r z o z o w s k a Z.A., *Rola carycy Marii-Ireny Lekapeny w recepcji elementów bizantyńskiego modelu władzy w pierwszym państwie bułgarskim*, "Vox Patrum" 66, 2016, p. 443–458.

B r z o z o w s k a Z.A., *Święta księżna kijowska Olga. Wybór tekstów źródłowych*, Łódź 2014.

B r z ó s t k o w s k a A., *Kroniki z kręgu Symeona Logotety*, [in:] *Testimonia najdawniejszych dziejów Słowian. Seria grecka*, vol. V, *Pisarze z X wieku*, ed. A. B r z ó s t k o w s k a, Warszawa 2009, p. 64–67.

B r u b a k e r L., *Memories of Helena: Patterns in Imperial Female Matronage in the 4th and 5th Centuries*, [in:] *Women, Men and Eunuchs*, ed. L. J a m e s, London–New York 1997, p. 52–75.

B r u b a k e r L., T o b l e r H., *The Gender of Money: Byzantine Empresses on Coins (324–802)*, "Gender & History" 12.3, 2000, p. 572–594.

B u r g e s s R.W., *The Accession of Marcian in the Light of Chalcedonian Apologetic and Monophysite Polemic*, "Byzantinische Zeitschrift" 86/87, 1993/1994, p. 47–68.

B u r i ć I., *Porodica Foka*, "Zbornik Radova Vizantološkogo Instituta" 17, 1976, p. 189–291.

B y l i n a S., *Bogomilizm w średniowiecznej Bułgarii. Uwarunkowania społeczne, polityczne i kulturalne*, "Balcanica Posnaniensia" 2, 1985, p. 133–145.

C a m e r o n Al., *Circus Factions. Blues and Grens at Rome and Byzantium*, Oxford 1976.

C a m e r o n Al., *Porphyrius the Charioteer*, London 1973.

C a m e r o n Av., *The Empress Sophia*, "Byzantion" 45, 1975, p. 8–15.

Catalogue of Byzantine Seals at Dumbarton Oaks and in the Fogg Museum of Art, eds. J. N e s b i t t, N. O i k o n o m i d e s, vol. I, *Italy, North of the Balkans, North of the Black Sea*, Washington 1991.

Catalogue of Byzantine Seals at Dumbarton Oaks and in the Fogg Museum of Art, eds. E. M c G e e r, J. N e s b i t t, N. O i k o n o m i d e s, vol. V, *The East (continued)*, Washington 2005.

C h r y s o s t o m i d e s J., *Byzantine Concepts of War and Peace*, [in:] *War, Peace and World Orders in European History*, eds. A.V. H a r t m a n n, B. H e u s e r, London–New York 2001, p. 91–101.

Č e š m e d ž i e v D., *Bułgarska tradycja państwowa w apokryfach: car Piotr w "Bułgarskiej kronice apokryficznej"*, transl. Ł. M y s i e l s k i, [in:] *Biblia Slavorum Apocryphorum. Novum Testamentum*, eds. G. M i n c z e w, M. S k o w r o n e k, I. P e t r o v, Łódź 2009, p. 139–147.

D a n i e l F r a n k f o r t e r A., *Amalasuntha, Procopius and a Woman's Place*, "Journal of Women's History" 8.2, 1996, p. 41–57.

D a u b e D., *The marriage of Justinian and Theodora. Legal and Theological Reflections*, "Catholic University of America Law Review" 16, 1967, p. 380–399.

D o b r e v I., *Sv. Ivan Rilski*, vol. I, Linz 2007.

D ö l g e r F., *Bulgarisches Cartum und byzantinisches Kaisertum*, "Известия на Българския Археологически Институт" 9, 1935, p. 57–68.

D r i j v e r s J., *Helena Augusta, the Mother of Constantine the Great and the Legend of Her Finding of the Cross*, Leiden–New York–København–Köln 1992.

D u j č e v I., *Relations entre Slaves méridionaux et Byzance aux Xe–XIIe siècles*, [in:] i d e m, *Medioevo bizantino-slavo*, vol. III, *Altrisaggi di storia, politica eletteraria*, Roma 1971, p. 175–221.

E v a n s J.A.S., *The Age of Justinian. The circumstances of Imperial power*, London–New York 1996.

F a l k o w s k i W., *Wielki król. Ideologiczne podstawy władzy Karola Wielkiego*, Warszawa 2011.

F e a t h e r s t o n e J., *Ol'ga's Visit to Constantinople*, "Harvard Ukrainian Studies" 14, 1990, p. 293–312.

F e a t h e r s t o n e J., *Olga's Visit to Constantinople in De Cerimoniis*, "Revue des études byzantines" 61, 2003, p. 241–251.

F e r l u g a J., *John Scylitzes and Michael of Devol*, [in:] i d e m, *Byzantium on the Balkans. Studies on the Byzantine Administration and the Southern Slavs from the VIIth to the XIIth Centuries*, Amsterdam 1976, p. 337–344.

F i n e J.V.A., *The Early Medieval Balkans: a Critical Survey from the Sixth to the Late Twelfth Century*, Ann Arbor 1983.

F o s s C., *The Empress Theodora*, "Byzantion" 72, 2002, p. 141–176.

F r e n d W.H.C., *The Rise of the Monophysite Movement. Chapters in the History of Church in Fifth and Sixth Centuries*, Cambridge 1972.

G a j e k J.S., *U początków świętości Rusi Kijowskiej*, [in:] *Chrystus zwyciężył. Wokół chrztu Rusi Kijowskiej*, eds. J.S. G a j e k, W. H r y n i e w i c z, Warszawa 1989, p. 95–105.

G a r l a n d L., *Byzantine Empresses. Women and Power in Byzantium AD 527–1204*, London–New York 1999.

G e o r g i e v a S., *The Byzantine Princesses in Bulgaria*, "Byzantinobulgarica" 9, 1995, p. 163–201.

G k a n t z i o s D r á p e l o v á P., *Byzantine Empresses on Coins in the Early Byzantine Period (565–610): a Survey of the Problems of Interpretation and Identification*, "Byzantinoslavica" 74.1/2, 2016, p. 75–91.

G r e g o r y T.E., *Macedonia*, [in:] *Oxford Dictionary of Byzantium*, ed. A.P. K a z h d a n, New York–Oxford 1991, p. 1261–1262.

G r i e r s o n Ph., *Byzantine Coins*, London–Berkeley–Los Angeles 1982.

G r u m e l V., *Notes de chronologie byzantine*, "Echo d'Orient" 35, 1936.

H a h n W., *Moneta Imperii Byzantini: Rekonstruktion des Prägeaufbaues auf Synoptisch-Tabellarischer Grundlage*, vol. I, *Von Anastasius I. bis Justinianus I (491–565)*, Vienna 1973.

H a h n W., *Moneta Imperii Byzantini: Rekonstruktion des Prägeaufbaues auf Synoptisch-Tabellarischer Grundlage*, vol. II, *Von Justinus II. bis Phocas (565–610)*, Vienna 1975.

H a l d o n J., *Warfare, State and Society in the Byzantine World*, London 1999.

H i l l B., *Imperial Women in Byzantium 1025–1204. Power, Patronage and Ideology*, New York 1999.

H e r r i n J., *The Imperial Feminine in Byzantium*, "Past and Present" 169, 2000, p. 5–35 [=J. H e r r i n, *Unrivalled Influence: Women and Empire in Byzantium*. Princeton 2013, p. 161–193].

H e r r i n J., *Late Antique Origins of the 'Imperial Feminine': Western and Eastern Empresses Compared*, "Byzantinoslavica" 74.1/2, 2016, p. 5–25.

H e r r i n J., *The Many Empresses of the Byzantine Court (and All Their Attendants)*, [in:] e a d e m, *Unrivalled Influence. Women and Empire in Byzantium*, Princeton 2013, p. 219–237.

H e r r i n J., *Theophano. Considerations on the Education of a Byzantine Princess*, [in:] *The Empress Theophano. Byzantium and the West at the turn of the first millennium*, ed. A. D a v i d s, Cambridge 1995, p. 64–85 [= J. H e r r i n, *Unrivalled Influence. Women and Empire in Byzantium*, Princeton 2013, p. 238–260].

H e r r i n J., *Women in Purple. Rulers of Medieval Byzantium*, London 2002.

H i l s d a l e C.J., *Byzantine Art and Diplomacy in an Age of Decline*, Cambridge 2014.

H o l u m K.G., *Theodosian Empresses: Women and Imperial Dominion in Late Antiquity*, Los Angeles 1981.

H o m z a M., *Mulieres suadentes – Persuasive Women. Female Royal Saints in Medieval East Central and Eastern Europe*, Leiden 2017.

H o m z a M., *St. Olga. The Mother of All Princes and Tsars of Rus'*, "Byzantinoslavica" 63, 2005, p. 131–141.

H o m z a M., *The Role of the Imitatio Helenae in the Hagiography of Female Rulers until the Late Thirteenth Centuries*, [in:] Бългaрия, Бългaрите и Европа – мит, истоpия, съвремие, vol. III, Велико Търново 2009, p. 128–158.

H o m z a M., *The Role of Saint Ludmila, Doubravka, Saint Olga and Adelaide in the Conversions of their Countries (The Problem of Mulieres Suadentes, Persuading Women)*, [in:] *Early Christianity in Central and East Europe*, ed. P. U r b a ń c z y k, Warszawa 1997, p. 187–202.

H o w a r d - J o h n s o n J., *A short piece of narrative history: war and diplomacy in the Balkans, winter 921/2 – spring 924*, [in:] *Byzantine Style, Religion and Civilization. In Honour of Sir Steven Runciman*, ed. E. J e f f r e y s, Cambridge 2006, p. 340–360.

J a m e s L., *Empresses and Power in Early Byzantium*, Leicester 2001.

J e n k i n s R.J.H., *A "Consolatio" of the Patriarch Nicholas Mysticus*, "Byzantion" 35, 1965, p. 159–166.

J e n k i n s R.J.H., *The Peace with Bulgaria (927) Celebrated by Theodore Daphnopates*, [in:] *Polychronion. Festschrift F. Dölger*, ed. P. W i r t h, Heidelberg 1966, p. 287–303.

J o n e s A.H.M, M a r t i n d a l e J.R., M o r r i s J., *The Prosopography of Later Roman Empire*, vol. I, A.D. 260–395, Cambridge 1971.

J o r d a n o v I., *Corpus of Byzantine Seals from Bulgaria*, vol. III/1, Sofia 2009.

K a r a y a n n o p o u l o s J., *Les causes des luttes entre Syméon et Byzance: un réexamin*, [in:] *Сборник в чест на акад. Димитър Ангелов*, ed. В. В е л к о в, София 1994, p. 52–64.

K a r l i n-H a y t e r P., L e r o y-M o l i n g h e n A., *Basileopator*, "Byzantion" 38, 1968, p. 278–281.

K a z h d a n A., *Romanos I Lekapenos*, [in:] *Oxford Dictionary of Byzantium*, vol. III, Oxford 1991, p. 1806.

K i j a s A., *Chrzest Rusi*, Poznań 2006.

K i j a s A., *Stosunki rusko-bułgarskie do XV w. ze szczególnym uwzględnieniem stosunków kulturalnych*, "Balcanica Posnaniensia" 2, 1985, p. 146–180.

K o m p a A., *Konstantynopolitańskie zabytki w Stambule*, [in:] *Z badań nad wczesnobizantyńskim Konstantynopolem*, eds. M.J. L e s z k a, K. M a r i n o w, A. K o m p a, Łódź 2011 [= "Acta Universitatis Lodziensis. Folia historica" 87], p. 123–214.

K o s i ń s k i R., *The Emperor Zeno. Religion and Politics*, Cracow 2006.

K o t s i s K., *Defining Female Authority in Eighth-Century Byzantium: the Numismatic Images of the Empress Irene (797–802)*, "Journal of Late Antiquity" 5.1, 2012, p. 185–215.

K o t s i s K., *Empress Theodora: A Holy Mother*, [in:] *Virtuous or Villainess: The Image of the Royal Mother form the Early Medieval to the Early Modern Era*, eds. C. F l e i n e r, E. W o o d a c r e, Basingstoke 2016, p. 11–36.

L e n s k i N., *Failure of Empire. Valens and the Roman State in the Fourth Century AD*, Berkeley–Los Angeles–London 2002.

L e s z k a M.B., L e s z k a M.J., *Bazylisa. Świat bizantyńskich cesarzowych IV–XV w.*, Łódź 2017.

L e s z k a M.J., *Aelia Zenonis, żona Bazyliskosa*, "Meander" 57, 2002, p. 87–93.

L e s z k a M.J., *Bunt Michała przeciw carowi Piotrowi (?930)*, "Slavia Antiqua" 58, 2017 (in press)

L e s z k a M.J., *Cesarzowa Ariadna*, "Meander" 54, 1999, p. 267–278.

L e s z k a M.J., *Cesarzowa Martyna, żona Herakliusza*, "Meander" 58, 2003, p. 447–458.

L e s z k a M.J., *Konstantyna, żona cesarza Maurycjusza*, "Przegląd Nauk Historycznych" 1.1, 2002, p. 21–32.

L e s z k a M.J., *Lupicyna–Eufemia – żona Justyna I*, "Meander" 54, 1999, p. 555–562.

L e s z k a M.J., *The Monk versus the Philosopher. From the History of the Bulgarian-Byzantine War 894–896*, "Studia Ceranea. Journal of the Waldemar Ceran Research Centre for the History and Culture of the Mediterranean Area and South-East Europe" 1, 2011, p. 55–70.

L e s z k a M.J., *Rola cara Piotra (927–969) w życiu bułgarskiego Kościoła. Kilka uwag*, "Vox Patrum" 66, 2016, p. 429–442.

L e s z k a M.J., *Rola cesarzowej Teofano w uzurpacjach Nicefora Fokasa (963) i Jana Tzymiskesa (969)*, [in:] *Zamach stanu w dawnych społecznościach*, ed. A. S o ł t y s i k, Warszawa 2004, p. 227–235.

L e s z k a M.J. *Spisek Jana przeciw carowi Piotrowi (928) – raz jeszcze*, "Balcanica Posnaniensia" 23, 2016, p. 5–13.

L e s z k a M.J., *Symeon I Wielki a Bizancjum. Z dziejów stosunków bułgarsko-bizantyńskich w latach 893–927*, Łódź 2013.

L e s z k a M.J., *Uzurpacje w cesarstwie bizantyńskim w okresie od IV do połowy IX w.*, Łódź 1999.

L e s z k a M.J., *Wizerunek władców pierwszego państwa bułgarskiego w bizantyńskich źródłach pisanych (VIII–pierwsza połowa XII w.)*, Łódź 2003.

L e s z k a M.J., *Zoe, o oczach czarnych jak węgiel, czwarta żona Leona VI Filozofa*, [in:] *Kobiety i władza w czasach dawnych*, eds. B. C z w o j d r a k, A. K l u c z e k, Katowice 2015, p. 95–112.

L e s z k a M.J., M a r i n o w K., *Carstwo bułgarskie. Polityka – społeczeństwo – gospodarka – kultura. 866–971*, Warszawa 2015.

L i l i e R.-J., *Byzanz unter Eirene und Konstantine VI (780–802). Mit einem Kapitel über Leon IV (775–780)*, Frankfurt am Main 1996.

L o s k a E., *Sytuacja aktorów i aktorek w rzymskim prawie małżeńskim*, "Zeszyty Prawnicze UKSW" 12, 2012, p. 81–100.

Ł a b u ń k a M., *Od Olgi do Włodzimierza. Sytuacja religijna na Rusi Kijowskiej w okresie poprzedzającym oficjalną chrystianizację*, [in:] *Teologia i kultura duchowa Starej Rusi*, eds. J.S. G a j e k, W. H r y n i e w i c z, Lublin 1993, p. 41–54.

M a i o r o v A.V., *Eufrozyna Halicka. Córka imperatora bizantyńskiego na Rusi Halicko-Wołyńskiej (ok. 1176/1180–po 1253)*, ed. D. D ą b r o w s k i, transl. R. S z p a k, Kraków 2016.

M a k s i m o v i c h K., *Byzantine Law in Old Slavonic Translations and the Nomocanon of Methodius*, "Byzantinoslavica" 65, 2007, p. 9–18.

M a l a m u t E., *L'impératrice byzantine et le cérémonial (VIIIe–XIIe siècle)*, [in:] *Le saint, le moine et le paysan: Mélanges d'histoire byzantine offerts à Michel Kaplan*, eds. O. D e l o u i s, S. M e t i v i e r, P. P a g e s, Paris 2016, p. 329–374.

M a r i n o w K., *Hémos comme barrière militaire. L'analyse des écrits historiques de Léon le Diacre et de Jean Skylitzès au sujet de la campagne de guerre des empereurs byzantins Nicéphore II Phocas en 967 et de Jean I Tzymiscès en 971*, "Bulgaria Mediaevalis" 2, 2011, p. 443–466.

M a r i n o w K., *In the Shackles of the Evil One. The Portrayal of Tsar Symeon I the Great (893–927) in the Oration On the treaty with the Bulgarians*, "Studia Ceranea. Journal of the Waldemar Ceran Research Centre for the History and Culture of the Mediterranean Area and South-East Europe" 1, 2011, p. 157–190.

M a r i n o w K., *Peace in the House of Jacob. A Few Remarks on the Ideology of Two Biblical Themes in the Oration On the Treaty with the Bulgarians*, "Bulgaria Mediaevalis" 3, 2012, p. 85–93.

M a r i n o w K., *Zadania floty cesarskiej w wojnach bizantyńsko-bułgarskich (VII–XI w.)*, [in:] *Byzantina Europaea. Księga jubileuszowa ofiarowana Profesorowi Waldemarowi Ceranowi*, eds. M. K o k o s z k o, M.J. L e s z k a, Łódź 2007, p. 381–392.

M a r t i n d a l e J.R., *The Prosopography of Later Roman Empire*, vol. II, A.D. 395–527, Cambridge 1980; vol. III, A.D. 527–641, Cambridge 1992.

M a s l e v S., *Die staatsrechtliche Stellung der byzantinischen Kaiserinnen*, "Byzantinoslavica" 27, 1966, p. 308–343.

M c C l a n a n A., *Representations of Early Byzantine Empresses. Image and Empire*, New York 2002.

M c C l a n a n A., *Ritual and Representation of the Byzantine Empress' Court at San Vitale, Ravenna*, [in:] *Acta XIII Congressus Internationalis Archaelogiae Christianae*, eds. M. C a m b i, E. M a r t i n, vol. II, Citta del Vaticano–Split 1998, p. 11–20.

M e n z e V., *Justinian and the Making of the Syriac Orthodox Church*, Oxford 2008.

M i n c z e w G., *Remarks on the Letter of the Patriarch Theophylact to Tsar Peter in the Context of Certain Byzantine and Slavic Anti-heretic Texts*, "Studia Ceranea. Journal of the Waldemar Ceran Research Centre for the History and Culture of the Mediterranean Area and South-East Europe" 3, 2013, p. 113–130.

M i n c z e w G., *Słowiańskie teksty antyheretyckie jako źródło do poznania herezji dualistycznych na Bałkanach*, [in:] *Średniowieczne herezje dualistyczne na Bałkanach. Źródła słowiańskie*, eds. G. M i n c z e w, M. S k o w r o n e k, J.M. W o l s k i, Łódź 2015, p. 13–57.

Missiou D., *Über die Institutionele Rolle der Byzantinischen Kaiserin*, "Jahrbuch der Österreichischen Byzantinistik" 32, 1982, p. 489–498.

Moravcsik G., *Byzantium and the Magyars*, Budapest 1970.

Moravscik G., *Zur Geschichte des Herrschertitels "caesar>царь"*, "Zbornik Radova Vizantološkog Instituta" 8, 1963, p. 229–236.

Moszyński L., *Staro-cerkiewno-słowiańskie apelatywy określające osoby będące u władzy*, "Balcanica Poznaniensia" 2, 1985, p. 43–48.

Nikolov A., *Making a New Basileus. The Case of Symeon of Bulgaria (893–927). Reconsidered*, [in:] *Rome, Constantinople and Newly-Converted Europe. Archaeological and Historical Evidence*, vol. I, eds. M. Salamon et al., Kraków–Leipzig–Rzeszów–Warszawa 2012, p. 101–108.

Obolensky D., *The Bogomils*, Cambridge 1948.

Oikonomides N., *A Collection of Dated Byzantine Lead Seals*, Washington 1986.

Oikonomides N., *Le kommerkion d'Abydos, Thessalonique et la commerce bulgare au IXᵉ siècle*, [in:] *Hommes et richesses dans l'Empire byzantin*, vol. II, *VIIᵉ –XVᵉ siècle*, eds. V. Kravari, J. Lefort, C. Morrisson, Paris 1991, p. 241–248.

Oikonomidès N., *Les listes de préséance byzantines des IXᵉ et Xᵉ siècles*, Paris 1972.

Ostrogorski G., *Avtokrator i samodržac*, [in:] idem, *Vizantija i Sloveni*, Beograd 1970, p. 281–364.

Pac G., *Kobiety w dynastii Piastów. Rola społeczna piastowskich żon i córek do połowy XII w. – studium porównawcze*, Toruń 2013.

Parani M.G., *Reconstructing the Reality of Image. Byzantine Material Culture and Religious Iconography (11ᵗʰ–15ᵗʰ Centuries)*, Leiden–Boston 2003.

Parani M.G., *The Romanos Ivory and the New Tokali Kilise: Imperial Costume as a Tool for Dating Byzantine Art*, "Cahiers archéologiques. Fin de l'antiquité et moyen-âge" 49, 2001, p. 15–28.

Paroń A., *Pieczyngowie. Koczownicy w krajobrazie politycznym i kulturowym średniowiecznej Europy*, Wrocław 2015.

Paroń A., *"Trzeba, abyś tymi oto słowami odparł i to niedorzeczne żądanie" – wokół De administrando imperio Konstantyna VII*, [in:] *Causa creandi. O pragmatyce źródła historycznego*, eds. S. Rosik, P. Wiszewski, Wrocław 2005, p. 345–361.

Penkov S., *Bulgaro-Byzantine Treaties during the Early Middle Ages*, "Palaeobulgarica" 5.3, 1981, p. 40–52.

Pirivatrić S., *Some Notes on the Byzantine-Bulgarian Peace Treaty of 927*, "Byzantinoslovaca" 2, 2008, p. 40–49.

P o d s k a l s k y G., *Chrześcijaństwo i literatura teologiczna na Rusi Kijowskiej (988–1237)*, transl. J. Z y c h o w i c z, Kraków 2000.

P o h l s a n d e r H.A., *Helena. Empress and Saint*, Chicago 1995.

P o p p e A., *La naissance du culte de Boris et Gleb*, "Cahiers de civilisation médiévale" 24, 1981, p. 29–53.

P o p p e A., *Once Again Concerning the Baptism of Olga, Archontissa of Rus'*, "Dumbarton Oaks Papers" 46, 1992, p. 271–277.

P o p p e A., *Państwo i Kościół na Rusi w XI w.*, Warszawa 1968.

P o p p e A., *The Political Background to the Baptism of Rus': Byzantine-Russian Relations between 986–989*, "Dumbarton Oaks Papers" 30, 1976, p. 195–244.

P o p p e A., *Przyjęcie chrześcijaństwa na Rusi w opiniach XI w.*, [in:] *Teologia i kultura duchowa Starej Rusi*, eds. J.S. G a j e k, W. H r y n i e w i c z, Lublin 1993, p. 89–104.

P o p p e A., *Ruś i Bizancjum w latach 986–989*, "Kwartalnik Historyczny" 85.1, 1978, p. 3–23.

P o p p e A., *Walka o spuściznę po Włodzimierzu Wielkim 1015–1019*, "Kwartalnik Historyczny" 102.3/4, 1995, p. 3–22.

P o p p e D., P o p p e A., *Dziewosłęby o Porfirogenetkę Annę*, [in:] *Cultus et cognitio. Studia z dziejów średniowiecznej kultury*, eds. S.K. K u c z y ń s k i et al., Warszawa 1976, p. 451–468.

P o t t e r D., *Theodora. Actress, Empress, Saint*, Oxford 2015.

P r i n z i n g G., *Entstehung und Rezeption der Justiniana Prima-Theorie im Mittelalter*, "Byzantinobulgarica" 5, 1978, p. 269–278.

P r i t s a k O., *When and Where was Ol'ga Baptized?*, "Harvard Ukrainian Studies" 9, 1985, p. 5–24.

Prosopographie der mittelbyzantinischen Zeit. Erste Abteilung (641–867), vol. I, ed. F. W i n k e l m a n n et al., Berlin –New York 1999; vol. III, ed. F. W i n k e l m a n n et al., Berlin–New York 2000; vol. IV, ed. F. W i n k e l m a n n et al., Berlin–New York 2001.

Prosopographie der mittelbyzantinischen Zeit. Zweite Abteilung (867–1025), vol. I–VI, ed. F. W i n k e l m a n n et al., Berlin–Boston 2013.

P r y o r J.H., J e f f r e y s E.M., *The age of dromon. The Byzantine Navy ca 500–1204*, Leiden–Boston 2006.

R i n g r o s e K., *The Perfect Servant. Eunuchs and Social Construction of Gender in Byzantium*, Chicago 2003.

R u n c i m a n S., *The Emperor Romanus Lecapenus and His Reign. A Study of Tenth-Century Byzantium*, Cambridge 1969.

R u n c i m a n S., *The History of the First Bulgarian Empire*, London 1930.

R u n c i m a n S., *The Medieval Manichee. A Study of the Dualist Heresy*, Cambridge 1982.

R u n c i m a n S., *Some Notes on the Role of the Empress*, "Eastern Churches Review" 4, 1972, p. 119–124.

S c h m i n c k A., *"Frömmigkeit ziere das Work". Zur Datierung der 60 Bücher Leons VI*, "Subseciva Groningana" 3, 1989, p. 79–114.

S c h u l z e H.K., *Die Heiratsurkunde der Kaiserin Theophanu. Die griechische Kaiserin und das römisch-deutsche Reich 972–991*, Hannover 2007.

S e i b t W., Z a r n i t z M.L., *Das Byzantinische Bleisiegel als Kunstwerk. Katalog zur Ausstellung*, Wien 1997.

S h e p a r d J., *Bulgaria. The Other Balkan "Empire"*, [in:] *New Cambridge Medieval History*, vol. III, ed. T. R e u t e r, Cambridge 2000, p. 567–585.

S h e p a r d J., *A marriage too far? Maria Lekapena and Peter of Bulgaria*, [in:] *The Empress Theophano. Byzantium and the West at the turn of the first millennium*, ed. A. D a v i d s, Cambridge 1995, p. 121–149.

S h e p a r d J., *Symeon of Bulgaria-Peacemaker*, [in:] i d e m, *Emergent elites and Byzantium in the Balkans and East-Central Europe*, Farnham–Burlington 2011, p. 1–53.

S m o r ą g R ó ż y c k a M., *Bizantyńsko-ruskie miniatury Kodeksu Gertrudy. O kontekstach ideowych i artystycznych sztuki Rusi Kijowskiej XI w.*, Kraków 2003.

S m o r ą g R ó ż y c k a M., *Cesarzowa Teofano i królowa Gertruda. Uwagi o wizerunkach władczyń w sztuce średniowiecznej na marginesie rozważań o miniaturach w Kodeksie Gertrudy*, [in:] *Gertruda Mieszkówna i jej rękopis*, ed. A. A n d r z e j u k, Radzymin 2013, p. 123–134.

S p e c k P., *Kaiser Konstantin VI. Die Legitimation einer fremden und der Versuch einer eigenen Herrschaft. Quellenkritische Darstellung von 25 Jahren byzantinischer Geschichte nach dem ersten Ikonoklasmus*, Münich 1978.

S t o k e s B., *The Background and Chronology of the Balkan Campaigns of Svyatoslav Igorevich*, "The Slavonic and East European Review" 40/94, 1961, p. 44–57.

S t o y a n o v Y., *The Other God. Dualist Religions from Antiquity to the Cathar Heresy*, New Haven 2000.

S t r ä s s l e P.M., *Krieg und Frieden in Byzanz*, "Byzantion" 74, 2004, p. 110–129.

S w o b o d a W., *Bułgaria a patriarchat konstantynopolitański w latach 870–1018*, [in:] *Z polskich studiów slawistycznych*, vol. IV, *Historia*, Warszawa 1972, p. 47–65.

S w o b o d a W., *Damian*, [in:] *Słownik starożytności słowiańskich. Encyklopedyczny zarys kultury Słowian od czasów najdawniejszych do schyłku XII w.*, vol. VIII, eds. A. G ą s i o r o w s k i, G. L a b u d a, A. W ę d z k i, Wrocław 1991, p. 13–14.

S w o b o d a W., *Kontynuacja Georgiosa*, [in:] *Słownik starożytności słowiańskich. Encyklopedyczny zarys kultury Słowian od czasów najdawniejszych do schyłku XII w.*, vol. II, eds. W. K o w a l e n k o, G. L a b u d a, T. L e h r-S p ł a w i ń s k i, Wrocław 1965, p. 468.

S w o b o d a W., *Symeon Logotheta*, [in:] *Słownik starożytności słowiańskich. Encyklopedyczny zarys kultury Słowian od czasów najdawniejszych do schyłku XII w.*, vol. V, eds. W. K o w a l e n k o, G. L a b u d a, T. L e h r-S p ł a w i ń s k i, Wrocław 1975, p. 506–507.

Š e v č e n k o I., *Byzanz und der Westen im 10. Jahrhundert*, [in:] *Kunst im Zeitalter der Kaiserin Theophanu. Akten des Internationalen Colloquiums veranstaltet vom Schnütgen-Museum*, eds. A. v o n E u w, P. S c h r e i n e r, Köln 1993, p. 5–30.

T i n n e f e l d F., *Byzantinische auswärtige Heiratspolitik vom 9. zum 12 Jahrhundert*, "Byzantinoslavica" 54.1, 1993, p. 21–28.

T i n n e f e l d F., *Die Russische Fürstin Olga bei Konstantin VII. und das Problem der "Purpurgeborenen Kinder"*, "Russia mediaevalis" 6, 1987, p. 30–37.

T i n n e f e l d F., *Zum Stand der Olga–Diskussion*, [in:] *Zwischen Polis, Provinz und Peripherie. Beiträge zur byzantinischen Geschichte und Kultur*, eds. L.M. H o f f-m a n n, A. M o n c h i z a d e h, Wiesbaden 2005, p. 531–567.

T o u g h e r S., *The Eunuch in Byzantine History and Society*, London 2008.

T o u g h e r S., *The Reign of Leo VI (886–912). Politics and People*, Leiden–New York–Köln 1997.

T u r l e j S., *Justiniana Prima: An Underestimated Aspect of Justinian's Church Policy*, Kraków 2016.

T w a r d o w s k a K., *Cesarzowe bizantyńskie 2 poł. V w. Kobiety a władza*, Kraków 2009.

W a l k e r A., *Numismatic and Metrological Parallels for the Iconography of Early Byzantine Marriage Jewelry. The Question of the Crowned Bride*, "Travaux et Mémoires" 16, 2010, p. 849–863.

W a s i l e w s k i T., *Bizancjum i Słowianie w IX w. Studia z dziejów stosunków politycznych i kulturalnych*, Warszawa 1972.

W h i t b y M., *The Successors of Justinian*, [in:] *The Cambridge Ancient History*, vol. XIV, *Late Antiquity. Empire and Successors AD 425–600*, eds. Av. C a m e r o n, B. W a r d - P e r k i n s, M. W h i t b y, Cambridge 2000, p. 86–111.

W o l i ń s k a T., *Armeńscy współpracownicy Justyniana Wielkiego*, II, *Wielka kariera eunucha Narsesa*, "Przegląd Nauk Historycznych" 4.1, 2005, p. 29–50.

W o l i ń s k a T., *Justynian Wielki*, Kraków 2003.

W o l i ń s k a T., *Justynian Wielki, cesarzowa Teodora i upadek Jana z Kapadocji*, "Piotrkowskie Zeszyty Historyczne" 1, 1998, p. 5–29.

W o l i ń s k a T., *Konstantynopolitańska misja Liudpranda z Kremony (968)*, [in:] *Cesarstwo bizantyńskie. Dzieje. Religia. Kultura. Studia ofiarowane Profesorowi Waldemarowi Ceranowi przez uczniów na 70-lecie Jego urodzin*, eds. P. K r u p c z y ń s k i, M.J. L e s z k a, Łask–Łódź 2006, p. 201–223.

Ziemscy aniołowie, niebiańscy ludzie. Anachoreci w bułgarskiej literaturze i kulturze, ed. G. M i n c z e w, Białystok 2002.

А н г е л о в Д., *Богомилство*, София 1993.

А н г е л о в Д., *Богомилството в България*, София 1961.

А н г е л о в Д., К а ш е в С., Ч о л п а н о в Б., *Българска военна история от античността до втората четвърт на X в.*, София 1983.

А н г е л о в П., *Духовници-дипломати в средновековна България*, "Studia Balcanica" 27, 2009, p. 143–150.

А н д р е е в Й., *Иван Рилски*, [in:] i d e m, И. Л а з а р о в, П. П а в л о в, *Кой кой е в средновековна България*, София 2012, p. 270–275.

А н и с и м о в а Т.В., *Хроника Георгия Амартола в древнерусских списках XIV–XVII вв.*, Москва 2009.

А т а н а с о в Г., *Инсигниите на средновековните български владетели. Корони, скиптри, сфери, оръжия, костюми, накити*, Плевен 1999.

А т а н а с о в Г., *Печатите на българските владетели от IX–X в. в Дръстър (Силистра)*, [in:] *От тука започва България. Материали от втората национална конференция по история, археология и културен туризъм "Пътуване към България", Шумен 14–16.05. 2010 година*, ed. И. Й о р д а н о в, Шумен 2011, p. 286–293.

А т а н а с о в Г., *Първата българска патриаршеска кафедра в Дръстър и патриарх Дамян*, [in:] *Изследвания по българска средновековна археология. Сборник в чест на проф. Рашо Рашев*, ed. П. Г е о р г и е в, Велико Търново 2007, p. 179–196.

А т а н а с о в Г., *Християнският Дуросторум-Дръстър. Доростолската епархия през късната античност и Средновековието IV–XIV в. История, археология, култура и изкуство*, Варна 2007.

Б а к а л о в Г., *Средновековният български владетел. Титулатура и инсигнии*, ²София 1995.

Б а к а л о в Г., *Царската промулгация на Петър и неговите приемници в светлината на българо-византийските дипломатически отношения след договора от 927 г.*, "Исторически преглед" 39.6, 1983, p. 35–44.

Б и л я р с к и И., *Покровители на Царство. Св. Цар Петър и св. Параскева-Петка*, София 2004.

Б и л я р с к и И., *Фискална система на средновековна България*, Пловдив 2010.

Б и л я р с к и И., Й о в ч е в а М., *За датата на успението на цар Петър и за култа към него*, [in:] *Тангра. Сборник в чест на 70-годишнината на акад. Васил Гюзелев*, София 2006, p. 543–557.

Б л а г о е в Н.П., *Българският цар Роман*, "Македонски преглед" 6.3, 1930, p. 15–34.

Б л а г о е в Н.П., *Критичен поглед върху известията на Лъв Дякон за българите*, "Македонски преглед" 6.1, 1930, p. 25–48.

Б о б р о в А.Г., *К вопросу о времени и месте создания Летописца Еллинского и Римского второй редакции*, "Труды Отдела древнерусской литературы" 55, 2004, p. 82–90.

Б о ж и л о в И., *Българската архиепископия XI–XII в. Списъкът на българските архиепископи*, София 2011.

Б о ж и л о в И., *Византийският свят*, София 2008.

Б о ж и л о в И., *Цар Симеон Велики (893–927): Златният век на Средновековна България*, София 1983.

Б о ж и л о в И., Г ю з е л е в В., *История на средновековна България. VII–XIV в.*, София 2006.

Б р а й ч е в с к и й М.Ю., *Утверждение Христианства на Руси*, Киев 1989.

В а к л и н о в а М., Щ е р е в а И., *Княз Борис I и владетелската църква на Велики Преслав*, [in:] *Християнската култура в средновековна България. Материали от национална научна конференция, Шумен, 2–4 май 2007 г., по случай 1100 години от смъртта на св. Княз Борис-Михаил (ок. 835–907 г.)*, ed. П. Г е о р г и е в, Велико Търново 2008, p. 185–194.

В а ч к о в а В., *Понятието "Запад" в историческата аргументация на средновековна България*, "Studia Balcanica" 25, 2006, p. 295–303.

В а ч к о в а В., *Симеон Велики. Пътят към короната на Запада*, София 2005.

В и л к у л Т., *Літопис і хронограф. Студії з домонгольського київського літописання*, Київ 2015.

В о й н о в М., *Промяната в българо-византийските отношения при цар Симеон*, "Известия на Института на История" 18, 1967, p. 147–202.

Г е о р г и е в П., *Превратът през 927 г.*, "Преславска Книжовна Школа" 10, 2008, p. 424–438.

Г е о р г и е в П., *Титлата и функциите на българския престолонаследник и въпросът за престолонаследието при цар Симеон (893–927)*, "Исторически преглед" 48.8/9, 1992, p. 3–12.

Г е о р г и е в а С., *Жената в българското средновековие*, Пловдив 2011.

Г о р и н а Л.В., *Болгарский хронограф и его судьба на Руси*, София 2005.

Г р а б а р А., *Император в византийском искусстве*, Москва 2000.

Г ю з е л е в В., *Значението на брака на цар Петър (927–969) с ромейката Мария-Ирина Лакапина (911–962)*, [in:] *Културните текстове на миналото – носители, символи, идеи*, vol. I, *Текстовете на историята, история на текстовете. Материали от Юбилейната международна конференция в чест на 60-годишнината на проф. д.и.н. Казимир Попконстантинов, Велико Търново, 29–31 октомври 2003 г.*, София 2005, p. 27–33.

Д а н и л е в с к и й И., *Повесть временных лет: герменевтические основы изучения летописных тестов*, Москва 2004.

Д и м и т р о в Х., *Българо-унгарски отношения през средновековието*, София 1998.

Д и м и т р о в Х., *История на Македония*, София 2004.

Д о б р е в И., *Българите за руския народ, държава и култура*, София 2011.

Д у й ч е в И., *Българският княз Пленимир*, "Македонски преглед" 13.1, 1942, p. 13–20.

Д у й ч е в И., *Рилският светец и неговата обител*, София 1947.

З в е з д о в С., *Българо-византийските отношения при цар Петър*, "Минало" 2016, 3, p. 11–18.

З в е з д о в С., *Българо-византийските отношения при цар Петър I*, София 2016.

З в е з д о в С., *Договорът от 927 година между България и Византия*, "History. Bulgarian Journal of Historical Education" 23.3, 2015, p. 264–277.

З л а т а р с к и В.И., *История на българската държава през средните векове*, vol. 1/2, *Първо българско Царство. От славянизацията на държавата до падането на Първото царство (852–1018)*, София 1927.

И в а н о в С.А., *Византийско-болгарские отношения в 966–969 гг.*, "Византийский Временник" 42, 1981, p. 88–100.

И г н а т о в В., *Българските царици. Владетелките на България от VII до XIV в.*, София 2008.

История на българската средновековна литература, ed. А. М и л т е н о в а, София 2008.

Й о р д а н о в И., *Корпус на печатите на Средновековна България*, София 2001.

Й о р д а н о в И., *Корпус на средновековните български печати*, София 2016.

Й о р д а н о в И., *Печати на Василий Лакапин от България*, [in:] *Средновековният българин и "другите". Сборник в чест на 60-годишнината на проф. дин Петър Ангелов*, eds. А. Н и к о л о в, Г.Н. Н и к о л о в, София 2013, p. 159–166.

Й о р д а н о в И., *Печати на Симеон, василевс на Ромеите (?–927)*, "Bulgaria Mediaevalis" 2, 2011, p. 87–97.

К а ж д а н А.П., *Хроника Симеона Логофета*, "Византийский Временник" 15, 1959, p. 125–143.

К а й м а к а м о в а М., *Българска средновековна историопис*, София 1990.

К а й м а к а м о в а М., *Власт и история в средновековна България VIII–XIV в.*, София 2011.

К а й м а к а м о в а М., *Култът към цар Петър (927–969) и движещите идеи на българските освободителни въстания срещу византийската власт през XI–XII в.*, "Bulgaria Mediaevalis" 4/5, 2013/2014, p. 417–438.

К а р п о в А.Ю., *Владимир Святой*, Москва 2004.

К а р п о в А.Ю., *Княгиня Ольга*, Москва 2012.

К а р ы ш к о в с к и й Р.О., *О хронологии русско-византийской войны при Святославе*, "Византийский Временник" 5, 1952, p. 127–138.

К л о с с Б.М., *К вопросу о происхождении Еллинского летописца второго вида*, "Труды Отдела древнерусской литературы" 27, 1972, p. 370–379.

К о л е д а р о в П., *Македония*, [in:] *Кирило-методиевска енциклопедия*, vol. II, ed. П. Д и н е к о в, София 1995, p. 592–593.

К о л е д а р о в П., *Политическа география на средновековната българска държава*, vol. I, *От 681 до 1018 г.*, София 1979.

К о л е д а р о в П., *Цар Петър I*, "Военно-исторически сборник" 51, 1982, p. 192–207.

К о л е с о в В.В., *Заметки о языке Летописца Еллинского и Римского второй редакции (К вопросу о месте и времени составления)*, "Труды Отдела древнерусской
литературы" 55, 2004, p. 91–97.

К о л п а к о в а Г., *Искусство Древней Руси. Домонгольский период*, Санкт-
Петербург 2007.

К о т л я р Н.Ф., *Древняя Русь и Киев в летописных преданиях и легендах*, Киев 1986.

К р ъ с т а н о в Т., *Испански бележки за translatio на Justiniana Prima с българската
църква преди 1018 г.*, "Шуменски Университет Епископ Константин Преславски.
Трудове на Катедрите по история и богословие" 6, 2004, p. 80–84.

К р ъ с т а н о в Т., *Титлите екзарх и патриарх в българската традиция от IX
до XIX в. Св. Йоан Екзарх от Рим и патриарх на българските земи*, [in:] *Държава
& Църква – Църква & Държава в българската история. Сборник по случай
135-годишнината от учредяването на Българската екзархия*, eds. Г. Г а н е в,
Г. Б а к а л о в, И. Т о д е в, София 2006, p. 73–86.

К р ъ с т е в К.С., *България, Византия и Арабският свят при царуването на
Симеон I Велики*, "Bulgaria Mediaevalis" 3, 2012, p. 371–378.

К ъ н е в Н., *Византийската титла патрикия-зости (IX–XI в.). Приносът на сфрагистиката за попълване на листата на носителките на титлата*, "Историкии"
4, 2011, p. 173–198.

К ъ н е в Н., *Стремял ли се е българският владетел Симеон I Велики (893–927 г.)
към ранг на визатийски василеопатор?*, [in:] i d e m, *Византинобългарски
студии*, Велико Търново 2013, p. 111–119.

К ъ н е в Н., *Четири непубликувани оловни печата от района на Шумен*,
"Историкии" 5, 2012, p. 61–67.

Л е ш к а М.Й., *Образът на българския цар Борис II във византийските извори*,
"Studia Balcanica" 25, 2006, p. 145–152.

Л и т а в р и н Г.Г., *Византия, Болгария, Древняя Русь (IX–начало XII в.)*, Санкт-
Петербург 2000.

Л и т а в р и н Г.Г., *Константин Багрянородный о Болгарии и Болгарах*, [in:] *Сборник
в чест на акад. Димитър Ангелов*, ed. В. В е л к о в, София 1994, p. 30–37.

Л и т а в р и н Г.Г., *Принцип наследственности власти в Византии и в Болгарии
в VII–XI вв.*, [in:] *Славяне и их соседи*, vol. I, Москва 1988, p. 31–33.

Л и т а в р и н Г.Г., *Путешествие русской княгини Ольги в Константинополь.
Проблема источников*, "Византийский Временник" 42, 1981, p. 35–48.

Литаврин Г.Г., *Христианство в Болгарии 927–1018 гг.*, [in:] *Христианство в странах восточной, юго-восточной и центральной Европы на пороге второго тысячелетия*, ed. Б.Н. Ф л о р я, Москва 2002, p. 133–189.

Литвина А.Ф., Успенский Ф.Б., *Выбор имени у русских князей в X–XVI вв. Династическая история сквозь призму антропонимики*, Москва 2006.

Лихачев Д.С., *Еллинский летописец второго вида и правительственные круги Москвы конца XV в.*, "Труды Отдела древнерусской литературы" 6, 1948, p. 100–110.

Малахов С.Н., *Концепция мира в политической идеологии Византии первой половины X в.: Николай Мистик и Феодор Дафнопат*, "Античная Древность и Средние Века" 27, 1995, p. 19–31.

Матвеенко В., Щеголева Л., *Временник Георгия Монаха (Хроника Георгия Амартола). Русский текст, комментарий, указатели*, Москва 2000.

Мещерский Н.А., *Источники и состав древней славяно-русской переводной письменности IX–XV вв.*, Ленинград 1978.

Михайлова Т., *Печат на "Мария Василиса" от Преслав*, "Нумизматика, сфрагистика и епиграфика" 3.2, 2007, p. 39–42.

Молчанов А.А., *Владимир Мономах и его имена. К изучению княжеского именника Рюриковичей X–XII вв.*, "Славяноведение" 2004, 2, p. 80–87.

Мутафчиев П., *История на българския народ (681–1323)*, София 1986.

Назаренко А.В., *Древняя Русь на международных путях. Междисциплинарные очерки культурных, торговых, политических связей IX–XII вв.*, Москва 2001.

Назаренко А.В., *Когда же княгиня Ольга ездила в Константинополь?*, "Византийский Временник" 50, 1989, p. 66–84.

Никитенко Н.Н., *Крещение Руси в свете данных Софии Киевской*, "Софія Київська: Візантія. Русь. Україна" 3, 2013, p. 415–441.

Никитенко Н.Н., *Русь и Византия в монументальном комплексе Софии Киевской. Историческая проблематика*, Киев 2004.

Никитенко Н.Н., *София Киевская и ее создатели. Тайты истории*, Каменец-Подольский 2014.

Николаев В.Д., *Значение договора 927 г. в истории болгаро-византийских отношений*, [in:] *Проблемы истории античности и средних веков*, ed. Ю.М. Сапрыкин, Москва 1982, p. 89–105.

Николов А., *"Великият между царете". Изграждане и утвърждаване на българската царска институция през управлението на Симеон I*, [in:] *Българският*

златен век. Сборник в чест на цар Симеон Велики (893–927), eds. В. Г ю з е л е в,
И.Г. И л и е в, К. Н е н о в, Пловдив 2015, p. 149–188.

Н и к о л о в А., *Политическа мисъл в ранносредновековна България (средата на
IX–края на X в.)*, София 2006.

Н и к о л о в А., *Старобългарският превод на "Изложение на поучителни глави към
император Юстиниан" от дякон Агапит и развитието на идеята за достойнството на българския владетел в края на IX–началото на X в.*, "Palaeobulgarica"
24.3, 2000, p. 76–105.

Н и к о л о в Г., *Български царици от Средновековието в "ангелски образ"*, "Годишник
на Софийския университет Св. Климент Охридски" 93(12), 2003, p. 299–315.

Н и к о л о в Г., *Прабългарската традиция в християнския двор на средновековна
България (IX–XI в.). Владетел и престолонаследие*, [in:] *Бог и цар в българската история*, ed. К. В а ч к о в а, Пловдив 1996, p. 124–130.

Н и к о л о в а Б., *Монашество, манастири и манастирски живот в средновековна
България*, vol. I, *Манастирите*, София 2010; vol. II, *Монасите*, София 2010.

Н и к о л о в а Б., *Печатите на Михаил багатур канеиртхтин и Йоан
багатур канеиртхтин (?). Проблеми на разчитането и атрибуцията*, [in:]
*Средновековният българин и "другите". Сборник в чест на 60-годишнината на
проф. Дин Петър Ангелов*, eds. А. Н и к о л о в, Г.Н. Н и к о л о в, София 2013,
p. 127–135.

Н и к о л о в а Б., *Устройство и управление на българската православна църква
(IX–XIV в.)*, София 2017.

Н и к о л о в а Б., *Цар Петър и характерът на неговия култ*, "Palaeobulgarica"
33.2, 2009, p. 63–77.

О в ч а р о в Н., *Една хипотеза за българо-византийските отношения през
912–913 г.*, "Археология" 31.3, 1989, p. 50–57.

О с т р о г о р с к и й Г., *Славянский перевод хроники Симеона Логофета*, "Seminarium
Kondakovianum" 5, 1932, p. 17–37.

П а в л о в П., *Братята на цар Петър и техните заговори*, "История" 7.4/5, 1999,
p. 1–6.

П а в л о в П., *Векът на цар Самуил*, София 2014.

П а в л о в П., *Години на мир и "ратни беди" (927–1018)*, [in:] А т а н а с о в Г.,
В а ч к о в а В., П а в л о в П., *Българска национална история*, vol. III, *Първо
българско царство (680–1018)*, Велико Търново 2015, p. 403–479.

П а в л о в П., *Стефан*, [in:] i d e m, И. Л а з а р о в, П. П а в л о в, *Кой кой е в сред-новековна България*, София 2012, p. 625.

П а в л о в П., *Християнското и имперското минало на българските земи в ойку-меничната доктрина на цар Симеон Велики (893–927)*, [in:] *Източното пра-вославие в европейската култура. Международна конференция. Варна, 2–3 юли 1993 г.*, ed. Д. О в ч а р о в, София 1999, p. 111–115.

П о л ы в я н н ы й Д.И., *Царь Петр в исторической памяти болгарского средневе-ковья*, [in:] *Средновековният българин и "другите". Сборник в чест на 60-годиш-нината на проф. дин Петър Ангелов*, eds. А. Н и к о л о в, Г.Н. Н и к о л о в, София 2013, p. 137–145.

П о п к о н с т а н т и н о в К., *Епиграфски бележки за Иван, Цар Симеоновият син*, "Българите в Северното Причерноморие" 3, 1994, p. 71–80.

П у ш к а р е в а Н.Л., *Женщины Древней Руси*, Москва 1989.

П ч е л о в Е.В., *Генеалогия древнерусских князей IX–начала XI в.*, Москва 2001.

Р а е в М., *Переяславец на Дунав – мит и действителност в речта на княз Святослав в Повесть временных лет*, "Годишник на Софийския Университет. Научен цен-тър за славяно-византийски проучвания 'Иван Дуйчев'" 95.14, 2006, p. 193–203.

Р а е в М., *Преслав или Переяславец на Дунае? (Предварительные замечания об одном из возможных источников ПВЛ и его трансформации)*, "Наукові запис-ки з української історії: Збірник наукових статей" 20, 2008, p. 37–40.

Р а ш е в Р., *"Втората война" на Симеон срещу Византия (913–927) като лите-ратурен и политически факт*, [in:] i d e m, *Цар Симеон Велики. Щрихи към личността и делото му*, София 2007, p. 84–96.

Р а ш е в Р., *Княз Симеон и император Александър*, [in:] i d e m, *Цар Симеон Велики. Щрихи към личността и делото му*, София 2007, p. 32–41.

Р а ш е в Р., *Цар Симеон – "нов Мойсей" или "нов Давид"*, [in:] i d e m, *Цар Симеон Велики. Щрихи към личността и делото му*, София 2007, p. 60–72.

Р ы к о в Ю.Д., *Новонайденный фрагмент Летописца Еллинского и Римского вто-рой редакции*, "Труды Отдела древнерусской литературы" 55, 2004, p. 71–81.

Р ы ч к а В., *Чью славу переял Переяслав?*, "Наукові записки з української історії: Збірник наукових статей" 16, 2005, p. 129–134.

С а л м и н а М.А., *Хроника Константина Манассии как источник Русского хроно-графа*, "Труды Отдела древнерусской литературы" 32, 1978, p. 279–287.

С а х а р о в А.Н., *Дипломатия Святослава*, Москва 1982.

Свердлов М.Б., *Домонгольская Русь. Князь и княжеская власть на Руси VI–первой трети XIII вв.*, Санкт-Петербург 2003.

Симеонова Л., *Щрихи към историята на тайната дипломация, разузнаването и контраразузнаването в средновековния свят*, [in:] *Тангра. Сборник в чест на 70. годишнината на Акад. Васил Гюзелев*, eds. М. Каймакавова et al., София 2006, p. 499–530.

Славова Т., *Владетел и администрация в ранносредновековна Бълагария. Филологически аспекти*, София 2010.

Славова Т., *Юридическа литература*, [in:] *История на българската средновековна литература*, ed. А. Милтенова, София 2008, p. 194–202.

Сотникова М.П., Спасский И.Г., *Тысячелетие древнейших монет России. Сводный каталог русских монет X–XI вв.*, Ленинград 1983.

Среднеболгарский перевод Хроники Константина Манассии в славянских литературах, eds. Д.С. Лихачев, И.С. Дуйчев, София 1988.

Стоименов Д., *Към договора между България и Византия от 927 г.*, "Векове" 17.6, 1988, p. 19–23.

Творогов О.В., *Древнерусские хронографы*, Ленинград 1975.

Творогов О.В., *Летописец Еллинский и Римский*, [in:] *Словарь книжников и книжности Древней Руси (вторая половина XIV–XVI в.)*, ed. Д.С. Лихачев, vol. II, Ленинград 1989, p. 18–20.

Творогов О.В., *Летописец Еллинский и Римский: текстологические проблемы*, "Труды Отдела древнерусской литературы" 52, 2001, p. 47–78.

Творогов О.В., *Паралипомен Зонары: текст и комментарий*, [in:] *Летописи и хроники. Новые исследования. 2009–2010*, ed. О.Л. Новикова, Москва–Санкт-Петербург 2010, p. 3–101.

Творогов О.В., *Хроника Георгия Амартола*, [in:] *Словарь книжников и книжности Древней Руси (XI – первая половина XIV в.)*, ed. Д.С. Лихачев, Ленинград 1987, p. 469–470.

Тодоров Т., *България през втората и третата четвърт на X век: политическа история*, София 2006 [unpublished PhD thesis].

Тодоров Т., *Владетелският статут и титла на цар Петър I след октомври 927 г.: писмени сведения и сфрагистични данни (сравнителен анализ)*, [in:] *Юбилеен сборник. Сто години от рождението на д-р Васил Хараланов (1907–2007)*, Шумен 2008, p. 93–108.

Т о д о р о в Т., *Вътрешнодинастичният проблем в България от края на 20-те-началото на 30-те години на X в.*, "Историкии" 3, 2008, p. 263–279.

Т о д о р о в Т., *За едно отражение на съвладетелската практика в Първото българско царство през втората половина на IX–първите десетилетия на X в.*, [in:] *България, българите и Европа – мит, история, съвремие*, vol. IV, *Доклади от Международна конференция в памет на проф. д.и.н. Йордан Андреев "България, земя на блажени...", В. Търново, 29–31 октомври 2009 г.*, ed. И. Л а з а р о в, Велико Търново 2011, p. 173–181.

Т о д о р о в Т., *Константин Багренородни и династичният брак между владетелските домове на Преслав и Константинопол от 927 г.*, "Преславска книжовна школа" 7, 2003, p. 391–398.

Т о д о р о в Т., *Към въпроса за престолонаследието в Първото българско царство*, "Плиска–Преслав" 8, 2000, p. 202–207.

Т о д о р о в Т., *"Слово за мир с българите" и българо-византийските отношения през последните години от управлението на цар Симеон*, [in:] *България, българите и техните съседи през векове. Изследвания и материали од научна конференция в памет на д-р Христо Коларов, 30–31 октомври 1998 г.*, Велико Търново, ed. Й. А н д р е е в, Велико Търново 2001, p. 141–150.

Т о д о р о в а-Ч а н е в а С., *Женският накит от епохата на Първото българско царство. VII–XI в.*, София 2009.

Т о т е в К., *За една група печати на цар Симеон*, [in:] *Общото и специфичното в Балканските народи до края на XIX в. Сборник в чест на 70-годишнината на проф. Василика Тъпкова-Заимова*, ed. Г. Б а к а л о в, София 1999, p. 107–112.

Т у р и л о в А.А., *К вопросу о болгарских источниках Русского хронографа*, [in:] *Летописи и хроники. Сборник статей*, Москва 1984, p. 20–24 [=*Межславянские культурные связи эпохи Средневековья и источниковедение истории и культуры славян. Этюды и характеристики*, Москва 2012, p. 704–708].

Т ъ п к о в а-З а и м о в а В., *Дюканжов списък*, "Palaeobulgarica" 24.3, 2000, p. 21–49.

Т ъ п к о в а-З а и м о в а В., *Падане на Североизточна България под византийска власт*, [in:] *История на България*, vol. II, *Първа българска държава*, София 1981, p. 389–397.

Т ъ п к о в а-З а и м о в а В., *Превземането на Преслав в 971 г. и проблемите на българската църква*, [in:] *1100 години Велики Преслав*, vol. I, ed. Т. Т о т е в, Шумен 1995, p. 172–181.

Христодулова М., *Титул и регалии болгарской владетельницы в эпоху средне-вековья (VII–XIV вв.)*, "Études Balkaniques" 1978, 3, p. 141–148.

Цанкова-Петкова Г., *Първата война между България и Византия при цар Симеон и възстановяването на българската търговия с Цариград*, "Известия на Института за История" 20, 1968, p. 167–200.

Чешмеджиев Д., *За времето на пренасяне на мощите на св. Иоанн Рилски от Рила в Средец*, "Bulgaria Mediaevalis" 6, 2015, p. 79–89.

Чешмеджиев Д., *Култовете на българските светци през IX–XII в. Автореферат*, Пловдив 2016.

Чешмеджиев Д., *Култът към български цар Петър I (927–969): монашески или държавен?*, [in:] *5. International Hilandar Conference, 8–14 September 2001, Raska, Jugoslavija. Love of learning and devotion to God in orthodox monasteries*, Beograd–Columbus 2006, p. 245–257.

Шандровская В.С., *Печати титулованных женщин Византии*, "Античная древность и средние века" 33, 2002, p. 89–101.

Щапов Я.Н., *Древнерусские княжеские уставы XI–XV вв.*, Москва 1976.

Щапов Я.Н., *Княжеские уставы и церковь в Древней Руси XI–XIV вв.*, Москва 1972.

Янин В.Л., *Актовые печати Древней Руси X–XV вв.*, vol. I, *Печати X – начала XIII в.*, Москва 1970.

Indices

Index of People

Index of Ethnic and Geographic Names

Illustrations

1. Christ crowning Otto II and Theophano, ivory, Byzantium, ca. 980. Musée national du Moyen Âge, Thermes et hôtel de Cluny, Paris. Phot. T. Wolińska

2. The Church of St. Sophia (Divine Wisdom) in Kiev, first half of 11th century. Phot. Z.A. Brzozowska

3. Empress Theodora surrounded by ladies of the court. Mosaic from the Church of San Vitale in Ravenna, 547. Phot. T. Wolińska

4. Empress Ariadne (?), Italy, end of 5th / beginning of 6th century. Santa Maria Antiqua museum, Rome. Phot. T. Wolińska

5. The column of Constantine I the Great, Istanbul.
Phot. M.J. Leszka

6. Follis with an image of Justin II and Sophia. From the collection of
prof. Ireneusz Milewski

7. The church of emperor Romanos I Lekapenos in Myrelaion and the early Byzantine rotunda upon which the palace (later monastery) stood. Phot. A. Kompa

8. The Golden Church, Preslav. Phot. K. Marinow

9. The throne room, 10th century, Preslav. Phot. K. Marinow

10. Part of the residential complex of Bulgarian rulers, 9th/10th century, Preslav. Phot. K. Marinow

11. The Church of the Assumption of St. John of Rila, 10th century (restored in the 19th century). Phot. M.J. Leszka

12. The Church of St. Sophia (Divine Wisdom), Mesembria (modern-day Nesebar). Phot. T. Pietras

BYZANTINA LODZIENSIA
1997–2017

I.

Sławomir Bralewski, *Imperatorzy późnego cesarstwa rzymskiego wobec zgromadzeń biskupów*, Łódź 1997, pp. 197.

[*Les empereurs du Bas-Empire romain face aux conciles des évêques*]

II.

Maciej Kokoszko, *Descriptions of Personal Appearance in John Malalas' Chronicle*, Łódź 1998, pp. 181.

III.

Mélanges d'histoire byzantine offerts à Oktawiusz Jurewicz à l'occasion de Son soixante-dixième anniversaire, red. **Waldemar Ceran**, Łódź 1998, pp. 209.

IV.

Mirosław Jerzy Leszka, *Uzurpacje w cesarstwie bizantyńskim w okresie od IV do połowy IX wieku*, Łódź 1999, pp. 149.

[*Usurpations in Byzantine Empire from the 4th to the Half of the 9th Century*]

V.

Małgorzata Beata Leszka, *Rola duchowieństwa na dworze cesarzy wczesnobizantyńskich*, Łódź 2000, pp. 136.

[*The Role of the Clergy at the Early Byzantine Emperors Court*]

VI.

Waldemar Ceran, *Historia i bibliografia rozumowana bizantynologii polskiej (1800–1998)*, tom I–II, Łódź 2001, pp. 786.

[*History and bibliography raisonné of Polish Byzantine studies (1800–1998)*]

VII.

Mirosław Jerzy Leszka, *Wizerunek władców pierwszego państwa bułgarskiego w bizantyńskich źródłach pisanych (VIII – pierwsza połowa XII wieku)*, Łódź 2003, pp. 169.

[*The Image of the First Bulgarian State Rulers Shown in the Byzantine Literary Sources of the Period from the 8th to the First Half of the 12th Centuries*]

VIII.

Teresa Wolińska, *Sycylia w polityce cesarstwa bizantyńskiego w VI–IX wieku*, Łódź 2005, pp. 379.

[*Sicily in Byzantine Policy, 6th–9th Century*]

IX.

Maciej Kokoszko, *Ryby i ich znaczenie w życiu codziennym ludzi późnego antyku i wczesnego Bizancjum (III–VII w.)*, Łódź 2005, pp. 445.

[*The Role of Fish In Everyday Life of the People of Late Antiquity and Early Byzantium (3rd–7th c.)*]

X.

Sławomir Bralewski, *Obraz papiestwa w historiografii kościelnej wczesnego Bizancjum*, Łódź 2006, pp. 334.

[L'image de la papauté dans l'historiographie ecclésiastique du haut Empire Byzantin]

XI.

Byzantina Europaea. Księga jubileuszowa ofiarowana Profesorowi Waldemarowi Ceranowi, red. **Maciej Kokoszko**, **Mirosław J. Leszka**, Łódź 2007, pp. 573.

[Byzantina Europaea. Studies Offered to Professor Waldemar Ceran]

XII.

Paweł Filipczak, *Bunty i niepokoje w miastach wczesnego Bizancjum (IV wiek n.e.)*, Łódź 2009, pp. 236.

[The Riots and Social Unrest in Byzantine Cities in the 4th Century A.D.]

XIV.

Jolanta Dybała, *Ideał kobiety w pismach kapadockich Ojców Kościoła i Jana Chryzostoma*, Łódź 2012, pp. 480.

[The Ideal of Woman in the Writings of the Cappadocian Fathers of the Church and John Chrysostom]

XV.

Mirosław J. Leszka, *Symeon I Wielki a Bizancjum. Z dziejów stosunków bułgarsko-bizantyńskich w latach 893–927*, Łódź 2013, pp. 368.

[Symeon I the Great and Byzantium: Bulgarian-Byzantine Relations, 893–927]

XVI.

Maciej Kokoszko, Krzysztof Jagusiak, Zofia Rzeźnicka, *Dietetyka i sztuka kulinarna antyku i wczesnego Bizancjum (II–VII w.)*, część I, *Zboża i produkty zbożowe w źródłach medycznych antyku i Bizancjum (II–VII w.)*, Łódź 2014, pp. 671.

[Dietetics and Culinary Art of Antiquity and Early Byzantium (2ⁿᵈ–7ᵗʰ c.), part I, Cereals and Cereal Products in Medical Sources of Antiquity and Early Byzantium (2ⁿᵈ–7ᵗʰ c.)]

XVII.

Andrzej Kompa, Mirosław J. Leszka, Teresa Wolińska, *Mieszkańcy stolicy świata. Konstantynopolitańczycy między starożytnością a średniowieczem*, Łódź 2014, pp. 490.

[Inhabitants of the Capital of the World: The Constantinopolitans between Antiquity and the Middle Ages]

XVIII.

Waldemar Ceran, *Artisans et commerçants à Antioche et leur rang social (secondo moitié du siècle de notre ère)*, Łódź 2013, pp. 236.

XIX.

Dietetyka i sztuka kulinarna antyku i wczesnego Bizancjum (II–VII w.), część II, *Pokarm dla ciała i ducha*, red. **Maciej Kokoszko**, Łódź 2014, pp. 607.

[Dietetics and Culinary Art of Antiquity and Early Byzantium (2ⁿᵈ–7ᵗʰ c.), part II, Nourishment for the Body and Soul]

XX.

Maciej Kokoszko, Krzysztof Jagusiak, Zofia Rzeźnicka, *Cereals of antiquity and early Byzantine times: Wheat and barley in medical sources (second to seventh centuries AD)*, Łódź 2014, pp. 516.

XXI.

Błażej Cecota, *Arabskie oblężenia Konstantynopola w VII–VIII wieku. Rzeczywistość i mit*, Łódź 2015, pp. 213.

[*The Arab Sieges of Constantinople in the 7th and 8th Centuries: Myth and Reality*]

XXII.

Byzantium and the Arabs: the Encounter of Civilizations from Sixth to Mid--Eighth Century, ed. **Teresa Wolińska, Paweł Filipczak**, Łódź 2015, pp. 601.

XXIII.

Miasto na styku mórz i kontynentów. Wczesno- i średniobizantyński Konstantynopol jako miasto portowe, red. **Mirosław J. Leszka, Kirił Marinow**, Łódź 2016, pp. 341.

[*Metropolis between the Seas and Continents: Early and Middle Byzantinine Constantinople as the Port City*]

XXIV.

Zofia A. Brzozowska, *Sofia – upersonifikowana Mądrość Boża. Dzieje wyobrażeń w kręgu kultury bizantyńsko-słowiańskiej*, Łódź 2015, pp. 478.

[*Sophia – the Personification of Divine Wisdom: the History of the Notion in the Byzantine-Slavonic Culture*]

XXV.

Błażej Szefliński, *Trzy oblicza Sawy Nemanjicia. Postać historyczna – autokreacja – postać literacka*, Łódź 2016, pp. 342.

[*Three Faces of Sava Nemanjić: Historical Figure, Self-Creation and Literary Character*]

XXVI.

Paweł Filipczak, *An introduction to the Byzantine administration in Syro--Palestine on the eve of the Arab conquest*, Łódź 2015, pp. 127.

XXVIII.

Zofia Rzeźnicka, Maciej Kokoszko, *Dietetyka i sztuka kulinarna antyku i wczesnego Bizancjum (II–VII w.)*, part III, *Ab ovo ad γάλα. Jajka, mleko i produkty mleczne w medycynie i w sztuce kulinarnej (I–VII w.)*, Łódź 2016, pp. 263.

[*Dietetics and Culinary Art of Antiquity and Early Byzantium (2nd–7th c.), part III, Ab ovo ad γάλα: Eggs, Milk and Dairy Products in Medicine and Culinary Art (1st–7th c. A.D.)*]